The Evolving Canadian Crown

Edited by Jennifer Smith and
D. Michael Jackson

Institute of Intergovernmental Relations
School of Policy Studies, Queen's University
McGill-Queen's University Press
Montreal & Kingston • London • Ithaca

Library and Archives Canada Cataloguing in Publication

The evolving Canadian crown / edited by Jennifer Smith and D. Michael Jackson.

Based on papers presented at the conference: The Crown in Canada : Present Realities and Future Options, held in Ottawa, Ont., from June 9-10, 2010.
Includes bibliographical references.
Includes chapter abstracts in French.
ISBN 978-1-55339-202-6

    1. Monarchy—Canada. 2. Constitutional history—Canada. 3. Canada—Politics and government—2006-. I. Smith, Jennifer, 1950- II. Jackson, D. Michael III. Queen's University (Kingston, Ont.). Institute of Intergovernmental Relations

JL88.E96 2011   320.471   C2011-907402-8

CONTENTS

ACKNOWLEDGEMENTS

The Institute of Intergovernmental Relations at Queen's University and Friends of the Canadian Crown wish to acknowledge the assistance of the following:

**Conference on the Crown in Canada, June 2010,
The Senate, Ottawa:**

Canadian Study of Parliament Group
Johnson-Shoyama Graduate School of Public Policy in the University
  of Saskatchewan and the University of Regina

Sponsors: The Walter and Duncan Gordon Foundation
        The Honourable Henry N.R. Jackman, OC, O.Ont, CD, LLD
        The Canadian Bar Association

Conference Advisory/Organizing Committee:
        Dr. Paul Benoit
        Rudyard Griffiths
        Dr. Christopher McCreery, MVO
        Senator Lowell Murray, PC, LLD
        Dr. David E. Smith, FRSC
        Caterina Ciavaglia, Office of Senator Segal
        Jonathan Aiello, Institute of Intergovernmental Relations
        Mary Kennedy, Institute of Intergovernmental Relations
        Nadia Verrelli, Institute of Intergovernmental Relations

Co-Chairs: Senator Serge Joyal, PC, OC, OQ
        Senator Hugh Segal, CM, LLD

Secretary: Dr. D. Michael Jackson, CVO, SOM, CD

Session Chairs: Dr. Paul Benoit
Dr. Richard Clippingdale
John Fraser, CM
Jodi White

Publication of this book:

The Honourable Hilary Weston, CM, O.Ont.
Mr. Galen Weston, OC
John Fraser, CM
Massey College in the University of Toronto

André Juneau, Institute of Intergovernmental Relations
Nadia Verrelli, Institute of Intergovernmental Relations
Mark Howes, School of Policy Studies, Queen's University
Valerie Jarus, School of Policy Studies, Queen's University
Carla Douglas, Copy Editor
McGill-Queen's University Press

Editorial Committee: Dr. Jennifer Smith (Editor)
Dr. D. Michael Jackson
Dr. Paul Benoit
Senator Serge Joyal
Dr. Christopher McCreery
Senator Lowell Murray
Senator Hugh Segal
Dr. David E. Smith

FOREWORD

The high-profile Canadian tour of the Queen and the Duke of Edinburgh in 2010 and the subsequent appointment of David Johnston as governor general drew renewed attention to the institution of the Crown in this country. The royal tour – like that of the Prince of Wales and Duchess of Cornwall in 2009 – could not be dismissed as a flash in the pan, a nostalgic retro to the days of Empire. Nor could the public interest in the wedding of Prince William and Catherine (the Duke and Duchess of Cambridge) in 2011 and the brilliant success of their Canadian tour shortly thereafter. There was something deeper at stake here. The Crown in Canada, long dismissed as irrelevant by skeptics, including many academics, has been re-awakening interest among scholars, politicians and the public alike. The Queen's Diamond Jubilee in 2012 can only heighten this awareness.

The renewed interest in the Crown can be traced back to the publication in 1995 of *The Invisible Crown: The First Principle of Canadian Government* by respected political scientist David E. Smith of the University of Saskatchewan, one of the contributors to this book. Dr. Smith's seminal work challenged those who dismissed the Crown as a colonial relic irrelevant to modern Canada. On the contrary, Dr. Smith maintained, constitutional monarchy was at the heart of how Canadians governed themselves and was crucial to the federal dimension of the country. His 1999 work, *The Republican Option in Canada, Past and Present*, underscored how, unlike Australia, republicanism had failed to make major inroads into the Canadian consciousness.

In the same year as David E. Smith's second book appeared, the appointment of Adrienne Clarkson as governor general, after twenty lacklustre years of former politicians in the job, revived public interest in the national vice-regal office. It followed positive developments in the office of lieutenant governor over the same twenty-year period, thanks to successful appointments to the provincial vice-regal positions. Through her energy, intellect, and artistic and literary talent, Adrienne Clarkson transformed the role of the governor general. Michaëlle Jean, with her personal charisma, empathy and media skills, built on Madame Clarkson's foundation to popularize the governor generalcy even more. Furthermore, the circumstances of minority government for both these incumbents of Rideau Hall, and the dissolution and prorogation controversies in 2008 and 2009, drew renewed attention to the constitutional reserve powers of the governor general. There was, on the other hand, a regrettable dimension to both tenures at Rideau Hall: the persistent drive to promote the governor general as head of state and downplay the Sovereign (and the lieutenant governors) as somehow discordant with the institution of the Canadian Crown. With this view, Friends of the Canadian Crown and the contributors to this book emphatically differ. It is gratifying that the tone at Rideau Hall has changed since David Johnston's appointment as governor general.

The monarchical system is subtle, nuanced and low-key. Perhaps this explains why there has been so little public awareness that it is fundamental to Canada's system of government and that it is legally and historically a key element of the provinces' autonomy within Confederation. Quebec public opinion, influenced since the 1960s by sovereigntist rhetoric, conveniently forgets that the Crown, dating back to British royal governors James Murray (1764–68), who implemented the *Quebec Act*, and Lord Elgin (1847–54), who granted responsible government, has been a powerful instrument of francophone particularity in North America. Those dismissing the monarchy also conveniently forget its vital importance to Canada's First Nations ever since King George III's landmark Royal Proclamation of 1763.

Evidently Stephen Harper's Conservative government does not share this approach to the Crown, the consequence of decades of benign and not-so-benign neglect of the institution in official Ottawa. The Queen's presence at the 90th anniversary of Vimy Ridge in France in 2007; the publication of the educational booklet *A Crown of Maples / La Couronne canadienne* in 2008 and a new citizenship guide, featuring the Crown, in 2009; the above-mentioned royal tours; and the restoration of the historic names Royal Canadian Navy and Royal Canadian Air Force in 2011 – all demonstrate that Crown and constitutional monarchy are very much alive in Canada in the 21st century.

The 2010 conference on the Crown held at the Senate in Ottawa, of which this book is a direct outcome, was therefore both welcome and timely. As co-chairs of Friends of the Canadian Crown, we express our thanks to all who supported and participated in the conference and to those who contributed to this book. Particular appreciation is owed to Senator Serge Joyal and Senator Hugh Segal, co-chairs of the conference; to the Institute of Intergovernmental Relations at Queen's University for its key role as organizing partner; and to the Honourable Hilary Weston and Mr. Galen Weston, whose financial support made the book possible.

John Fraser, Massey College, Toronto
D. Michael Jackson, University of Regina
January 2012

PREFACE

The Crown in Canada, as this book shows, is fundamental to our country's governance and has been an integral part of Canada's political culture since the first European settlements. More recently, the prorogation debate of 2008 served as a reminder of the importance of the reserve powers of the governor general.

It was therefore timely that a conference on the Crown should be held in the Parliament Buildings in Ottawa in June 2010. Entitled "The Crown in Canada: Present Realities and Future Options," it was co-chaired by Quebec Senator Serge Joyal and Ontario Senator Hugh Segal. The conference was an initiative of Friends of the Canadian Crown, an informal cross-Canada network of academics, policy-makers, writers and others interested in the Crown, formed in 2005 to promote better understanding of the institution. The Institute of Intergovernmental Relations was asked to organize it and we were pleased to do so in light of our continuing interest in the role of our institutions in the Canadian federation.

The Institute is now pleased to publish *The Evolving Canadian Crown*, largely based on the conference. We thank Dr. Jennifer Smith for editing this volume and Dr. D. Michael Jackson for assisting her. We trust that the book will assist Canadians in assessing the present and future roles of the Crown.

André Juneau
Director, IIGR

Contributors

DAVID ARNOT — Chief Commissioner of the Saskatchewan Human Rights Commission; former Treaty Commissioner for Saskatchewan

PAUL BENOIT — Government relations consultant; former university lecturer, senior aide to federal ministers, and Senate Committee Clerk

PETER BOYCE — Honorary Research Fellow, School of Government, University of Tasmania, Australia; former Vice-Chancellor of Murdoch University

NOEL COX — Head of the Department of Law and Criminology, Aberystwyth University, Wales; former Professor of Constitutional Law at Auckland University of Technology, New Zealand

JOHN FRASER — Master of Massey College, University of Toronto; author and journalist; co-chair, Friends of the Canadian Crown

LYNDA M. HAVERSTOCK — President and CEO of Tourism Saskatchewan; former Lieutenant Governor of Saskatchewan; former Leader of the Saskatchewan Liberal Party

ROBERT E. HAWKINS — Professor of Law, Johnson-Shoyama Graduate School of Public Policy, and former President, University of Regina; former Vice-President, Nipissing University

ANDREW HEARD — Associate Professor, Department of Political Science, Simon Fraser University

D. MICHAEL JACKSON — Research Fellow at the University of Regina; former Chief of Protocol of Saskatchewan; co-chair, Friends of the Canadian Crown

SERGE JOYAL — Senator, author, patron of the arts; former Secretary of State of Canada; co-chair of the 2010 Conference on the Crown

CHRISTOPHER MCCREERY — Private Secretary to the Lieutenant Governor of Nova Scotia; historian and commentator; former assistant to the Speaker and the Government Leader of the Senate

PATRICK J. MONAHAN — Professor and former Dean of Law at Osgoode Hall Law School and Provost, York University

JACQUES MONET — Historian, The Jesuit Archive of Canada; former President of Regis College and the University of Sudbury

HUGH SEGAL — Senator; Senior Policy Fellow, School of Policy Studies, Queen's University; co-chair of the 2010 Conference on the Crown

JENNIFER SMITH — Formerly Eric Dennis Memorial Professor of Government & Political Science, now Professor Emeritus, Dalhousie University

DAVID E. SMITH — Senior Policy Fellow, Johnson-Shoyama Graduate School of Public Policy, Universities of Saskatchewan and Regina; Emeritus Professor of Political Studies, University of Saskatchewan

1

INTRODUCTION

JENNIFER SMITH

La Couronne revêt une énorme importance symbolique et institutionnelle pour l'État canadien et la vie politique du pays. Cet ouvrage est le fruit de la conférence « La Couronne au Canada : réalités actuelles et choix futurs », tenue à Ottawa en juin 2010 sous la commandite des Amis de la Couronne canadienne, de l'Institut des relations intergouvernementales de l'Université Queen's, du Groupe canadien d'étude des questions parlementaires et de l'École d'études supérieures en politiques publiques Johnson-Shoyama des universités de la Saskatchewan et de Regina.

L'ouvrage vise les objectifs suivants : suppléer à l'extrême rareté des textes sur la Couronne dans les livres et documents servant à l'enseignement des régimes politiques ; mettre à jour les connaissances sur les récents développements qui touchent la Couronne ; examiner l'évolution des liens entre la Couronne et le gouverneur général, le pouvoir exécutif et le Parlement ; envisager enfin la Couronne dans sa dimension symbolique et sous l'angle des questions constitutionnelles.

La première section traite des aspects concrets de la Couronne et la deuxième de ses pouvoirs de réserve. Consacrée aux rapports entre la Couronne et la société civile, la troisième section aborde les questions de la liturgie, des titres honorifiques et des Premières Nations, avant de proposer une analyse comparative de la Couronne dans certains pays et un examen des enjeux actuels qui la concernent. Signalons que chacun des textes de l'ouvrage est brièvement décrit à la fin de l'introduction.

The fact that Canada is a constitutional monarchy is no small thing. The Canadian Crown is steeped in symbolism, to be sure, and in many respects it is this symbolic face that the public sees and knows. More than that, however, the institution is tightly woven into the fabric of the Canadian constitution and parliamentary system of government, itself loosely patterned on the British model. The symbolic light of the Crown illuminates many of the formal processes of parliamentary government. It also engages the conduct of government and politics.

Attentive to these matters, many people attended a conference held in Ottawa in June 2010 on "The Crown in Canada: Present Realities and

Future Options," an initiative of the Friends of the Canadian Crown in partnership with the Institute of Intergovernmental Relations at Queen's University. The Canadian Study of Parliament Group and the Johnson-Shoyama Graduate School of Public Policy at the Universities of Saskatchewan and Regina were co-sponsors of the event. This book is an outcome of the conference.

Neither was the conference, nor is the book, an exercise in debating the merits of a constitutional monarchy versus a republican government. Instead, the effort is to gain a comprehensive understanding of the Canadian Crown today from multiple perspectives: governmental, political, social and comparative. From the standpoint of the general public, there is a pressing need for such an effort. R. MacGregor Dawson's *The Government of Canada*, the last edition of which was issued in 1963, devoted a full chapter to "The Monarchy and the Governor General," the first of four on the executive. The standard textbooks used in universities today do not dwell on the subject, if they bother with it at all. Worse, the scant attention that is paid to it is focused on the "reserve" powers of the Crown, a subject invariably muddled by the authors. A young person bent on working out the mystery of the Crown in Canada has to resort to specialist literature.

The years of no coverage or misleading coverage supply a second reason for this book – getting up to date. Governmental institutions evolve, especially parliamentary institutions, which in many respects are governed by conventional understandings of the ways to do things as opposed to written rules. Why would anyone suppose that the institutional relationships of the Canadian Crown with the Canadian government have stood still? Of course they have not. Changes occur – some minor, some less so. Since the media take little notice of these matters, the upshot is that an important aspect of governance in Canada is evolving in the dark, as it were, instead of in the light of day. This book shines the light on the Crown in Canada, in the course of which exercise are revealed some institutional tensions. Here is yet a third reason for the book. Outside of the public glare, there is some jockeying going on between elected and appointed officials about the boundaries that distinguish the sphere of the prime minister from the sphere of the governor general, on the one hand, and the Queen, on the other. Several of the articles probe these tensions.

Finally, there is much-needed reflection in these pages on the meaning of the Crown in Canada. It is present *en passant*, for instance, in the articles that engage the constitutional role of the Crown. In others, however, it is the central purpose of the exercise, and a section of the book is devoted to them. For these reasons – recovering older understandings, tracking recent developments, analyzing current problems and ruminating on the symbolism of the Crown in our day – this book is long overdue. Accordingly, it is organized in a manner that first takes the reader through some concrete aspects of the Canadian Crown with which he or she might well be unaware, and then to a question with which there is bound to be some familiarity, the use of the reserve power, lately in the news. Next, the reader is invited to consider the relationship between the Crown and civil society in the matters of liturgy, honours and First Nations. Then the perspective shifts to the Crown in Australia and New Zealand in an effort to give the reader a comparative look at the institution. The articles in the final section engage the reader on issues that perplex the Crown in Canada today.

In the first section, the *Canadian* Crown is on offer. In "The Crown in the Provinces: Canada's Compound Monarchy," authors D. Michael Jackson and Lynda M. Haverstock remind us that the Canadian Crown is not confined to the national government but is also very much part of the provincial experience. Indeed, they use the phrase "provincial Crown" in their study of the evolution of the institution at this level of government. They demonstrate that the Crown and the Crown's representative for provincial purposes, the lieutenant-governor, were central to the effort of the provinces to secure independence in relation to the subjects assigned to them under the Constitution, and they draw some interesting parallels between this development and the role that the Crown could play in integrating a third order of aboriginal government in Confederation.

Shifting to the federal level of government, Christopher McCreery sets us straight on the *Letters Patent* that were issued by King George VI in 1947. They were the culmination of a long process whereby successive governors general were given increasing ability to act in the place of the Sovereign and exercise the royal prerogative without direct consultation with the king or queen of the day. As he points out, while King George VI thereby delegated considerable authority to the governor general, the action was accomplished in the form of enabling legislation, and particular areas of the royal prerogative were outlined as being beyond the scope of the governor general's duties, except in the most exceptional circumstances such as a regency or the incapacity or capture of the Sovereign by a foreign power. As McCreery emphasizes, the *Letters Patent* constitute a *delegation* of most powers, not a blanket abdication of the Sovereign's role in the Canadian state. It hardly needs to be said that there is food for thought in this observation.

The next section on the Crown and the Canadian Parliament opens with an article by David E. Smith, in which he asks a provocative question – does the Crown sustain Canadian democracy? The question is a complex one. Smith's answer takes the form of careful and erudite argumentation, and cannot be easily disclosed here. It awaits discerning readers. Suffice it to say that in the course of the analysis he pays close attention to the evolution of the office of the governor general, an office which, in his view, remains impartial in the eyes of the public and the politicians, even through the rigours of the prorogation crisis in 2008. Mention of the prorogation crisis, of course, raises the issue of the reserve powers of the Crown, a vital one that has long been a preoccupation of students of responsible, parliamentary government. And it is the preoccupation of the remaining three articles in the section.

Patrick Monahan, Andrew Heard and Robert Hawkins tackle the reserve powers, each from a different vantage point. In "The Constitutional Role of the Governor General," Monahan asks whether a governor general can refuse to act on the advice she receives from the prime minister – in other words, whether a governor general still possesses reserve powers. Having arrived at a positive answer to the question, he turns to the specific case of Governor General Jean's decision to accept Prime Minister Harper's 2008 request to prorogue Parliament and outlines the reasons why he thinks she was right to do so. Finally, while he does not support the idea of legislating restrictions on the ability of the prime minister to request prorogation of Parliament in the future, he sees merit in the creation of an authoritative statement of constitutional conventions similar to the Cabinet Manual in New Zealand.

Heard agrees with Monahan about there being a discretion in the office of the governor general to refuse to act on the advice of the prime minister, but he approaches the 2008 prorogation incident from a different angle. In "The Reserve Powers of the Crown: The 2008 Prorogation in Hindsight," he focuses on the issue of the viable alternative government. As he points out, rejection of Prime Minister Harper's request for prorogation would have exposed his government to a vote of loss of confidence in the House a mere two months after the general election, thereby generating the need for an alternative government without resorting to the polls. What is involved, he asks, in the effort to gauge whether a viable alternative government is available? He acknowledges that the ultimate collapse of the opposition coalition following the 2008 prorogation highlights the difficulties in assessing that viability, but at the same time explains why these alleged difficulties are overblown. And he stresses that we not lose sight of the central role of the House in generating and sustaining governments.

For his part, Hawkins sees in the 2008 prorogation controversy the vital question articulated in the title of his article, "Written Reasons and Codified Conventions in Matters of Prorogation and Dissolution." He notices that some analysts used the occasion to argue for the need to trim the discretion of the governor general by legislating rules to follow in specified circumstances. In other words, they want to codify what are now conventional rules of conduct. A notable proposal is to require that the governor general give reasons to explain the exercise of discretion. These publicized reasons would then be available for the purpose of holding the governor general accountable – in some fashion or other – and they would also serve as precedents to govern future occasions of the use of discretion. Hawkins doubts that the proposal is a good one. In analyzing it he makes a number of penetrating observations about the importance of maintaining the office of the governor general apart from the political arena and warns how easy it would be – unintentionally – to compromise the office in the name of reform.

In the third section of the book the point of departure is social and cultural rather than constitutional and political, beginning with Paul Benoit's meditation on "State Ceremonial: The Constitutional Monarch's Liturgical Authority." Discussions of the symbolism of the Crown today are cursory, to say the least. Not so Benoit's. In it he probes the basis of the attachment of citizens to their country, that is, their subjective engagement with it. In this inquiry, the state looms large. Benoit begins by sketching the historical arc through which states in the West came to differentiate themselves from organized religion and then came to play a religious or quasi-religious role in the sense of binding people together emotionally, even transporting them, however briefly, onto a higher plane of existence. He asks, what are the conventions that should govern this modern secular form of worship? By way of response, he makes some practical suggestions to enhance the two most important state ceremonies in Canada, the installation of the governor general and the opening of Parliament. He also suggests ways to refine the celebration of the three statutory holidays that pertain to constitutional development and defence, namely, Canada Day, Victoria Day and Remembrance Day. As he points out, these ceremonies and holidays involve the monarch as the embodiment of the state, and warrant the development of more thoughtful protocols that would help to stimulate a richer sense of Canadian citizenship.

Moving from the collective to the individual, Christopher McCreery writes about "The Crown and Honours: Getting It Right." As McCreery reminds us, the role of the Crown as the fount of all official honours in Canada is as old as its place in our constitutional structure. Since the days of Louis XIV, residents of Canada have been honoured by the Crown for their services with a variety of orders, decorations and medals. The position of the Crown in the modern Canadian honours system, he continues, remains firmly entrenched, notwithstanding attempts to marginalize it in recent years. Through this system, individuals receive official recognition for what are deemed as good works or, in the modern context, exemplary citizenship. McCreery traces the development of the modern honours system, paying particular attention to the central role of the Crown and Sovereign in it. He also highlights aspects of the system that, in his view, are ripe for reform. He wants us to get it right. So too does David Arnot, although in his case the subject is First Nations.

As Arnot writes in "The Honour of the First Nations – the Honour of the Crown," First Nations entered into treaties with the Crown. In so doing, they engaged the honour of the Crown. Arnot stresses that the notion of the honour of the Crown, while longstanding, is not antiquated. It was resurrected by the Supreme Court of Canada in *Guerin v. R.* in 1984, in which the court stated that the federal government has a fiduciary duty towards First Nations that requires it to rise above mere political expediency and instead act in a manner that lends credibility and honour to the Crown. In Arnot's view, the federal government has not reached this standard in the implementation of treaties with First Nations, and his is a clarion call for the government to do so.

Peter Boyce and Noel Cox, whose articles are grouped in the fourth section, on the Crown in comparative perspective, offer readers a look at the subject from the vantage points of Australia and New Zealand respectively. Writing on the Australian case, Boyce says that the discussion on monarchy there is focused almost exclusively on whether it should be abandoned; few express an interest in ways of enhancing public respect for the institution or strengthening its effectiveness within the system of government. At the same time, and in the wake of the failure of the constitutional referendum held in 1999 on the proposal to introduce a republican form of government, republican zeal currently languishes. In his account of the state of play on the Crown in Australia, Boyce makes a number of observations, among them that Australians appear to accept the need for a head of state with access to the reserve power and that their preference is an elected head of state. The country's political leaders, by contrast, do not find the idea of a directly elected president – an obvious competitor to themselves – to be an inviting prospect. Evidently the shift from a constitutional monarchy to a republic is not clear sailing. Meanwhile, according to Cox, in New Zealand the sails are not even hoisted.

According to Cox, the republican movement in New Zealand is fairly quiescent, and a clear majority supports the status quo of the constitutional monarchy, at least for now. Cox traces the evolution of a distinct New Zealand Crown (Queen Elizabeth as the Queen of New Zealand) and the nationalization of the office of the governor general marked by the appointments of New Zealanders to it. In his account, the three principal roles of the office involve community leadership, ceremonial duties and constitutional responsibilities. An interesting contrast between New Zealand and Canada emerges on the last role. According to Cox, the powers of the office in New Zealand flow largely from legislative enactments and regulations rather than the royal prerogative, as is the case in Canada. Cox is an unapologetic monarchist whose main fear for the Crown in New Zealand is its eventual demise at the hand of what he terms the "inevitability" argument, or the idea that the end of the monarchy is inevitable.

Readers head back to Canada, in the final section, to find Hugh Segal, Jacques Monet and Serge Joyal writing on issues that concern the Canadian Crown today. Segal's subject is Royal Assent, which is the third and final stage of the process in which a bill that has been passed by the House of Commons and the Senate becomes law. In the traditional ceremony, he says, the governor general, representing the Sovereign, is seated in the Senate chamber and there indicates approval for bills in the presence of the senators and members of the House who are summoned to the chamber to witness the event. In fact, he continues, Royal Assent often is executed by a judge of the Supreme Court of Canada. But Royal Assent is not the same thing as judicial assent, and Segal argues that pretending otherwise is problematic for two reasons, institutional and ceremonial. On the institutional front, he points out, the principle of judicial independence should preclude judges from standing in for the governor general and giving assent to a bill that later might comprise part of a dispute before them. On the ceremonial front, he continues, the use of judges is incoherent, since judges are not themselves part of the formal law-making process. He has some proposals to remedy a problem which might appear arcane, but in fact arises out of carelessness about the need to square ceremony with constitutional monarchy and responsible parliamentary government.

Monet's ceremonial and institutional concerns, by contrast, are painted on a very large canvas, since they involve the relationship between the Sovereign, the governor general and the prime minister. Monet would like to see the Sovereign play a larger role in the ceremonies of parliamentary government. He also sees a need to strengthen the office of the governor general in relation to the prime minister and in the eyes of the public, and suggests that this can be accomplished in several ways. One is to include more participants in the process by which the governor general is appointed rather than leaving it in the hands of the prime minister, where it stands now. Another is to lengthen the term of office of the governor general. And a third is to get prime ministers today to revert to the practice of their predecessors of paying regular visits to the governor general, visits that Monet is convinced are of value to both.

While Monet's recommendations on these issues imply a degree of optimism on the future of the Canadian Crown, Joyal's article that concludes the book strikes a more sombre note. Indeed, at the very outset he writes: "An institution like the Canadian Crown that is continually depreciated, either by design or through ignorance, will eventually atrophy. It will wither and die and with it an integral part of our constitution." Joyal cites evidence of two developments that support this observation. One is that the Queen herself rarely exercises any of the powers and prerogatives that are hers by right under the *Constitution Act, 1867*. The other is that the governor general, who does exercise these powers in her stead, is not always treated by the prime minister of the day with the respect that the office deserves. For example, like Monet, Joyal is concerned that prime ministers neglect to advise the governor general on the nation's business on anything like a regular basis.

After reviewing the evidence that Joyal assembles to demonstrate that the Crown – an essential element of the Constitution and a counterweight to the power of the prime minister – is a diminishing force, readers might be forgiven for wondering how to reconcile this pessimistic account with the more optimistic assessments present elsewhere in the book. I can offer no solution to that conundrum. However, armed with these articles, readers will find themselves better informed on the historical, institutional, ceremonial and symbolic dimensions of the Canadian Crown. Thus equipped, they can see for themselves the significance of the Canadian Crown in Canadian governance and in Canadian civil society. And they can scrutinize more critically any allegedly easy options on offer to replace the Canadian Crown with something else.

THE CROWN
IN CANADIAN
PERSPECTIVE

2

THE CROWN IN THE PROVINCES: CANADA'S COMPOUND MONARCHY

D. MICHAEL JACKSON AND LYNDA M. HAVERSTOCK

Si le texte original de l'Acte de l'Amérique du Nord britannique faisait des provinces des unités subordonnées dans une quasi-fédération, l'interprétation judiciaire du document a donné lieu à un régime fédéral plus authentique où les provinces forment en réalité des territoires co-souverains. Et c'est la reconnaissance des lieutenants-gouverneurs au titre de représentants directs de sa Majesté qui a été une des clés de cette évolution.

Après avoir graduellement perdu de son lustre pendant une bonne partie du XXe siècle, la charge de lieutenant-gouverneur a aujourd'hui retrouvé l'essentiel de son prestige et de son influence. Examinant le triple rôle constitutionnel, symbolique et collectif du lieutenant-gouverneur, ce chapitre propose des moyens d'enrichir la charge vice-royale provinciale. Par l'entremise du lieutenant-gouverneur, estiment en effet les auteurs, la Couronne provinciale est indispensable au statut constitutionnel des provinces. C'est d'ailleurs pourquoi il est erroné de qualifier le gouverneur général de « chef de l'État ».

L'institution de la Couronne relève conjointement des gouvernements central et provinciaux. Elle représente un intérêt vital pour la Province de Québec et une promesse de gouvernance pour les Premières Nations. Aussi les Canadiens doivent-ils se méfier des répercussions centralisatrices d'une forme républicaine de gouvernement.

Canada: a "compound monarchy" (Smith 1995, 11). This succinct phrase of David E. Smith, dean of Canadian scholars of the Crown, neatly sums up a key dimension of the constitutional monarchy in Canada. The Crown is an institution belonging jointly to the central and provincial governments and is crucial to the co-sovereign status of the provinces in Confederation. It is, therefore, of vital interest to the Province of Quebec and holds promise for First Nations' governance. This aspect of our nation's constitutional monarchy merits far more examination by scholars and policy makers than it has received.

Recent attention to the Crown in Canada has focused primarily on the office of the governor general. In part, this stems from a spotlight on the federal vice-regal reserve powers of dissolution and prorogation in 2008 and 2009 (Russell and Sossin 2009). In addition, there has been debate in the media about the appropriateness of using the term "head of state" in reference to the governor general. Few commentators have drawn attention to the Crown in the provinces and the lieutenant governors who embody it. In most cases, those who call for the end of the monarchy ignore its vital provincial dimension.

This chapter concerns the development of the provincial Crown in Canada's federal system. We make the case that the provincial Crown is integral to how Canada has evolved into a fascinating federation and that to ignore its significance diminishes thoughtful discourse on the nation's strengths.

THE PROVINCIAL CROWN – FROM SUBORDINATE TO COORDINATE

It is well known that the first prime minister of Canada, Sir John A. Macdonald, wanted a centralized state with most of the levers of power controlled by Ottawa. This was reflected in the text of the *British North America Act, 1867*, now the *Constitution Act, 1867*. The colonial governors had exercised most of the Sovereign's powers in the British North American colonies. But the new lieutenant governors lost some of those prerogatives. They were – and still are – appointed and removable by the governor general, not the Queen, on the advice of the federal prime minister and with no input from the provinces. They were and are paid by the federal government. True, they exercised some of the royal prerogative in their provinces: reading the speech from the throne, granting royal assent to legislation in the name of the Queen (not the governor general), signing orders-in-council, formally appointing the premier and swearing in the cabinet. Yet they were not considered as directly representing the Queen but rather as subordinate to the governor general and intended to function as federal officers. This role was reflected in their power of "reservation" of royal assent for the governor general (i.e., the federal cabinet) – a vice-regal equivalent of the federal power of disallowance of provincial legislation.

The nineteenth century historian Goldwin Smith was caustic about the monarchical institution in the Dominion and particularly its provincial manifestation. "The King who reigns and does not govern is represented by a Governor-General who does the same, and the Governor-General solemnly delegates his impotence to a puppet Lieutenant-Governor in each province" (Smith 1971, 118). Less bluntly, J.R. Mallory also noted the original subservience of the lieutenant governors to Ottawa:

> The office [of lieutenant governor] was conceived by the federal government as an important element in preserving the dominant role of Ottawa over

the provinces. Canadian federalism in the beginning was, in Sir Kenneth Wheare's phrase, "quasi-federal." It was clearly based on the old colonial model, with the government in Ottawa playing the role previously played by the British government … (Mallory 1991, 43).[1]

This quasi-colonial provincial vice-regal status was evident in symbols. Instead of the 21-gun salute to which the colonial governors had been and now the governor general was entitled on formal occasions, the lieutenant governors received a 15-gun salute, a respect grudgingly conceded by the British Admiralty only in 1905. Instead of the title "Excellency" enjoyed by their colonial predecessors and the governor general, the lieutenant governors had to be content with the half-baked "Your Honour," also used by magistrates.

Canada has changed considerably from the quasi-centralized state that was envisaged in 1867 – and so has the provincial vice-regal office. David E. Smith makes the important historical point that "although Canada's federation was conceived as a highly centralized form of government, the provinces inherited cohesive societies that pre-dated Confederation and monarchical forms of government to give those societies institutional expression" (Smith 1991, 471). To the "question of how to reconcile monarchy and federalism, a constitutional form pioneered by Canada in 1867," says Smith, "[t]he answer was to create a federation of compound monarchies, each province of which within its jurisdiction might claim the statutory and prerogative power necessary to realize its constitutional objectives" (Smith 2007, 27).

Judicial Activism

From the earliest days of Confederation, the courts had to rule on numerous federal-provincial disagreements over their respective powers. The delineation of legislative powers between Parliament and the provinces was reasonably clear in the *British North America Act*, although not clear enough to prevent frequent federal-provincial litigation. On the other hand, the delineation of prerogative and executive powers was not so clear. It was up to the courts to sort it out and this they did, generally asserting the co-ordinate, not subordinate, status of the provinces in the federation. While judgments of the provincial superior courts and the Supreme Court of Canada tended in this direction, it was the Judicial Committee of the Privy Council (JCPC) in London that most forcefully asserted provincial co-sovereignty.

---

[1] Mallory then notes, however, that this "'colonial' model was replaced by a more balanced federal system in which the provinces emerged as co-equal units in a 'classical' model of federalism" (ibid).

The legal cases referred to the Judicial Committee involved curious and apparently trivial matters such as alcohol and saloons, escheats, and the right to appoint Queen's Counsel. Between the 1880s and the 1920s, especially under the leadership of Lord Watson, and then of Viscount Haldane, the Judicial Committee interpreted the *British North America Act* in a way that tilted Canadian federalism from the centralized model of Sir John A. Macdonald to a much more decentralized form where the provinces enjoyed genuine autonomy. In describing this evolution, John Saywell points out that by the end of the nineteenth century "the principle of coordinate federalism was generally accepted" by the courts and that the Judicial Committee had "authoritatively asserted the independent status of the lieutenant governor as the representative of the crown for all purposes of provincial government"(Saywell 2002, 114). In short, provincial autonomy revolved around the office of lieutenant governor.

In 1883, a landmark ruling by the JCPC in *Hodge v. The Queen* established that provincial legislatures were co-sovereign and not delegates of parliament, and that provincial legislation was not subordinate to federal legislation.[2] But if the *legislative* autonomy of the provinces was settled fairly early after Confederation, their *executive* sovereignty was far slower to be affirmed. Initially, like the Canadian Supreme Court, the Judicial Committee and British officials were reluctant to concede the status of the provincial executive. Just as they were unwilling to grant the lieutenant governors 21-gun salutes, so they at first "refused to admit that such officials could exercise the prerogative powers of the Crown – powers symbolic of sovereignty" (Romney 1999, 111). The arguments were based on the fact that, under the *British North America Act,* lieutenant governors were appointed by the federal governor-in-council and not by the Queen, as had been the case with the colonial governors (and has, since 1901, been the appointment process with Australian governors). Therefore the contention was that the lieutenant governor, unlike the governor general, did not directly represent the Sovereign and could not exercise the royal prerogative in her name.

It was not a minor point – on the contrary – and provincial autonomists quickly grasped its importance. As Saywell puts it, "[i]f the crown was represented directly within the provincial government, coordinate rather than subordinate status would be achieved in the executive branch as it was in the legislative" (Saywell 2002, 50). The protracted dispute over the right to confer the honour of Queen's Counsel (QC) on the legal profession illustrates, at one and the same time, the basic tension between the centralist and provincial perspectives on federalism, the key role in that dispute of the office of lieutenant governor, and the apparently trivial nature of

---

[2] "Within these limits [of section 92 of the BNA Act] the local legislature is supreme" (Olmsted 1954, I, 199).

issues leading to constitutional litigation. In an 1879 split decision, *Lenoir v. Ritchie*, the Supreme Court of Canada declared that Nova Scotia legislation of 1874 providing for the provincial appointment of QCs was *ultra vires* "because the lieutenant-governor had no right to exercise, and the legislature had no right to confer, this prerogative power" (Vipond 1991, 66). The lieutenant governor, the court declared, was a federal officer and not a personal representative of the Sovereign; furthermore, the Queen did not form part of the provincial legislatures and the provinces were subordinate to the Dominion. For the defenders of provincial autonomy, it was imperative to challenge *Lenoir v. Ritchie*.

The opportunity arose in 1888: the premier and attorney general of New Brunswick, A.G. Blair, argued in *The Provincial Government of New Brunswick v. The Liquidators of the Maritime Bank* that the provincial Crown had the prerogative right of precedence over other creditors in the case of the failed Maritime Bank. The executive prerogative in the person of the lieutenant governor, he maintained, was co-extensive with the division of powers between federal and provincial jurisdictions. The Supreme Court of New Brunswick agreed.

The case was appealed to the Supreme Court of Canada. Surprisingly, in view of that court's recent record, it upheld the New Brunswick ruling in 1889. The case then proceeded to the Judicial Committee of the Privy Council. The resulting judgement in 1892 of the JCPC, in *Liquidators of the Maritime Bank v. Receiver General of New Brunswick*, was as much a landmark ruling as *Hodge v. The Queen* had been nine years earlier. Lord Watson stated that the "object of the [BNA] Act was neither to weld the provinces into one nor to subordinate provincial governments to a central authority" (Olmsted 1954, I, 268). He "summarily dismissed" the argument that "Confederation had severed the connection between the crown and the provinces" (Saywell 2002, 127) and ruled conclusively that, "a lieutenant-governor, when appointed, is as much a representative of Her Majesty, for all purposes of provincial government as the Governor General himself is, for all purposes of Dominion government" (Olmsted 1954, I, 270). In a somewhat anticlimactic JCPC decision six years later, Lord Watson finally confirmed that the prerogatives of the provincial Crown did indeed include the right to appoint Queen's Counsel as had been asserted since 1872 by the Province of Ontario and confirmed in a unanimous judgement of the Ontario Court of Appeal in 1896. As late as this date, in appealing the Ontario decision, the attorney general of Canada claimed that "the Lieutenant-Governor of Ontario does not entirely represent the Crown in respect of the prerogative right of the Crown" (ibid., I, 412). The JCPC disagreed: "Their Lordships [...] do not entertain any doubt that the Parliament of Ontario had ample authority to give the Lieutenant-Governor power to confer precedence by patent upon such members of the bar of the province as he may think fit" (ibid., I, 416–17). Ontario's fierce defence of its right to appoint Queen's Counsel is ironic, given that the province abolished appointments of QCs in the 1980s.

In an interesting decision in 1919, Watson's successor, Viscount Haldane, ruled that Manitoba's *Initiative and Referendum Act* was invalid because it conflicted with the lieutenant governor's powers: "the Lieutenant-Governor who represents the Sovereign is part of the Legislature." [...] "[The law] compels him to submit a proposed law to a body of voters totally distinct from the Legislature of which he is the constitutional head" (ibid., II, 111). Contrary to the centralist view that the lieutenant governor was a subordinate officer of the dominion, Lord Haldane referred to "his position as directly representing the Sovereign in the province" – hence "the exclusion of his office from the power conferred on the Provincial Legislature to amend the constitution of the Province" (ibid., II, 110).

The culmination of the JCPC's pro-provincial jurisprudence came in 1925, in *Toronto Electric Commissioners v. Snider*, where Lord Haldane went so far as to say that the provinces were "in a sense like independent kingdoms with very little Dominion control over them" (*Snider*, 116) and "should be autonomous places as if they were autonomous kingdoms" (ibid., 166). This would be music to the ears of the Quebec nationalists today, if they supported the monarchy!

Decline and Revival of the Lieutenant Governor

It is ironic that, in the eighty years or so following the *Liquidators of the Maritime Bank* case, the prestige and profile of the lieutenant governors steadily declined despite their enhanced juridical status. There was even talk, especially in the Depression years of the 1930s, of abolishing the office of lieutenant governor as redundant and useless, although this was a constitutional non-starter.

The framers of Confederation and the *British North America Act* had expressly identified the lieutenant governor as a federal officer, a role in their view more significant than that of provincial representative of the Crown. Their power of reservation of royal assent for the pleasure of the governor general was a clear centralizing device to permit the federal government to override provincial legislation. And it was by no means an idle threat. Saywell records that between 1867 and 1937 sixty-nine provincial bills were reserved, usually, though not always, on the instruction of the federal government, the *ultra vires* legislation of William Aberhart's Social Credit government in Alberta being the last target (Saywell 1986, 192–227). After this, reservation was considered obsolete – though in 1961, there was a one-time revival of the power in Saskatchewan (Jackson 2001, 53–54).[3]

---

[3] *Reservation* is not to be confused with the vice-regal power of *refusing* royal assent. Royal assent has never been refused by a Canadian governor general since Confederation. However, lieutenant governors cast their vice-regal veto no less than 38 times between 1870 and 1945 – but almost always on the advice or with the concurrence of their cabinets as a handy tool to avoid awkward legislation. There was one exception, when the lieutenant

During the early years of Confederation the lieutenant governors could, and frequently did, act as the eyes and ears and agents of the federal government. Yet this activist role on Ottawa's behalf all but disappeared early in the twentieth century. Prime ministers were able to use their national parties and their own ministers, senators and members of parliament, as well as the media, to communicate their policies. Eventually, intergovernmental conferences and bureaucracies provided formal channels for federal-provincial relations. The role of the lieutenant governor as federal agent was eclipsed even more quickly than that of the instrument of reservation of royal assent. By the mid-twentieth century, the lieutenant governor had caught up in fact and perception to the legal definition in the 1892 *Maritime Bank* JCPC decision: the provincial representative of the Sovereign.

What did not change was the federal government's *appointment* of the lieutenant governor. It has always been a jealously guarded prerogative of the prime minister who, for many decades, usually named supporters of his own party as a reward for past services or loyalty. In the early years of Confederation, when the office of lieutenant governor was relatively powerful, it was therefore seen as more prestigious, worth seeking, and characterized by high-profile appointees. A century later, with the office less coveted, it was no longer as desirable among those with political ambition. Current or former politicians predominated among the nominees. Accordingly, they were often treated as federal interlopers rather than as impartial viceroys by provincial governments, especially those whose political stripe differed from the party in power in Ottawa. Although the vice-regal position was protected by the *British North America Act*, some premiers showed overt hostility to it. The notorious Mitch Hepburn in Ontario threatened to starve out the lieutenant governor and closed Toronto's Government House, Chorley Park, in 1937. Alberta's William Aberhart did the same in Edmonton in 1938, no doubt in retaliation for Ottawa's use of disallowance and reservation. Saskatchewan's first CCF premier, T.C. Douglas, closed Government House in Regina in 1945[4] and Saskatchewan became thereafter one of the most negative provinces with respect to the vice-regal office (Jackson 2001 and 2009). By the 1960s, the office was dwindling in significance in most provinces.

But the 1970s saw a shift: the lieutenant governors started recovering from obscurity. This coincided with the increased clout of the provinces

---

governor of Prince Edward Island withheld assent from a bill on his own initiative in 1945 – and that was, interestingly, given the legislation referred to the JCPC in the 1880s, a liquor bill! It was the last time the power has been used (Saywell 1986, 221–23).

    [4] Ironically, Quebec maintained its Government House until 1997, when the Parti Québécois administration of Lucien Bouchard closed it. La "Maison Dunn" had been purchased for the vice-regal residence as recently as 1967 by Union Nationale Premier Daniel Johnson to replace historic Bois-de-Coulonge, which had been destroyed by fire in 1966.

in Confederation, at least those in central and western Canada. Perhaps the relatively low profile of the governors general following Roland Michener's tenure (1967–74) provided the climate for raised visibility of the lieutenant governors. A key factor, however, appeared to be the people selected for the office. Individuals from varied backgrounds were appointed, many without ties to the governing party in Ottawa. By 1974, the first woman was appointed in Ontario and by 2010, all provinces except Newfoundland and Labrador had had female appointees. One observer considers that the appointment of women, starting in Canada two decades earlier than Australia, "has helped transform both the image and the priorities of a lieutenant-governor" (Boyce 2008, 97).

THE CONTEMPORARY ROLE OF THE LIEUTENANT GOVERNOR

The Constitutional Role

In Canada, "[s]overeignty is vested in one individual, the reigning monarch, acting in Parliament for some purposes and in the provincial Legislatures for others" (Jackson 2001, 49). Thus, the lieutenant governor is at the constitutional apex of the province, holding royal prerogative powers in the name of the Queen, and is, so to speak, the legal incarnation of provincial autonomy in Confederation. And he or she acts as a constitutional umpire and guarantor – the role emphasized by recent commentators on the office of governor general.

The Reserve Powers

The vice-regal reserve powers of dissolution, prorogation, and dismissal, like other aspects of the provincial Crown, have not received much attention. Nor have these powers been used as frequently by Canadian lieutenant governors as by their Australian counterparts (Boyce 2008). However, Saywell (1986) recounts a number of examples of dismissal or refusal of dissolution in the early decades of Confederation. The reserve powers came into play in two minority government situations (Saskatchewan, 1929 and Ontario, 1985), where the lieutenant governor called on the leader of another party to form government rather than dissolving the legislature and springing another election.

Presently, provincial vice-regal intervention is usually low key and confidential. But a lieutenant governor of British Columbia, David Lam, was evidently prepared to use the prerogative of dismissal if a disgraced and compromised premier did not resign. This occurred in 1991. With his government nearing the end of its legal five-year mandate, Premier William Vander Zalm was investigated for allegedly having contravened his own conflict-of-interest guidelines. The premier was contemplating a request for dissolution to out-manoeuvre a cabinet revolt. Discreet pressure was applied by the office of the lieutenant governor and Premier Vander Zalm visited Dr. Lam to resign after conclusions of the investigation were made public. It is a telling example of how the vice-regal office can play an effective constitutional role.[5]

To be Consulted, to Encourage, and to Warn

The nineteenth century British constitutional expert, Walter Bagehot, made the well-known and oft-cited statement that the Sovereign (and thus her representative) has three rights: to be consulted, to encourage, and to warn – presumably through regular meetings with the first minister. The Sovereign meets weekly with the prime minister in the United Kingdom. In Canada, governors general met regularly with the prime ministers in the 1960s and 1970s, but the practice seems to have fallen into abeyance. Practices in the Canadian provinces and the Australian states vary considerably. In Australia, the governor of Queensland and the administrator of the Northern Territory only meet with their respective premiers as and when required. However, the governor of Western Australia meets with the premier every two months and since 1995 the governors of Tasmania have enjoyed regular monthly meetings.

In Canada, the lieutenant governors of British Columbia and Nova Scotia meet regularly with their premiers. In Prince Edward Island, the two meet quarterly. By contrast, Manitoba lieutenant governors and premiers have not had meetings since the 1960s. Nor do regular meetings occur in Ontario, Quebec or Alberta. A similar disconnect once existed between premiers and lieutenant governors in Saskatchewan. However, after Roy Romanow assumed office as Saskatchewan premier in 1991, Lieutenant Governor Sylvia Fedoruk asked to see him to discuss a problem over granting special warrants. The issue cemented the relationship between lieutenant governor and premier, with regular monthly meetings becoming the norm. Subsequent premiers have had no hesitation in continuing the practice. Brad Wall, premier since 2007, has praised the meetings as an opportunity to seek "solace and counsel" from the lieutenant governor (Jackson 2009, 21).

The Community and Ceremonial Role

In Canada, as in Australia and New Zealand, the vice-regal office has increasingly focused on civic or moral leadership and in the promotion

---

[5] The episode has been described to the authors by a private source and is summarized in McWhinney 2005, 110–12. An analogous intervention of the governor of Queensland, Australia, is recounted in ibid., 112–14. Other examples of the exercise of vice-regal discretion in Australia can be found in Boyce 2008.

of what are perceived as national values. Canadian lieutenant governors have extended their reach into "civil society," the intricate web of non-governmental organizations and worthy causes. Lieutenant governors in Saskatchewan and Ontario have emphasized outreach to Aboriginal peoples. The vice-regal affinity for the First Nations derives, in part, from their traditionally close connection with the Crown dating back to the nineteenth century treaties with Queen Victoria. Although this relationship has been primarily with the monarch, and with the federal Crown represented by the governor general, the lieutenant governors have been playing a more prominent role.

James Bartleman, lieutenant governor of Ontario from 2002 to 2007 and himself a First Nations person, organized a highly successful campaign to promote literacy among Aboriginal youth in northern Ontario by collecting books for them from across the province. In Saskatchewan, Lynda Haverstock, lieutenant governor there from 2000 to 2006, noted community health issues arising from the large number of stray dogs in northern Aboriginal communities. She organized a spay-neutering program, obtaining *pro bono* veterinary services and engaging local youth to participate in pre- and post-operative care. Her successor, Gordon Barnhart, launched a Lieutenant Governor's Leadership Forum for youth in 2007. The Forum introduces promising young people from across the province to major figures in the public and private sectors. Half of the participants are from northern Saskatchewan where Aboriginals predominate.

Honours – More than One Crown?

The Crown plays another leadership role by virtue of another royal prerogative – presenting honours to deserving citizens. In a monarchy, the Sovereign is the "fount of honours." This means that in Canada, the Queen is the ultimate source of recognition by the state. Given the dynamics of Canadian federalism, it was not surprising that, following the creation of the Order of Canada in 1967, the provinces entered the field of honours. This occurred despite active opposition by the federal government, especially through the Chancellery of Honours at Rideau Hall. Hearkening back to the legal struggles over the royal prerogative a century earlier, Saskatchewan argued that provinces could, indeed, create honours of the Crown and that the office of queen's counsel, confirmed, as we have seen, by the Judicial Committee of the Privy Council for the provinces, was the first nationally recognized provincial honour (Jackson 2009, 25–27).

Ontario established the first modern provincial honour in 1973 – the Ontario Medal for Good Citizenship. This was soon followed by the Ontario Police and Firefighters Bravery Medals, all with insignia bearing the Crown and presented by the lieutenant governor despite objections from Ottawa. Quebec established the first provincial order, *l'Ordre national du Québec* in 1984; the Saskatchewan Order of Merit followed in 1985, the

Order of Ontario in 1986, and the Order of British Columbia in 1989. All ten provinces now have orders and half of them – Ontario, Saskatchewan, Alberta, British Columbia, and Newfoundland and Labrador – have decorations and medals as well. In all provinces except Quebec, provincial honours come under the aegis of the Crown and are presented by the lieutenant governor. They have had the indubitable effect of raising the profile of the vice-regal representatives and that of the provincial Crown (McCreery 2005, 121–40, Jackson 2007, 115–19, and Haverstock 2007, 158–61). More importantly, they have ensured that worthy individuals receive appropriate recognition for their outstanding contributions to society.

IMPROVEMENTS TO THE PROVINCIAL VICE-REGAL OFFICE

In the light of the positive developments noted above, could the provincial vice-regal office be improved or reformed?

The first issue is the selection and appointment of the lieutenant governor. As previously noted, this is entirely the prerogative of the federal prime minister. The provinces have no official role to play in the choice of their own vice-regal representative. At most, they may be informally consulted before a final decision is made. Although the Australian system of appointment of governors by the Queen on the advice of the premiers may seem appealing (Twomey 2006), it is impractical in Canada. No one has the appetite for seeking a constitutional amendment to make this happen, even if Buckingham Palace could be convinced to accept it. Instead, we suggest that the federal and provincial governments work out a genuine and mutually acceptable method of consultation on the appointment.

The provinces could present a short list of potential names to the prime minister. This list should be prepared through consultation between the premier and, for example, the leader of the opposition, the speaker of the legislative assembly, chief justices and chief judge, senior Aboriginal leaders, and possibly former lieutenant governors, acting as a "college of elders." A promising development occurred in 2009 when Prime Minister Stephen Harper publicly announced that, in selecting Philip Lee as lieutenant governor of Manitoba, he had directly consulted with the premier and leader of the opposition, both of whom expressed their support. The prime minister pursued this policy in the appointment of Graydon Nicholas as lieutenant governor of New Brunswick later the same year. Harper's pragmatic, inclusive approach may well be the solution to the conundrum of provincial vice-regal appointments.

The symbols of the provincial vice-regal offices should also reflect today's reality that lieutenant governors are royal representatives in co-sovereign jurisdictions in Confederation. Lieutenant governors should be entitled to a twenty-one gun salute. They should also have the title

"Excellency." Both of these simply require administrative decisions like the one made by the federal government in the 1980s to grant the title "Your Honour" to the spouse of the lieutenant governor.

These changes are the prerogative of the federal government. Internally, what could the provinces do to enhance their vice-regal offices? First, lieutenant governors need more resources. Peter Boyce points to the practical constraints on the Canadian vice-regal offices in terms of budget and staff. Lieutenant governors' private secretaries lack the bureaucratic status of the Australian official secretaries. The smallest Australian vice-regal establishment has a bigger budget than the largest Canadian one. This limited support means that Canadian lieutenant governors are restricted in "the quality of available in-house advice on constitutional matters, as well as an understanding of important precedents in protocol" (Boyce 2008, 113). Furthermore, in the past, individuals appointed to the positions of governor general or lieutenant governor were financially independent. This is no longer the norm and some would say that the result has enhanced rather than diminished the role. There are monetary considerations when a vice-regal representative leaves such a high profile post and cannot simply resume "life as usual."

The relationship of vice-regal representatives with their first ministers is, or should be, a vital one. As has been noted, regular meetings have continued between four Saskatchewan lieutenant governors and three premiers since 1991, a practice that has been publicly recognized as of immense value to both parties. Commenting on the monthly meetings between the governors and premiers of Tasmania in Australia, the vice-regal official secretary in that state said that three recent governors "have each been eminently qualified to provide reasoned, impartial advice."[6] It is unfortunate that so few provincial governments have followed the examples of Saskatchewan and Tasmania. We submit that it would greatly enhance not only the vice-regal office but the entire political process if they did.

THE CROWN AND FEDERALISM

Strengthening the provincial vice-regal office as suggested above is a logical concomitant of the status of the provinces in Canada's compound monarchy. Given the constitutional evolution led by, but not limited to, the Judicial Committee of the Privy Council, the Crown in Canada is not the exclusive preserve of the federal parliament – far from it. Even if centralists hostile to the monarchy try to discount the long-standing

---

[6] Letter to the authors from Anne Parker, Official Secretary to the Governor of Tasmania, 9 December 2009.

provincial role in the Crown, the more recent confirmation of that role in the *Constitution Act, 1982* is conclusive. The *Act* specifies in section 41 that any constitutional amendment "in relation to the Office of the Queen, the Governor-General and the Lieutenant-Governor of a province" requires the agreement of both Houses of Parliament and the legislatures of all ten provinces. "The plain intent of section 41 is to signal that the Crown in Canada is owned jointly by the country and the provinces," said Ian Holloway, then Dean of Law at the University of Western Ontario.[7] "For the federal government [on its own] to try to republicanize Canada through the back door," he adds, "would be [...] contrary to the inferred principles underlying section 41" (Valpy 2009, A19).

If, as we have argued, the Crown is essential to the status of the provinces in Confederation, the provinces are equally essential to the status of the Crown in Canada. The Canadian Crown is a "50-50 deal" and the provinces are one-half of that deal. What then does the term "head of state" signify in Canada?

Who Is the "Head of State"?

The longstanding debate about the Canadian "head of state" surfaced again in 2009, when Governor General Michaëlle Jean referred to herself as such in a speech in Paris. In response to media inquiries, Rideau Hall maintained that the governor general was *de facto* head of state and cited the 1947 Letters Patent of King George VI as evidence.

Indeed, these letters have been interpreted by some as making the governor general the Canadian head of state. But a more nuanced view of the Letters Patent seems appropriate. For one thing, the Letters Patent do not assert that the governor general is "head of state." Rather, they empower that person to *exercise* the powers of the Sovereign, who presumably remains their source of legitimacy. In other words, the powers are delegated.[8] It is more accurate to say, in the words of a recent federal government publication, that the Letters Patent "authorized and empowered the Governor General to *exercise most of the royal prerogatives in right of Canada* [our emphasis]" (MacLeod 2008, 35).

While the Letters Patent apply to the Sovereign in right of Canada as a whole, *the governor general does not and cannot exercise the royal prerogative in provincial jurisdiction*. In Canada, the "headship of state" is tripartite. When Rideau Hall promotes the governor general as "head of state," it is effectively pushing the Queen out and the lieutenant governors down. This Ottawa-style centralization of the Crown is not the Canadian way:

---

[7] Communication to the authors.

[8] See the chapter by Christopher McCreery in the present volume, "Myth and Misunderstanding: The Origins and Meaning of the Letters Patent Constituting the Office of the Governor General, 1947."

the genius of the Crown is that it balances the roles of Sovereign, governor general and lieutenant governor to incarnate Canada's federal and parliamentary polity. Smith points out that the term head of state in any case "is inappropriate where there is a sovereign. The concept of state may be fine in France, but legally it does not apply to a monarchical system such as ours" (Smith 2010, 3). In his thesis on the Crown in New Zealand, Noel Cox elaborates on the "theory of sovereignty" in a constitutional monarchy: "The Crown is important legally in the Westminster constitutional system because it holds the conceptual place held by the State in those legal systems derived from or influenced by the Roman civil law" (Cox 2008, 35). Ironically, but not surprisingly, in 1978 Quebec Premier René Lévesque was at the forefront of the premiers in resisting the Trudeau government's Bill C-60, which purported to make the governor general to all intents and purposes the head of state.

The Conundrum of Quebec

The office of lieutenant governor in Quebec has had a rocky road in recent years, with concerted attempts made by sovereigntists to discredit the office and little or no effort by federalists to defend it. In our view, this is unfortunate, not only for the institution of the provincial Crown but also for the best interests of Quebec.

Historically, going back as far as the British conquest of 1759, the Crown was, at first grudgingly, then more positively, viewed as an instrument of survival for francophones isolated on an anglophone continent. It was under the umbrella of the Crown – it was thanks to the flexible, adaptable, evolving system of constitutional monarchy – that democratic government eventually prevailed in nineteenth century Canada without the convulsions of revolution or civil war. And monarchy in Quebec was scarcely a British innovation. Franco-Ontarian historian Jacques Monet, writing of the surrender of New France in 1760 by the last French royal governor, Pierre de Vaudreuil, to the first British governor, Jeffrey Amherst, says "... il lui légua l'idéal et les anciennes traditions de notre patrimoine monarchique." The second British governor, James Murray, "accepta ce legs de la Nouvelle-France," while the third, Sir Guy Carleton, "travailla à le faire passer dans l'Acte du Québec, lequel allait garantir la nationalité et les institutions du Canada français" (Monet 1979, 27–29).

The *Constitutional Act* of 1791 provided Quebec with its first elected assembly ever, under the British Crown. Janet Ajzenstat notes how prominent French-Canadian leaders saw this British constitution as a prime asset for their own governance. Pierre Bédard was the first leader of the "French party" in the Lower Canada assembly and first editor of the journal of political opinion *Le Canadien*. Writing in 1805, he vigorously opposed the policies of British officials, which in his view subverted democratic institutions and free speech, and he was imprisoned at one point for his outspoken opposition. But Bédard "never relinquished his confidence in British institutions. After his release from jail, he argued that what had happened ought not to diminish French Canadians' admiration for their Constitution" (Ajzenstat 2007, 128). In 1808, while "urging his constituents to stand firm on their rights under the Constitution to elect representatives who would foil the governor's political plots, he did not fail to remind them to honour and obey the governor as the king's representative" (ibid., 140).

Indeed, French-Canadians looked to the Crown as the protector of their minority rights – their identity, language, legal system and religion. A prominent Quebec leader, Hector Langevin, in 1849 hailed Lord Elgin "qui représente parmi nous notre auguste souverain et qui se fait le gardien de nos droits constitutionnels " (Monet 1969, 355). After all, it was Lord Elgin who, in implementing responsible government, "a donné de sa propre initiative, dès 1849, une sanction toute royale à l'utilisation officielle de la langue française au Canada" (Monet 1976, 30). In the 1860s, French-Canadian leaders showed complete solidarity with their English-speaking colleagues in wishing Canada to remain a monarchy under Queen Victoria at the time of Confederation. In the course of Canadian history, illustrious names like de Salaberry and Vanier have featured among the most loyal supporters of the Sovereign and the Crown.

This positive attitude towards the Crown has regrettably dissipated since the 1960s. Quebec opponents of the 1964 royal tour blamed Ottawa for using it as a centralizing tool to "détourner les sympathies provinciales pour les orienter vers Ottawa … La reine, instrument des centralisateurs!" (Smith 1999, 230). Jacques Monet commented in 1976 that "depuis une quinzaine d'années la Couronne est associée au Québec avec un colonialisme désuet et un ordre social démodé" (Monet 1976, 30). We respectfully ask Québécois to think again. Quebec has benefited enormously from the Canadian compound monarchy. The office of lieutenant governor is far from representing "un colonialisme désuet"; the Queen is far from being "un instrument des centralisateurs." On the contrary, the Crown in right of Quebec is a powerful instrument of co-sovereignty in Confederation.

The First Nations

Today, we are well aware of how Canada's indigenous inhabitants were displaced and marginalized by European colonization. Some are of the opinion that the ideal and intent of fair treatment for native peoples were always there, but thwarted by poor implementation and even interference. The ideal could be found in the Crown. The Royal Proclamation of 1763 issued by King George III recognized Aboriginal ownership of their lands. It firmly stated the principle that European settlement could only proceed by treaty with the First Nations. The Proclamation of 1763 is considered to this day by many First Nations, says David Arnot, "as their Magna Carta for inherent rights: it protected First Nations lands and recognized First Nations peoples as nations. It established that a treaty with the Crown was the sole means by which the British could acquire land and excluded private interests from such transactions" (Arnot 2009, 226).

A hundred years hence, based on that charter, came the series of nineteenth century treaties which defined the relationship between the First Nations and the settlers. The treaties were and are a solemn covenant, "the promise to reconcile differences between First Nations and the Queen through a treaty relationship made before the Creator in the name of the Queen and in the name of First Nations" (ibid., 236). The direct, treasured relationship between the First Nations and the Sovereign stems from the treaties. It is true that some aspects of those treaties are finally being recognized only today. Interestingly, though, the Crown has always been seen by First Nations as the symbol and guarantor of the treaties signed with Queen Victoria. A surprising number of First Nations fly the Union Jack at their ceremonies. A Saskatchewan lieutenant governor has the privilege of taking part in numerous treaty days, during which either the governor or a member of the RCMP in red serge uniform pays the symbolic annuity payment of five dollars in the name of the Queen to the members of the First Nation.

In New Zealand, Noel Cox emphasizes the vitally important relationship of the Maori people with the Crown through the landmark 1840 Treaty of Waitangi. This relationship is even more intense than that in Canada, because a single treaty encompasses all the indigenous peoples. Indeed, the Treaty of Waitangi is one of the constitutional building blocks of New Zealand, conferring legitimacy on the Crown – which, in turn, validates for the Maori people the legitimacy of the current legal and political system in their country. Says Cox: "It continues to be the case, and in fact this appears increasingly imperative to Maori, that *the Crown is not only something other than the government of the day* [our emphasis], but also that the Crown is able to function in such a manner as to hold the government to the guarantees made under the Treaty of Waitangi" (Cox 2008, 86). Any move to eliminate the monarchy would, therefore, very much impinge on the interests of the Maori in New Zealand, just as it would on First Nations in Canada.

In an interesting essay on Aboriginal self-government within the Canadian confederation, Greg Poelzer and Ken Coates believe that amidst conflicting and divisive opinions, the Crown offers a solution. "Institutions that predate Canada that Aboriginal and non-Aboriginal Canadians share, and that can serve as organizing principles for building a new future, do exist. In fact, the most elemental building block of Canadian political institutions, the Crown, may well provide the answer" (Poelzer and Coates 2006, 162). Echoing and emphasizing Smith's seminal work, the authors point out that "the existence of a divided Crown, federal and provincial, and of provinces led by their own powerful executives in possession of sovereignty in their own right, made Canada a compounded monarchy" (ibid., 163). This could be the key to finding a rightful and appropriate place for First Nations as a third order of government.

However, Poelzer and Coates assert that for such an approach to work, two things are required: non-Aboriginal Canadians must recognize the special relationship of the First Nations with the Crown; and Aboriginals must come to terms with the divided Crown and compound monarchy in Canada. This latter point is important. First Nations have a history of looking only to the imperial and then the federal Crown as their sole interlocutor, given that section 91 of the *British North America Act* assigns responsibility for Indians and their lands to Ottawa. Poelzer and Coates write that First Nations leaders "in many ways operate with a vision of Canada frozen in 1867" (ibid., 165) before the judicial-driven evolution to compound monarchy changed that vision. "However," they point out, "much of the authority that First Nations governments seek, whether concurrent, or concurrent with paramountcy, are actually provincial powers" (ibid., 165), such as Crown lands, natural resources, health and education. What has been called "treaty federalism" would involve "extending our current practice of federalism and of recognizing the common institution of the Crown" (ibid., 166).

This is a work in progress. Much more needs to be done as the federal government, the provinces and the First Nations grapple with the implications of a third order of government. However, the tried and proven flexibility of the Canadian compound monarchy holds much promise. First Nations are paying increasing attention to the lieutenant governor and the provincial Crown. The Province of British Columbia was a party to the Nisga'a Agreement and Saskatchewan has been a party to the treaty land entitlement process in that province. The traditional, historic, deeply rooted relationship of the First Nations with the Crown and the Sovereign is, then, not archaic folklore or mere sentimentality. It is the grounding of a dynamic future for the Aboriginal peoples in Confederation.

CONCLUSION

The Crown was instrumental in the evolution of the Canadian state towards true federalism. This was in spite of the initial constraints of the original constitutional texts and the centralizing thrust of the first federal governments and some subsequent ones. It is, in large measure, attributable to the Crown and the lieutenant governor that, through the courts, the provinces, and notably Quebec, secured their jurisdictional autonomy. The same potential now exists for integrating a "third order" of Aboriginal government in Confederation.

In Australia, hesitations associated with the adoption of a republican form of government come in part from a perceived threat to federalism.

David E. Smith quotes a former chief justice of the High Court, Sir Harry Gibbs, who contended that "[t]he legal complexities associated with the change to a republic involve difficult questions that go to the very heart of federation" (Smith 1999, 220). In Canada, "[w]hether or not tension between republicanism and federalism is endemic is not the point," says Smith. "For a country like Canada, where federalism is the bedrock of national existence, the possibility that the two systems are incompatible is enough to prompt unease" (ibid., 221).

Senator Serge Joyal, in his chapter in this volume, warns of the concentration of power in the office of the prime minister of Canada and its repercussions for the office of governor general. It is thus worth emphasizing that the autonomy of the provinces, anchored in the provincial Crown, serves as an essential counter-balance to this development. It is impossible to predict the fate of this balancing mechanism in a republican system.

For our part, we believe that Canadians should reject a change of this magnitude to Canada's political culture and institutions. Such a fundamental shift holds the risk of far-ranging, unintended consequences to the political order. Indeed, we assert that the advantages of the present system of constitutional monarchy far outweigh its defects. Given past history, the Canadian provinces, like the Australian states, should be very wary indeed of the centralizing implications of a republic.

REFERENCES

Ajzenstat, J. 2007. *The Canadian Founding: John Locke and Parliament.* Montreal and Kingston: McGill-Queen's University Press.

Arnot, D. 2009. "We Are All Treaty People." In *Saskatchewan Politics: Crowding the Centre,* ed. H.A. Leeson. Regina: Canadian Plains Research Center, University of Regina.

Boyce, P. 2008. *The Queen's Other Realms: The Crown and Its Legacy in Australia, Canada and New Zealand.* Sydney: The Federation Press.

Cox, N. 2008. *A Constitutional History of the New Zealand Monarchy: The Evolution of the New Zealand Monarchy and the Recognition of an Autochthonous Polity.* Saarbrücken: VDM Verlag Dr. Müller.

Haverstock, L.M. 2007. "Bestowing Honours – the Other Side." In *Honouring Commonwealth Citizens: Proceedings of the First Conference on Commonwealth Honours and Awards, Regina, 2006,* ed. D.M. Jackson. Toronto: Ontario Ministry of Citizenship and Immigration.

Jackson, D.M., ed. 2007. *Honouring Commonwealth Citizens: Proceedings of the First Conference on Commonwealth Honours and Awards, Regina, 2006.* Toronto: Ontario Ministry of Citizenship and Immigration.

— 2001. "Political Paradox: The Lieutenant Governor in Saskatchewan." In *Saskatchewan Politics: Into the Twenty-First Century,* H.A. Leeson, ed. Regina: Canadian Plains Research Center, University of Regina.

— 2009. "The Crown in Saskatchewan: An Institution Renewed." In *Saskatchewan Politics: Crowding the Centre,* H.A. Leeson, ed. Regina: Canadian Plains Research Center, University of Regina.

MacLeod, K.S. 2008. *A Crown of Maples: Constitutional Monarchy in Canada*. Ottawa: Department of Canadian Heritage.

Mallory, J.A. 1991. "Canada." In *Sovereigns and Surrogates,* D. Butler and D.A. Low, eds. London: Macmillan.

McCreery, C. 2005. *The Canadian Honours System*. Toronto: Dundurn Press.

McWhinney, E. 2005. *The Governor General and the Prime Ministers: The Making and Unmaking of Governments*. Vancouver: Ronsdale Press.

Monet, J. 1969. *The Last Cannon Shot A Study of French-Canadian Nationalism, 1837-1850*. Toronto: University of Toronto Press.

— 1976. "La Couronne du Canada", *Journal of Canadian Studies/Revue d'études canadiennes*, Vol. XI, No. 4.

— 1979. *La Monarchie au Canada*. Ottawa: Le Cercle du livre de France.

Olmsted, R.A., ed. 1954. *Decisions of the Judicial Committee of the Privy Council Relating to the British North America Act, 1867, and the Canadian Constitution, 1867–1854.* 3 volumes. Ottawa: Queen's Printer.

Poelzer, G. and K. Coates. 2006. "Aboriginal Peoples and the Crown in Canada: Completing the Canadian Experiment." In *Continuity and Change in Canadian Politics: Essays in Honour of David E. Smith*, H.J. Michelmann and C. de Clercy, eds. Toronto: University of Toronto Press.

Romney, P. 1999. *Getting It Wrong How Canadians Forgot Their Past and Imperilled Confederation*. Toronto: University of Toronto Press.

Russell, P.H. and L. Sossin, eds. 2009. *Parliamentary Democracy in Crisis*. Toronto: University of Toronto Press.

Saywell, J.T. 2002. *The Lawmakers: Judicial Power and the Shaping of Canadian Federalism*. Toronto: University of Toronto Press, for The Osgoode Hall Law Society.

— 1957. *The Office of Lieutenant Governor*. Toronto: University of Toronto Press. Rev. ed., Toronto: Copp Clark Pitman, 1986.

Smith, D.E. 1991. "Empire, Crown and Canadian Federalism." *Canadian Journal of Political Science* XXIV: 3.

— 1995. *The Invisible Crown: The First Principle of Canadian Government.* Toronto, Buffalo, London: University of Toronto Press.

— 1999. *The Republican Option in Canada, Past and Present*. Toronto: University of Toronto Press.

— 2007. *The People's House of Commons: Theories of Democracy in Contention*. Toronto: University of Toronto Press.

— 2010. "Re-examining the Canadian Constitution." Remarks to the Commonwealth Parliamentary Association, Regina, 16 July 2010.

Smith, G. 1891/1971. *Canada and the Canadian Question*. Toronto: Hunter Rose Co. New edition, ed. Carl Berger. Toronto: University of Toronto Press.

Twomey, A. 2006. *The Chameleon Crown: The Queen and Her Australian Governors*. Sydney: The Federation Press.

Valpy, M. 2009. "Offshore, but built-in." *The Globe and Mail*. 14 November, A19.

Vipond, R.C. 1991. *Canadian Federalism and the Failure of the Constitution*. Albany NY: State University of New York Press.

3

Myth and Misunderstanding: The Origins and Meaning of the Letters Patent Constituting the Office of the Governor General, 1947

Christopher McCreery

Depuis les gouverneurs de la Nouvelle-France, les lettres patentes et les commissions ont servi à définir autant qu'à restreindre les pouvoirs dévolus aux représentants de sa Majesté. Amplement commentées mais faiblement comprises, les Lettres patentes de 1947 *constituent le principal document établissant l'étendue des pouvoirs du gouverneur général par rapport à sa Majesté. Ce chapitre en retrace les origines et l'élaboration tout en décrivant le développement ultérieur des pratiques liées à l'exercice de l'autorité souveraine. Invariablement perçues comme un transfert global de cette autorité, les* Lettres patentes de 1947 *ont pourtant été élaborées dans le cadre d'un processus de modeste retrait entamé près de 20 ans auparavant, suivant lequel certaines prérogatives royales furent déléguées – et non transférées – au gouverneur général.*

It is not felt that the revised documents are revolutionary or startling in nature. They will, however, serve to bring the law abreast of the present constitutional position and practice.

> Louis St. Laurent to Cabinet
> March 11, 1946

There has long been a degree of myth and misunderstanding associated with the letters patent constituting the office of the governor general that were adopted by King George VI in 1947. In her memoir, *Heart Matters*, Adrienne Clarkson explained her own view of the document:

> There is much misunderstanding about the authority of the Governor General. Even many politicians don't seem to know that the final authority of the state was transferred from the monarch to the Governor General in the Letters Patent of 1947, thereby making Canada's government independent of Great Britain (Clarkson 2006, 190).

True, there is much misunderstanding surrounding the governor general's authority; however, the remainder of the statement is false and reveals a common misconception about the purpose and functions of the *Letters Patent 1947*. Well before 1947, Canada's government had become independent of Great Britain's through a series of achievements, most notably the *Statute of Westminster, 1931*. Indeed, since the resolution of the imperial conference of 1926, the Sovereign had acted in relation to Canadian matters on the advice of his Canadian ministers alone, and officials from the British government were largely reduced to playing messenger for Ottawa when it came to the King exercising the royal prerogative for his largest realm.

In the weeks leading up to her departure from Rideau Hall, Governor General Michaëlle Jean gave an interview to *More* magazine, where she built upon the Clarkson view of the *Letters Patent*: "from 1947, with what we call the letters patent, [t]he sovereign conferred the responsibilities of the head of state and all of the responsibilities are those of the head of state" (*More*, November 2010, 204). The interview also included an erroneous reference to the governor general becoming the commander-in-chief in 1947, a position held by successive governors general since 1905. That the two most recent holders of the office of the governor general have such a flawed understanding of the *Letters Patent* is cause for concern, especially since they employed the document to marginalize the role of the Sovereign.

In essence, the *Letters Patent 1947* constitute the office of the governor general and also regulate the delegation of the royal prerogative. They were the culmination of a long process whereby successive governors general were given increasing ability to act in the place of the Sovereign and exercise the royal prerogative without direct consultation with the king or queen of the day. As we shall see, while much authority was delegated by the King to the governor general, this was done in the form of enabling legislation, and particular areas of the royal prerogative were outlined as being beyond the scope of the governor general's duties, except in the most exceptional circumstances such as a regency or the incapacity or capture of the Sovereign by a foreign power. Thus, the *Letters Patent* constitute a *delegation* of most powers, not a blanket abdication of the Sovereign's role in the Canadian state.

While it is true that since 1947 some elements of the royal prerogative – notably those related to external relations – have been delegated by the Sovereign to the governor general, this has not limited the royal prerogative. In writing about the then newly adopted *Letters Patent*, R. MacGregor Dawson noted that, even with this delegation of powers, the governor general was still "not in quite the same position as the Sovereign in regard to the exercise of certain prerogative powers" (Dawson 1948, 160).

Indeed, the process by which some of the elements of the royal prerogative have been delegated by the Sovereign to the governor general serves as a window into the continuing potency of the person of the Sovereign and the Sovereign's ongoing role in some elements of the Canadian state, well beyond mere symbolism or social and cultural matters.

This chapter will examine the development, evolution and operation of the *Letters Patent 1947*. Whether by accident or by design, an overly simplistic view of the *Letters Patent* has developed. Little attention has been given to those elements of the royal prerogative that have been delegated to the governor general or how they came to be. The unfortunate impression is that the *Letters Patent 1947* signified a significant break with previous practice in terms of the role of the governor general, whereas in fact they were quite similar to the *Letters Patent, Commission and Royal Instructions* issued since 1931. The changes were more akin to provision for a *Regency Act*, via non-legislated means, than an overt desire to transfer all of the Sovereign's responsibilities to his personal representative in the dominion. The fact remains that, in addition to the appointment of extra senators under section 26 of the *Constitution Act, 1867*, there continue to exist certain elements of the royal prerogative that have never been exercised by the governor general. Nevertheless, a number of governors general have used the *Letters Patent* to expand their own role, failing to realize that their authority is reflective, that without the person of the Sovereign they are little more than ceremonial bureaucrats. Perhaps the most glaring use of the *Letters Patent* to marginalize the Sovereign came in 2004 when the name of the Queen was removed from the Letters of Credence issued to Canadian diplomats.

Surprisingly, not all of the works that examine the role and position of the governor general include reference to the *Letters Patent*. David Smith's *The Invisible Crown* notes that "the new Letters Patent in 1947 made a complete delegation of the monarch's powers to the Governor General" (Smith 1995, 45). Other works tend to place the *Letters Patent* in the same context as that espoused by Clarkson and her contemporaries: a document that transferred all authority from the Sovereign to the governor general – note the use of the word "transferred" as opposed to "delegate," a rather convenient interpretation for those seeking to marginalize the role of the Sovereign via extra-constitutional means.

In the most recent context, it was only during Michaëlle Jean's tenure as governor general, when almost every reference to the Queen was removed from the governor general's website, that the *Letters Patent 1947* were included in the website: "In 1947, the Letters Patent of King

George VI transferred all the duties of Head of State of Canada to the Governor General and the new Commission of Appointment referred to the Office of the Governor General and Commander-in-Chief in and over Canada" (archived Governor General's Website, 20 April 2009). During the October 2009 controversy over whether or not the governor general is Canada's head of state, officials from the office of the secretary to the governor general claimed that the *Letters Patent 1947* proved that the governor general is in fact the "head of state." Following the imbroglio that culminated in Prime Minister Stephen Harper forcefully reminding the governor general that Queen Elizabeth II is Canada's head of state, not the person holding the office of governor general, the website was corrected, making the Queen's position as head of state clear – as it had been on the same website previously back to its inception during Roméo LeBlanc's tenure as governor general. Throughout the entire controversy, the *Letters Patent 1947* were held up by officials at Rideau Hall as a sort of emancipation proclamation that transformed the governor general into a person holding all the powers of the Sovereign. It was a rather imaginative development that ignored sixty years of history and the original intent of the *Letters Patent 1947* as an ersatz regency act to delegate certain elements of the royal prerogative to the governor general – not a document that sought to remove the Sovereign from the operation of the Canadian state.

HISTORY OF LETTERS PATENT, COMMISSIONS AND ROYAL INSTRUCTIONS

The use of *Letters Patent, Commissions* and *Royal Instructions* to define duties and offices of the Crown is one that dates back to New France. Following the establishment of royal government in 1663, Jean-Baptist Colbert, France's controller-general of finances, who had responsibility for the kingdom's overseas possessions, sent his intendants to New France with *Letters Patent* in which they were "empowered to reconstitute this body [the Sovereign Council of New France]" (Eccles 1954, 27). The governors of New France were similarly issued with commissions of appointment and instructions which outlined their power to act in the place of the King, while *Letters Patent* defined their position as governor/governor general. Thus, it was this triumvirate of legal documents, *Letters Patent, Commissions* and *Royal Instructions*, which constituted offices, appointed people to offices and instructed them on their powers and duties. The British used the same three types of documents when it came to defining, appointing and instructing their governors and other senior offices of the Crown, a pattern that was duplicated throughout the entire British Empire and thus in all of the component parts of British North America.

With the advent of Confederation, a new set of *Letters Patent* constituting the office of the governor general was drawn up. As per custom, these were *Letters Patent* and a *Commission* in a single document and were accompanied by *Royal Instructions*. The new documents were very similar to those issued to Viscount Monck in 1861 when he became governor general of the Province of Canada. While the *Constitution Act, 1867* contains forty-nine references to the governor general, nowhere is the role or office defined. Indeed, no provision is made for the appointment of the governor general, as the *Constitution Act, 1867* assumed the pre-existence of a governor general (Heard 1991, 16). Sections 9 and 10 simply set out that executive government and authority are vested in the Queen and that the governor general is empowered to "carrying on the Government of Canada on behalf and in the Name of the Queen, by whatever Title he is designated" (*Constitution Act, 1867*).

From 1867 to 1878, every governor general was appointed by a new set of *Letters Patent* and *Commission* (in one document) appointing him specifically, as well as *Royal Instructions* for specific issues that might come up during his tenure. These documents delineated the role, authority and mandate of each governor general, and thus the office of the governor general was attached to each individual governor general until 1878.

The first section of the *Letters Patent* and *Commission* began by appointing the governor general to his position and defining his territory of responsibility. From here, the document transitioned to outlining the role and responsibilities of the office holder. This included empowering the governor general to the following:

a)   Use of the Great Seal of Canada
b)   Appoint judges
c)   Suspend or remove persons holding office by virtue of a commission or warrant issued by the governor general
d)   Grant pardons
e)   Assemble and prorogue Parliament
f)   Issue marriage licences, letters of administration and probate wills

The *Royal Instructions* dealt with more specific matters:

a)   The oaths the governor general was required to take to assume office
b)   Authority to administer oaths and delegation of this authority
c)   Provision of a copy of the royal instructions to the Queen's privy council for Canada
d)   Requirement for the governor general to summon meetings of the privy council
e)   Quorum requirements for meetings of the privy council
f)   Governor general's right to oppose decisions of the council (cabinet)
g)   Appoint a president of the privy council to serve in the absence of the governor general

h) Production of journals and minutes of all acts, proceedings, votes and resolutions of the privy council
i) Power to grant or withhold royal assent
j) Reservation for the Queen's assent to bills related to divorce, grants of land or money to the governor general, bills creating legal tender, bills imposing differential duties and other bills considered inconsistent with treaty obligations

The *Royal Instructions* also made provision for the appointment of deputies; delegation of the governor general's power and authorities to a lieutenant governor in case of incapacity or death (appointment of an administrator), or in the absence of such, the senior military officer in command of military forces in Canada; and lastly, a clause requiring all inhabitants of Canada to be obedient to, aid and assist the governor general.

The documents were not voluminous and left much to interpretation and convention. This would ultimately become an issue in relation to the prerogative of mercy/granting of pardons. In 1875 the colonial office proposed that permanent *Letters Patent* constituting the office of the governor general, separate from the commission, be drafted. This change came in large part out of a desire to standardize the role and authority of the various governors and governors general throughout the British Empire: the colonial office, that paragon of efficiency, was forever seeking to create uniform practice throughout Britain's overseas territories.

Beginning in 1879, the new form of *Letters Patent* was issued which "superceded an inconvenient mode by which, whenever a new governor was appointed, a commission was issued to him which appointed him to his office, defined his authority, reconstituted the legislature and gave him instructions as to the exercising of the powers which were further supplemented by an instrument of instructions" (Keith 1928, 80–81). The governor general's ability to grant pardons without the consent of the cabinet had become an issue in the colony of New South Wales as well as in Canada, on account of a number of high profile cases. Canada's minister of justice, Edward Blake, played an important role in the development and redrafting of the first *Letters Patent 1878*. Blake was anxious to "codify evolved conventions respecting the vice regal role" (Messamore 2006, 178).[1]

The *Letters Patent 1878* and *Royal Instructions* were significantly different from the previous documents. Most specifically, the various powers that had come under provincial jurisdiction at the time of Confederation but had remained in the pre-1878 documents were removed. The new documents also no longer implied that the governor general was required

---

[1] The development of the *Letters Patent 1878* is ably recounted in Barbara Messamore's *Canada's Governors General: Biography and Constitutional Evolution* (Toronto: University of Toronto Press, 2006).

to preside personally over meetings of the privy council, there was no longer a list of bills that the governor general was required to withhold assent to, and reference to the prerogative of mercy was moved to the *Royal Instructions*. Within the *Royal Instructions* it was clearly set out that the highly contentious prerogative of mercy was only to be exercised by the governor general in capital cases on the advice of the privy council, and for lesser offences a pardon could only be granted if the governor general had the consent of one minister of the Crown.

With this, three separate documents came into being: the *Letters Patent* defining the office of the governor general; the *Commission* appointing a person to the office of governor general and empowering him to act as such; and the *Royal Instructions* delineating how the governor general was to undertake certain decisions and deal with various matters of state. As Arthur Berriedale Keith and Barbara Messamore note, "the omission of these few clauses and the slight rewording of others, signified a real change in the written description of the governor general's role" (Messamore 2006, 213). The post-1878 system "is one of letters patent which are not varied for each Governor, but made applicable to him by the commission which appoints him to the office defined in the letters patent and regulated by the instructions" (Keith 1928, 81).

From 1878 to 1947 every governor general was issued with this triumvirate of documents, which underwent periodic revision. The *Letters Patent 1878* and *Royal Instructions 1878* set the foundation for all future documents, including the *Letters Patent 1947*. The *Letters Patent* were next amended in 1905 to vest the position of commander-in-chief in and over Canada in the person of the governor general, a position hitherto held by the senior officer commanding British military forces in Canada. While the position of commander-in-chief rests with the Sovereign, as outlined in section 15 of the *Constitution Act, 1867*, the title and authority have always been delegated. The 1905 *Letters Patent* also made the chief justice of Canada the administrator of the government of Canada, to act as governor general in the absence of the person holding that office.

The next revision of the *Letters Patent* and *Royal Instructions* came following the imperial conference of 1926, which saw the role of the governor general transformed from that of personal representative of the Sovereign and an agent of the British government to being simply that of the personal representative of the King. These *Letters Patent* were signed by King George V and brought into operation on April 4, 1931, in advance of passage of the *Statute of Westminster*.

In 1935 the *Letters Patent* were amended to include an article allowing the governor general to retain "all and every the powers vested in him" while he travelled outside of Canada. These were signed by King George V on September 25, 1935 and were sealed under the Great Seal of the realm.

Origins of the 1947 Letters Patent

The origins of the *Letters Patent 1947* can be found in a number of key events: the *Statue of Westminster 1931*, the British *Regency Act 1937*, and the Second World War. For this latter point, it was the fall of Denmark and ensuing ambiguity of the legal status of the government of Iceland that were of concern.

Following assent being granted to the *Statute of Westminster* in 1931, Canada's constitutional position vis-à-vis the United Kingdom was brought into line with Resolution IX of the imperial war conference, which recognized the dominions as being autonomous entities from the United Kingdom capable of conducting foreign relations, and the decisions taken at the imperial conferences of 1926 and 1930 that outlined that the governor general was henceforth the personal representative of the King and not an officer of the British government. The statute also noted "in accord with the established constitutional position that no law hereafter made by the Parliament of the United Kingdom shall extend to any of the said Dominions as part of the law of that Dominion otherwise than at the request and with the consent of the Dominion."

The then newly drafted *Letters Patent 1931, Commission* and *Royal Instructions* issued to Lord Bessborough upon his appointment as governor general brought the content of the documents into line with the *Statute of Westminster*, and the *Royal Instructions* now came directly from the King and not from the British government (colonial secretary). Nevertheless, there remained certain elements of the royal prerogative that were only exercised by the King on the advice of his Canadian prime minister; these included matters related to the appointment of representatives to Commonwealth and foreign countries, declarations of war, signing of peace treaties and matters touching specifically upon the Crown such as honours, and certain issues of protocol.

The *Letters Patent* issued in 1935 to Lord Tweedsmuir were altered to allow the governor general to retain all of the powers vested in him when he was out of Canada for less than a month. These were signed by George V and sealed under the Great Seal of the realm. Both the 1931 and 1935 *Letters Patent* were countersigned by Claude Schuster, the permanent secretary to the lord chancellor's office. Earlier documents had traditionally been signed by the secretary of state for the dominions and prior to the creation of that department, by the colonial secretary. So with the permanent secretary to the lord chancellor signing the documents there was an overt movement away from involving the colonial office; nevertheless, the *Letters Patent* were still not being countersigned by a Canadian.

Bessborough's commission was signed by the King and countersigned by the prime minister of Canada, R.B. Bennett; this was the first time that the Canadian prime minister's signature was included. Beginning with Lord Athlone, who was appointed governor general in 1940, the *Letters*

Patent as well as the *Commission* were countersigned by the prime minister of Canada and sealed under the Great Seal of the realm. The *Royal Instructions* were signed by the King alone. Given that the Great Seal of the realm is in effect the Great Seal of the United Kingdom, this detail of the documents was still not in line with Canada's constitutional position as being autonomous from the United Kingdom. We will see a gradual shift with these changes in not only the text of the *Letters Patent, Commission and Royal Instructions*, but also the signatures affixed and types of seals used.

Following the abdication of King Edward VIII and the accession of George VI to the throne, officials at the British cabinet office focused on the need for a new *Regency Act*. This was largely because the King's daughter, Princess Elizabeth, the heiress presumptive, was not yet 18 and was therefore incapable of discharging the duties as Sovereign in the event of her father's death, illness or extended absence from the United Kingdom. The act created a new body known as the council of state. Membership of the body consisted of the consort of the Sovereign and the next four people in the line of succession over the age of 21. The regent was to be the senior person in the line of succession over the age of 21. As the *Regency Act 1937* was adopted following the adoption of the *Statute of Westminster 1931*, it did not apply to Canada. British officials suggested that Canada should adopt its own *Regency Act*, and the deputy minister of justice, W. Stewart Edwards, wrote to the undersecretary of state for external affairs, O.D. Skelton, on this issue, noting that some elements of the royal prerogative "have not been delegated to the Governor General by his Commission or Instructions, include, amongst the more important, the issue of full powers and instruments of ratification, exequaturs to Consults, the appointment and recall of Governors General of Canada, and the issue of Letters of Credence." Edwards explained that "I think it is clearly essential that appropriate legislation should be enacted" (*Manual*, Vol 2, 842, Edwards to Skelton, 16 Feb 1937). In 1937 and again in 1941, consideration was given to the adoption of a Canadian regency act, but no such bill was ever presented to Parliament, and the absence of a mechanism to allow for the exercise of the elements of the royal prerogative that required the King's consent continued until the *Letters Patent 1947*. Nevertheless, the 1931 and 1935 *Letters Patent* and *Royal Instruction* were still robust documents in relation to the governor general's ability to exercise the royal prerogative. When Canada declared war on Germany in 1939, it was King George VI as Sovereign of Canada who signed the proclamation declaring that a state of war existed. Vincent Massey, the Canadian high commissioner, had to rush out to Windsor Castle to have the King sign the document on September 9 and, at 1:08 GMT, 8:08 a.m. Ottawa time, Canada was officially at war with the German Reich. In the days following the invasion of Poland, the governor general, Lord Tweedsmuir, and Prime Minister Mackenzie King had had a series of discussions about who should sign the proclamation declaring war. Tweedsmuir said "that he was only H.M.'s representative with respect to those matters the King was himself not in a position to perform" (Mackenzie King Diary, 9 September 1939) and King was inclined to agree, but not on the basis of law or convention. "I [Mackenzie King] said to him that it would stimulate I thought the pride of the country in its nationhood ... particularly after H.M's visit to Canada, there should be additional pride in having the proclamation issued in the name of our King" (ibid.). When the prime minister took the issue to cabinet it was the minister of justice, Ernest Lapointe, who first proposed that it should be the King who signed the document and the rest of the cabinet followed suit, although there was some lingering concern that the governor general might feel his status lessened by the King being given the lead in this role. It is interesting to note that the discussion of who should sign the proclamation was not a legal one but rather one focused on the symbolic importance of the moment.

The issues of the governor general's powers and the absence of a *Canadian Regency Act* were brought up in the House of Commons on February 17, 1947, when Prime Minister Louis St. Laurent was asked if the British council of state would act on behalf of the King in relation to Canadian affairs during his extended visit to South Africa and Southern Rhodesia. St. Laurent replied that the King would continue to act for Canada while abroad and that the *Regency Acts of 1937–43* did not apply to Canada.

While the tiny kingdom of Iceland seems a peculiar example to draw from, the situation that arose there became a cause of concern for Mackenzie King in relation to the possibility that Canada's King, George VI, could be captured in the event of an invasion of Britain by the Germans, which was a very real threat from 1939 to 1942. Despite a successful policy of neutrality dating back to the First World War, Denmark was invaded on April 9, 1940 and capitulated almost immediately to avoid bloodshed. The surrender caused a significant problem for Denmark's sister kingdom, Iceland. Christian X was in fact King of two separate countries, Denmark and Iceland (not unlike George VI in relation to Canada, Australia, New Zealand, South Africa and the Irish Free State). This arrangement had been arrived at in 1918 when an *Act of Union* between Iceland and Denmark was adopted. By this act, "Denmark recognized Iceland as a sovereign state in personal union with Denmark" (Kristinsson and Nordal 1975, 126). Iceland had control over all of its own affairs, although it left foreign relations to the Danish ministry of foreign affairs, which acted on the advice of the Icelandic cabinet in matters related to Iceland.

The invasion and surrender meant that Christian X was "almost hermetically sealed and separate" from Iceland throughout the occupation (Arnenson 1949, 97). Captive of an occupying power, the King was unable to carry out his duties as Iceland's head of state, which included granting royal assent to bills passed by Iceland's Parliament, the Althing, and carrying out other elements of the royal prerogative that related specifically to foreign relations.

The King of Iceland having been captured by the Germans, the Althing passed two resolutions "investing the Icelandic cabinet with the power of the head of state [Christian X] and declaring that Iceland would herself perform the duties hitherto carried out on her behalf by Denmark" (Lacey 1998, 130). Realizing that cabinet was a cumbersome body through which to execute the duties of the head of state, in June 1941 the Althing elected a regent, Sveinn Björnsson, who would later go on to become the first president of Iceland. Under the *Act of Union 1918* and the Icelandic constitution, all of this was illegal and constituted a very tidy *coup d'état* but, with no mechanism to allow the kingdom to function in the prolonged absence/incapacity of the head of state, there were no other options.

It was these diverse series of events that led to the government of Canada drafting new *Letters Patent* for the governor general. A host of familiar figures was involved in the process: King George VI; his private secretary, Sir Alan Lascelles, who had served as secretary to the governor general of Canada from 1931–35; William Lyon Mackenzie King; Louis St. Laurent; Lester B. Pearson; the governor general, Lord Alexander; and his secretary, Major-General H.F.G. Letson.

The war having come to a successful conclusion, the cabinet was in a position to turn its mind to peacetime issues. The impetus behind drafting new *Letters Patent* was the impending installation of Field Marshal Lord Alexander of Tunis as the new governor general. In February 1946, St. Laurent struck an interdepartmental committee to draft new *Letters Patent* in advance of the governor general's installation. The committee consisted of representatives from the department of justice, the department of external affairs, the clerk of the privy council and the law clerk of the house of commons.

The interdepartmental committee quickly drafted a new set of *Letters Patent* that also incorporated the *Royal Instructions*. St. Laurent presented the proposal to cabinet on March 12, 1946 and noted that the "texts reflect the present constitutional position and practice" (cabinet meeting minutes 12 March 1946, RG 2 A5a, Vol 2637) and that the most significant changes proposed were the inclusion of a clause conferring general powers upon the governor general, revocation of the former *Letters Patent* and instructions and incorporation of both documents into *Letters Patent*. The cabinet decided to delay the project until after Alexander was installed as governor general, as there was a need to "inform other Commonwealth governments, in advance, of any action in this connection" (ibid.).

Almost a year after Alexander was installed, the issue was again brought before cabinet by St. Laurent and it was agreed that "the matter would be taken up informally by the Prime Minister with the Governor General" (ibid.). Having developed a cordial relationship with the new governor general, Mackenzie King raised the issue with Alexander a few days after the cabinet meeting. The discussion was short and Mackenzie King agreed to send the draft documents to the governor general for review (Mackenzie King Diary, 25 March 1947). Two days later, Lester Pearson wrote to General Letson, enclosing the draft *Letters Patent* and seeking Alexander's informal comments. Pearson went on to explain that the *Letters Patent* and *Royal Instructions* were to be consolidated and reissued under the Great Seal of Canada, that the documents reflected the present constitutional position and practice and that the documents would be countersigned by the prime minister of Canada. Delving into the actual text of the draft *Letters Patent*, Pearson explained that "the Governor General is authorized to exercise all of His Majesty's powers and authority in respect of Canada. This does not, in theory, limit the Royal Prerogative submissions to the King" (Pearson to Letson, 27 March 1947). On 11 April, Letson replied to Pearson, "His Excellency has studied the proposals and has no objection to them" (Letson to Pearson 11 April 1947). Letson was most concerned about the provisions that required the governor general to seek the King's permission before departing Canada for any period of time and sought to have a blanket exemption to allow him to visit the United States or elsewhere "on the authority of the Prime Minister."

With the governor general's acquiescence, St. Laurent wrote Mackenzie King to suggest that the draft documents be submitted to the King for informal observations and a letter was subsequently sent to Sir Alan Lascelles on May 5. The prime minister explained the need for the revision and that "the only fundamental change ... would empower the Governor General to exercise all powers and authorities lawfully belonging to the King in respect of Canada." Perhaps the most interesting inclusion in the letter was that "[t]he Canadian Government is of the opinion that such 'enabling legislation' is necessary and desirable. ... However the Government has no present intention of altering the practice governing submissions to His Majesty ... save in exceptional circumstances, alter the existing practices without prior consultation with, or at any rate, prior notification to, the Governor General and the King" (Mackenzie King to Lascelles, 5 May 1947). The consolidation of the *Letters Patent*, as opposed to drafting a *Regency Act*, was seen as a more logical way to provide for unforeseen circumstances such as a regency because the King already had a representative in Canada – the governor general – who was capable of discharging most royal duties.

Lascelles discussed the matter with the King, and George VI fully approved of the new *Letters Patent*, although Lascelles stressed that the King was anxious that "it would only be in exceptional circumstances that any change would be made in the existing practice with regard to submissions to The King and that no such change will take effect without previous consultation" (Lascelles to Mackenzie King, 21 May 1947). In particular, the King was anxious that "no Canadian Ambassadors or Ministers should be appointed without a submission to himself" (ibid.). Mackenzie King replied to Lascelles and explained that there "may have been a slight misunderstanding. As to the sense of my letter of May 5 what

I had intended to convey was that, unless exceptional circumstances made it necessary to do so, it was not proposed by the Canadian Government to alter existing practices without prior consultation" (Mackenzie King to Lascelles, 6 June 1947). The formal submission was made to the King by Lord Alexander on August 30 after having received the draft documents from St. Laurent. The documents were received by George VI at Balmoral Castle and he signed the *Letters Patent* on September 8, with a coming into force date of October 1, 1947.

Before the ink on the new *Letters Patent* was even dry, Mackenzie King had to request a change to the "existing practice" in relation to Lord Alexander's concern about having to seek the permission of the King every time he travelled to the United States. On September 20 Mackenzie King requested that article XIV of the *Letters Patent* 1947, relating to the fact that the governor general could not quit Canada without "having first obtained leave from His Majesty through the Prime Minister," be altered. Alexander had proposed that he be allowed to travel to the United States for periods of not more than two weeks with the concurrence of the prime minister and that the governor general would inform the King when such visits were planned. The King approved this amendment to the *Letters Patent* on September 27, just days before the new document was due to come into force.

At 10 a.m. on October 1, the prime minister's office issued a press release announcing the changes and a proclamation was published in the *Canada Gazette*. The release focused on clause 2, which "authorizes the Governor General to exercise on advice ..., all of His Majesty's powers and authorities in respect of Canada. This does not limit the King's prerogatives" (PMO press release, 1 October 1947).

The elements of the royal prerogative that constituted part of the existing practice and required submission to the Sovereign for approval were as follows:

a) Signatures of full powers for the signing of treaties in the heads of state form, and signature of ratification of such treaties
b) Approval of the appointment of Canadian ambassadors and ministers to foreign countries, and signature of their letters of credence
c) Approval of the proposed appointment of foreign ambassadors and ministers to Canada (i.e., granting the *agrément*)
d) Authorizing declarations of war
e) Appointment of the governor general of Canada
f) Granting of honours (including the creation of)
g) Amendments to the letters patent constituting the office of the governor general
h) Alterations in the elements of the royal prerogative that were to be referred to the Sovereign, commonly referred to as "existing practice"
i) Alternations in the royal style and title

j)   Changes to the Canadian table of titles
k)   Changes in the Canadian table of precedence
l)   Granting of royal patronage
m)   Appointment of colonels-in-chief of Canadian regiments
n)   Designs for Canadian coinage bearing the Sovereign's effigy
o)   Appointment of the Canadian secretary to the Queen
p)   Permission for the inclusions of the Crown in Canadian grants of
      arms and badges

Some of the royal prerogatives constituting the "existing practice" existed long before 1947, but were only defined as the issues arose or required attention. This was the case for items (a) to (n) but not for (o) and (p). For instance, when the *Letters Patent* were brought into force in October 1947, there was no such person or office as the Canadian secretary to the Queen. This would not come into being until 1958 with the appointment of Lieutenant-General Howard Graham as the commissioner for the 1959 royal tour, a position that was subsequently renamed Canadian secretary to the Queen. Prior to the appointment, the prime minister seeks the consent of the Queen and then a commission is sealed under the Great Seal of Canada.

Elements of the royal prerogative contained in the list have come to be exercised by the governor general on a regular basis without direct consultation with the Sovereign. However, this has only been achieved after often lengthy discussions between an array of senior officials, culminating with the Queen and her Canadian prime minister.

The first attempt to delegate an element of the royal prerogative from the King to the governor general under the new *Letters Patent* came in December of 1947, when the minister of national defence, Brooke Claxton, requested that the governor general approve the creation of a new Canadian long service medal, which would become known as the Canadian Forces' Decoration (CD). Claxton wrote to the clerk of the privy council, Arnold Heeney, to ask that the prime minister write to the governor general and request that the CD be created. Heeney responded one week later, noting the authority and power to create new honours were to remain in the hands of the King and to be delegated to the governor general only in exceptional circumstances.

When George VI fell seriously ill in the fall of 1951, he issued *Letters Patent* in accordance with the *Regency Act 1937* delegating certain elements of the royal prerogative to counsellors of state on account of his illness. The King did not indicate that he was unable to continue discharging his duties in relation to Canada, but the government of Canada considered temporarily delegating all elements of the royal prerogative to the governor general for the duration of the King's illness. Prime Minister St. Laurent noted that "it would not be the wish of the Government of Canada to burden the King by asking His Majesty to sign documents which would ordinarily be submitted to The King for signature" (J.F. Delaute, Assistant Secretary to the Governor General, to Sir Allan Lascelles, 17 October 1951). By the time the government of Canada came to a decision on the issue, the King had recovered and "is now well enough to deal with all such documents ... His Majesty would prefer therefore that they should be sent to Buckingham Palace in the usual way" (Commonwealth Relations Office Telegram, 18 October 1951). Arnold Heeney, clerk of the privy council, resolved that in the event of future emergencies the governor general would perform the functions as necessary. Heeney went on to note that, despite various suggestions, there was no need for Canada to adopt a *Regency Act*, as the *Letters Patent 1947* had the same effect in relation to the Sovereign's position in Canada.

With these two episodes we see the development of what can best be characterized as "the theory of delay and inconvenience." That is, the submission of matters to the Sovereign will invariably result in a delay and cause inconvenience not only to the government of Canada, but also to the Sovereign. The theory has little validity. By the end of the Second World War there were daily flights between Britain and Canada, and it rarely took more than two days for the contents of the external affairs diplomatic bag to reach the King. In matters relating to the royal prerogative, no matter has ever been as time-sensitive as Canada's declaration of war in 1939 and there was no delay in having the King sign the proclamation. The second concept, that the Sovereign might be "inconvenienced" by Canadian matters, is another fallacy and presumes that Sovereigns do not take their role seriously, or that Canadian matters are of secondary importance. There is absolutely no evidence that this has ever been the case.

The process by which Queen Elizabeth II has delegated authority for exercising certain parts of the royal prerogative has been quite simple: informal discussion between the prime minister (or his delegate) and the Queen's private secretary, an exchange of letters between the clerk of the privy council and the Queen's private secretary, a face-to-face meeting between the Queen and her Canadian prime minister, and a formal letter from the Queen's private secretary to the clerk of the privy council outlining the change in "existing practice."

In 1966 Her Majesty agreed that changes in the table of titles (such as Right Honourable and Honourable) would henceforth be approved by the governor general "unless the Prime Minister or Governor General decided that the change was of such consequence that Her Majesty's pleasure ought to be ascertained." This was in relation to the discontinuation of a long tradition that saw certain senior office-holders appointed to Her Majesty's Most Honourable Privy Council, which was colloquially known as the Imperial Privy Council. Appointment to this body entitled an individual to carry the title "Right Honourable" and traditionally membership had been bestowed upon the governor general, prime minister, chief justice and other persons on the advice of the prime minister of Canada.

Beginning in 1966, those holding the office of governor general, prime minister and chief justice were automatically accorded the title "Right Honourable" upon assuming office. Other Canadians can be given the title on the advice of the prime minister.

In 1967 the Queen agreed to the governor general overseeing future changes to the Canadian table of precedence, with the same proviso that the Sovereign would not need to be consulted other than in relation to changes that altered the position of the Sovereign. This same year also witnessed the creation of the Order of Canada, and the Sovereign's consent for the creation of the Order – and indeed the entire Canadian honours system that would develop – was sought and ultimately signified in her signing the *Letters Patent* constituting various Canadian orders, decorations and medals since 1967.

The most significant changes to the elements of the royal prerogative delegated to the governor general for exercise on behalf of the Queen and in her name were related to external relations. These changes came in 1975 and 1977 respectively, at a time when the role of the Sovereign was being increasingly questioned and marginalized by federal bureaucrats. The first set of changes was initiated by Mitchell Sharp during his time as secretary of state for external affairs. Sharp wanted to see the responsibility for the approval of the appointment of Canadian ambassadors and ministers to foreign countries, signature of their letters of credence and the approval of the proposed appointment of foreign ambassadors and ministers to Canada (granting the *agrément*) delegated to the governor general (Sharp to Trudeau, 20 November 1970). These elements of the royal prerogative had hitherto been discharged by the Sovereign, with informal consent sought via telegram, formal advice tendered and then the formal documents sent for the Queen's signature. The entire process took between 48 and 72 hours to complete. Nevertheless, this was not quick enough for Sharp. With the consent of Prime Minister Trudeau, Sharp directed the Canadian high commissioner in London to speak with the Queen's private secretary, Sir Michael Adeane, on the delegation of these duties. It was reported back on February 3, 1971 that, while Adeane did not personally see any issue with these changes, he thought that, as these matters touched very directly upon the Queen's role as head of state, it would be best if the prime minister were to speak directly with the Queen during her impending visit to British Columbia.

Trudeau did not bring up the matter with the Queen during the BC visit in June 1971, although he did speak to Adeane about the proposed changes and Adeane again expressed his personal view that, while he thought that the Queen would have no issue with any of the proposed changes, he was hesitant to comment upon the proposal to have the governor general sign letters of credence and recall. He went further to note that, in cases of emergency or great urgency, there was no prohibition on the governor general signing the letters of credence. Reading between the lines, one has to assume that this was an element of the royal prerogative of which the Queen was not anxious to be relieved.

Trudeau wrote to Sharp noting that he had an indication from Sir Michael Adeane at that time that the Queen might well authorize the exercise by the governor general of the following functions on her behalf:

a) Granting of *agrément* to appointments of foreign ambassadors and ministers
b) The acceptance of letters of recall of the above
c) The appointment of Canadian ambassadors and ministers
d) The approval of establishment and severance of diplomatic relations
e) The signature of letters of credence of Canadian envoys in cases where it was specially urgent to do so (Trudeau to Sharp, 22 February 1972)

Trudeau went on to suggest that "my own thoughts [are that] we should ask Her Majesty to authorize the Governor General to sign all Letters of Credence on her behalf, regardless of circumstances" (ibid.). Rather ironically, many heads of mission preferred to have their letters of credence signed by the Queen as it was more prestigious than having the governor general sign.

Trudeau and Sharp being of the same mind, the clerk of the privy council, Gordon Roberson, wrote to Adeane to formally raise the issue. Robertson's letter offered a convoluted explanation for the change. Alluding to the great success of the Queen's recent tours and the high regard Canadians had for their Queen, he explained that "the Queen's participation in the formalities and the procedures relating to the conduct of Canada's external relations does not appear to have the same significance for [the general public] for whom the performance of such symbolic functions is rarely seen or reported" (Robertson to Adeane, 6 March 1972).

A response was received from Sir Martin Charteris, Adeane's successor, on April 5, 1972. Charteris informed Robertson that the Queen "has given considerable thought to the Prime Minister's suggestion regarding the performance, by the Governor-General, of certain of her prerogative functions" (Charteris to Robertson, 5 April 1972). It was noted that the letters of credence should continue to be signed by Her Majesty, but that they could be signed by the governor general when it was particularly urgent. (There are definite grounds to believe that the Queen preferred to retain the prerogative of signing the letters of credence and that it was with considerable reluctance that she eventually acceded to the prime minister's request.) Charteris went on to suggest that Trudeau should discuss the matter with the Queen, face to face, during his impending visit to Britain in December, and that until such a meeting had transpired there would be no alteration in the existing practice. In part this was because of the need for a personal discussion between the prime minister and the Queen, more than just a courtesy, and also the desire for a similar agreement to be reached with Australia to ensure a level of uniformity in the field of the external affairs of the Queen's realms. Barring any difficulties, the prime minister's office planned on making the announcement in early 1973. Despite all of the diligent planning, a leak on the issue delayed the entire process for years.

In December 1972, journalist Charles Lynch published the entire cabinet briefing note on the proposed changes to the royal prerogative and the resulting furor in the press over the perceived erosion of the Queen's position placed the entire project in abeyance. Following the leak, it was "deemed expedient not to implement the new measures at that time" (MacEachen to Trudeau, 29 November 1974). Shortly after becoming secretary of state for external affairs, Alan J. MacEachen asked the prime minister to reactivate the issue. On March 12, 1975, Trudeau met privately with the Queen at Buckingham Palace and they discussed the change in procedures. At this time it was agreed that the Queen would continue to sign the letters of credence and recall for Canadian ambassadors and the letters of commission and recall for Canadian high commissioners. The governor general would, henceforth, on the Queen's behalf and in the name of the Queen,

a)   grant *agrément* to appointments of foreign ambassadors and ministers;
b)   accept letters of recall of the above;
b)   appoint Canadian ambassadors and ministers;
b)   approve the establishment of and severance of diplomatic relations.

These changes were announced with little fanfare in a press release from the prime minister's office on December 30, 1975. Another proposal that was broached at the March meeting was changes to the royal style and title, from "Elizabeth the Second, by the Grace of God of the United Kingdom, Canada, Her Other Realms and Territories, Queen, Head of the Commonwealth, Defender of the Faith" to "Elizabeth the Second, Queen of Canada, Head of the Commonwealth." Such a change would have required the Queen's consent before a bill could be presented to Parliament. Australia and New Zealand had slightly altered the Queen's royal style and title in 1973 and 1974 respectively, but no change was made to the Canadian royal style and title. Trudeau dropped the entire idea following his meeting with the Queen.

The next group of changes was executed much more expeditiously. These changes were proposed by the governor general, Jules Léger, himself an experienced diplomat, having served as Canadian ambassador to Mexico, France, Italy and Belgium. Léger was anxious to see the role of the governor general expanded to include all matters touching upon external relations.

In early 1977, Léger wrote to the prime minister to explain that, having now been in office for more than two years, he had given a great deal of thought to the issue of signing the letters of credence and recall. Reflecting upon René Lévesque's stunning victory in the Quebec provincial election, the growth of separatism in Quebec, the increasing discussions of constitutional changes and a potential debate about the role of the Crown, he postulated that it would be advantageous, "Pour empêcher un tel débat de s'envenimer, ce qui ne ferait l'affaire de personne, on pourrait peut-être mettre notre propre maison en ordre" (Léger to Trudeau, March 1977). In advance of the Queen's Silver Jubilee visit, Léger believed it important to forestall any potential accusation that officials in Canada were unable to exercise all of the powers of the Crown and that it was now time to have the governor general exercise the remaining elements of the royal prerogative on behalf of the Queen. Léger was deeply concerned with the threat of separatism in Quebec and he thought that delegating the remaining elements of the royal prerogative related to external relations to the governor general would help to further demonstrate that the Crown and the principal representative of the Queen in Canada were fully capable of exercising all the functions of the head of state in Canada – to him it was the last step towards Canadianizing the Crown. His great fear was that the Crown would be used by Quebec nationalists as another reason for Quebeckers to vote to separate from Canada. While it may have been a pressing issue at the time, today it seems a minor point related to the mechanics of external relations, not a matter central to winning over sovereigntists.

Léger proposed that Trudeau take up the discussion directly with the Queen rather than leaving the matter to intermediaries, as in his estimation the reason the process achieved in 1975 was so slow was because there were too many interlopers muddying the waters.

A confidential internal memo from Léger to the noted historian of the Crown, Father Jacques Monet, who served as an adviser to Léger, noted:

> Autant pour permettre à l'Institution de mieux server l'unité nationale que pour désamorcer une situation qui risquerait de devenir explosive, je crois qu'il serait sage d'accroître l'indépendance sinon l'autorité du Gouverneur général vis-à-vis de la Reine, je parle ici d'enrichir des valeurs symboliques.

Monet played a more central role in the changes made in 1977 than would have usually been undertaken by an adviser, primarily because Léger had suffered a stroke six months after taking office in 1974 and as a result had impaired speech. It was Monet who undertook most of the background research and some of the discussions between Rideau Hall and the privy council and prime minister's office.

Trudeau met with the Queen at Rideau Hall on October 15, 1977. One of the key items they discussed was the delegation of the last of the elements of the royal prerogative related to external relations. Trudeau explained the ongoing situation in terms of Quebec separatism and the fear that the Crown could be used by separatists to say that Canada was not even an independent country and still had to go to London to have certain matters approved. The theory was that if the proposed changes were made, no such claim could be made, as all the functions of the Canadian Crown could be executed in Ottawa. The Queen was not opposed to the change, but she wanted the opportunity to allow Australia and New Zealand to consider similar changes. Léger then met with Sir Philip Moore, the Queen's private secretary, on October 16, when they discussed the same matter, and news of the Queen's consent was relayed to the governor general.

In his letter of December 28 to Michael Pitfield, clerk of the privy council, Moore confirmed that Her Majesty had no issue with the governor general exercising the following elements of the royal prerogative on her behalf:

a) The governor general will sign letters of credence and recall for Canadian ambassadors abroad, and letters of commission and recall for Canadian high commissioners to Commonwealth nations that do not recognize Her Majesty as head of state.
b) The governor general will authorize declarations of war and Canadian treaties of peace.
c) The governor general will provide his signature for full powers for signing treaties in head of state form and his signature for ratification of such treaties.

There is ample evidence to suggest that unlike previous changes, these matters were delegated to the governor general on the formal advice of the prime minister. The announcement of these changes was made by the prime minister's office on December 30, 1977. This time of year was chosen to minimize the level of potential public discontent. The briefing note given to the governor general and prime minister on the issue explained:

> Her Majesty retains "full power and authority," acting on the advice of her Canadian Prime Minister, to amend the *Letters Patent*. Likewise, it is understood that she retains the "power and authority," acting on like advice to approve and appoint the Governor General of Canada. There is nothing in the changes announced to suggest any alterations in Her Majesty's constitutional position as Queen of Canada, nor do they alter the position of the Crown as a vital part of Canada's parliamentary system (briefing note to Léger and Trudeau, December 1977).

The next significant change to the royal prerogative came in 1988, in the realm of honours. The Queen's power to grant coats of arms, badges and flags was delegated to the governor general with the creation of the Canadian Heraldic Authority (CHA) by *Letters Patent* in 1988. The CHA is part of the chancellery of honours administered by the office of the secretary to the governor general. Submissions of heraldic grants that include the royal crown continue to be made directly to the Queen for consent to use the crown. The *Letters Patent 1988* constituting the CHA saw the creation of a Canadian institution to administer the grant of symbols on behalf of the Crown in right of Canada. Previously, Canadians petitioned English and Scottish officials to be granted arms, and there remains significant doubt as to whether or not the College of Arms or Court of the Lord Lyon had any ability to act on behalf of the Queen in right of Canada. In essence, the creation of the CHA saw the patriation of one of the prerogatives of the Crown and the preservation of the Sovereign's role in matters that touched upon the granting of the symbol of the Crown.

In December 2004, changes were made to the format of the letters of credence and recall which had hitherto been signed by the governor general on the Queen's behalf. A new format was developed omitting reference to the Queen in the standard preamble that has traditionally been included in all federal *Letters Patent*, commissions and appointments. This preamble outlined the Queen's style and title as Queen of Canada, but this was replaced with the name of the governor general as of December 29, 2004. The announcement of the change was made by Prime Minister Paul Martin's office: "Letters of Credence and Recall presented by foreign High Commissioners and Ambassadors to Canada will now be addressed to the Governor General directly" (PMO Press Release, 29 December 2004). This removal of all reference to the Queen was made only after Martin had consulted with the Queen but, as in 1977, the change was only made after formal advice was tendered to the Sovereign by the Prime Minister – advice that she was bound to follow by constitutional convention. It was a change that resulted in much discussion in the press and Parliament following the initial announcement. In some ways this action mirrored steps taken by Eamon de Valera and the Irish Free State in 1937 through the *External Relations Act*, which effectively sought to remove all mention of the Sovereign without taking the final step towards becoming a republic at that time. The removal of the Queen's name from the letters of credence was a development that made absolutely no sense at all. The governor general's authority, both in law and symbolically, is derived from the person of the Sovereign and the broader institution that the Sovereign heads: the Canadian Crown. It was a blatant move to enhance further, then, Governor General Adrienne Clarkson's view of herself as Canada's head of state.

CONCLUSION

While the *Letters Patent 1947* do clearly delegate many of the Sovereign's powers to the governor general, we should remain mindful that this is done as enabling legislation, for use "in exceptional circumstances." There remain ten areas where the Sovereign continues personally to exercise the royal prerogative:

a) Appointment of the governor general
b) Amendments to the letters patent constituting the office of the governor general
c) Alteration of what matters will be referred directly to the Sovereign, commonly referred to as changes to the "existing practice"
d) Alterations in the royal style and title
e) Granting of honours (including the creation of)
f) Granting of royal patronage
g) Appointment of colonels-in-chief of Canadian regiments
h) Appointment of the Canadian secretary to the Queen
i) Designs for Canadian coinage
j) Permission for the inclusion of the crown in Canadian grants of arms and badges

The most recent of these matters to be brought before the Queen was the appointment of David Lloyd Johnston as governor general. The Queen's bestowal of the Royal Victorian Order upon twelve Canadians during her 2010 royal tour was another example of the Sovereign exercising the royal prerogative. Her Majesty also approved the creation of the Operational Service Medal while in Toronto during the same tour.

The fact that the Queen continues to exercise the royal prerogative in relation to the appointment of the governor general reveals her continuing paramountcy in the Canadian state. In the period leading up to the appointment of Michaëlle Jean as governor general in 2005, Paul Martin's government considered having the instrument signed by Governor General Adrienne Clarkson, but it was decided not to make this change, as it would require consultation with the Queen. While the governor general could indeed appoint his or her successor, this would only be logical if the Sovereign were held captive or incapacitated for an extended period of time. If anything, it would seem incredibly awkward to have a governor general involved in the process appointing a successor, simply because the appointment necessitates that the incumbent vacate the office. Excluding the Queen from the appointment would make it impossible to remove a governor general from office. In a constitutional crisis, how could any prime minister call upon a governor general to remove himself from office? Only the Queen can remove a governor general from office.

Although no Canadian prime minister has ever called upon the Sovereign to remove a governor general, the prorogation incident of 2008 clearly shows that adopting a narrow vision of what is possible in politics is risky. Having the Queen make the appointment ensures a level of accountability that can only be achieved by having the Sovereign as the final arbiter in such matters. Without this ability, a governor general could, in the extreme, decide not to accept a prime minister's advice to appoint a successor to Rideau Hall and remain in office for life.

As has been noted, there is nothing preventing the Queen from exercising the royal prerogative in any of the areas touched upon in this chapter. While there would be no legal impediment to delegating these elements of the royal prerogative from the Queen to the governor general, little would be gained by doing so. The speed of communication is now so efficient that consultation with the Sovereign can rapidly be achieved via telephone, fax and email, or even in person.

The path towards drafting the *Letters Patent 1947* and the development of practice surrounding the royal prerogative is one marked by delegation, not wholesale transfer of authority. The *Letters Patent 1947* are best viewed as an enabling document that allows for the delegation of the Sovereign's authority and a non-legislative mechanism to serve in place of a *Regency Act*, not a mechanism to transform the governor general into the Sovereign. By better understanding the origins, development and implementation of the *Letters Patent*, we gain a more comprehensive concept of the role of not only the governor general but of the Sovereign in relation to the royal prerogative and the legal role of the Sovereign in the Canadian state. We would be wise to consider how Louis St. Laurent, the main architect of the *Letters Patent 1947*, described them: "it is not felt the revised documents are revolutionary or startling in nature."

References

Arnenson, B.A. 1949. *The Democratic Monarchies of Scandinavia.* New York: D. Van Nostrand Co.

Canada. 1968. *Manual of Official Procedure of the Government of Canada.* Ottawa: Privy Council Office.

Clarkson, A. 2006. *Heart Matters.* Toronto: Viking Canada.

Dawson, R.M. 1948. *The Government of Canada.* Toronto: University of Toronto Press.

Eccles, W.J. 1964. *Canada Under Louis XIV, 1633-1701.* Toronto: McClelland and Stewart.

Evans, M.K. 1960. *Letters Patent, Instructions and Commissions of Canadian Governors General, 1867-1959.* Ottawa: Privy Council Office.

Heard, A. 1991. *Canadian Constitutional Conventions.* Toronto: Oxford University Press.

Keith, A.B. 1928. *Responsible Government in the Dominions.* 2nd ed. Oxford: Clarendon Press.

Kennedy, W.P.M. 1954. "The Regency Acts, 1937-1953." *University of Toronto Law Journal* 10(2): 248–54.

Library and Archives Canada. The Diaries of William Lyon Mackenzie King. Record Group 2, The Privy Council Office.

Kristinsson, V. and J. Nordal, eds. 1975. *Iceland 874–1974.* Reykjavik: Central Bank of Iceland.

Lacey, T.G. 1998. *Rising of Seasons: Iceland – Its Culture and History*. Ann Arbor: University of Michigan Press.

Messamore, B. 2006. *Canada's Governors General: Biography and Constitutional Evolution*. Toronto: University of Toronto Press.

Smith, D.E. 1995. *The Invisible Crown: The First Principle of Canadian Government*. Toronto: University of Toronto Press.

THE CROWN
AND
PARLIAMENT

4

THE CROWN AND THE CONSTITUTION: SUSTAINING DEMOCRACY?

DAVID E. SMITH

La Couronne peut-elle préserver la démocratie ? Si les principes monarchiques et démocratiques semblent à première vue incompatibles, la controverse suscitée par la récente prorogation du Parlement laisse entrevoir une convergence des intérêts qui en découlent. Chose certaine, jamais le public ne s'est autant intéressé au rôle de la Couronne (représentée au Canada par le gouverneur général) dans les questions constitutionnelles. L'auteur se demande si la Couronne vient en fait renforcer ou affaiblir la Constitution canadienne, avant de mesurer l'incidence des nouvelles technologies sur l'évolution des relations constitutionnelles. Reprenant les adjectifs employés il y a un siècle et demi par Walter Bagehot, il évoque pour le Canada la possibilité d'une Couronne certes moins « solennelle », mais plus « efficace ».

As one of the members of the planning committee that helped organize the 2010 conference on the Crown, and especially one who had a hand in designating the topics of the panels that make up the program, it would be presumptuous, if not irrational, to quarrel with the title assigned to me. Nor do I intend to do that. I do, however, want to say a few words about the topic of "The Crown and the Constitution: Sustaining Democracy?"

Let me say at the outset what, to my mind, this topic is not about. It is not about the comparative merits of monarchy and republicanism. Until there is some agreement, or even understanding, about the meaning of the Canadian monarchy, it is premature, and a recipe for failure were it tried, to balance its strengths and weaknesses against those of a republican constitution. (As an aside, the ingredients of a republican constitution are themselves not self-evident, but that is for another conference.) One indication of the uncertainty and unease that accompany the subject of the Canadian monarchy is the infrequency with which that phrase appears. The reason for this deserves examination, although whatever the explanation, it will embrace a rationale articulated more than sixty years ago by Gordon Robertson, then a member of the Cabinet Secretariat: "I don't think Canadians will like the term 'King of Canada,' no matter how logical it may be. Whatever the legal facts are, most Canadians ... have not thought of themselves as citizens of either a republic or a monarchy" (LAC. Reid Papers, Gordon Robertson comment, 27 July 1949). There is still much truth to that comment, and it goes far in explaining the ambivalence Canadians display when talking about the Crown and the constitution (and the lassitude they exhibit when discussing a republican alternative). Nor should this attitude be surprising. Canada, like Australia and New Zealand, and a handful of much smaller states, possesses a unique constitutional status, of which the surrogate representative of the Sovereign as local Crown is a fundamental element. In itself, that constitutional arrangement does not explain the ambivalence, but combined with historical and geographic features (proximity to the United States, for example), it reinforces the sentiment.

Another topic omitted from this paper is Walter Bagehot's trinity of rights due the Sovereign or her representative: to be consulted, to encourage, and to warn. (As one scholar has recently commented, that historic formulation has been altered to read: "to advise, encourage and warn." The substitution of the right to advise for the original right "to be consulted" is a large change indeed, and yet another topic that requires examination (Hicks 2009, 69)). Silence on this matter is not because these rights are unimportant. On the contrary, they are essential to legitimizing the relationship that continues to exist, as it did in Bagehot's time, between the dignified and efficient parts of Parliament. In this context it should be noted that the chapters in Bagehot's famous volume, *The English Constitution*, deal only with the three parts of Parliament, while the meaning of the word constitution, as used in the title of this paper, extends well beyond Parliament. This enhanced meaning deserves attention in any discussion of the Crown in Canada.

One reason for the elision of the familiar trinity is because it is so familiar to students of the parliamentary system of government. Where there may be room for debate and re-evaluation is the reputation its author holds as master interpreter of the constitutional position of the Crown. The attributions associated with this by now classic interpretation are increasingly subject to review. For instance, in Australia it has been said that "the law is coming to reflect the political reality that executive power does not descend from the Crown, but flows up from the electorate ..."(Curtis 1983, 6–7). In Canada, a similar, electoral democratic political culture appears to be emerging. At the time of the imminent legislative defeat of the Harper government and its replacement by a coalition of opposition parties, Professor Tom Flanagan argued that "only voters have the right to decide on the coalition" and, by inference, the transition of power (Flanagan 2009, A13). Dissent from this view on the grounds that sovereignty rests not with the people but with the Crown-in-Parliament, as demonstrated by the convention that political authority is monopolized by those who command the support of the House of Commons, has been strongly voiced (Russell and Sossin 2009). In turn, this orthodox interpretation has generated its own unorthodox response (Potter 2009).

Like the English, the Canadian constitutional formula links the public to the executive power through Parliament. It is for this reason that Parliament, specifically the House of Commons, has the indisputable authority to make and unmake governments. That many members of the public and representatives of the media in 2008 seemed to be confused about this bedrock foundation of parliamentary government was treated by scholars as a matter both perplexing and disturbing. Perhaps, but it should not have been viewed as surprising: in the midst of what quickly was labelled a "constitutional crisis," Ipsos Reid reported that "half of Canadians (51percent) believe the prime minister is directly elected by voters" (Ipsos Reid 2008). How this view can be held in a country that for more than 150 years has had responsible government under a constitutional monarchy is a puzzle.

When it is said, as the Friends of the Canadian Crown have said, that the public and the media need to be better informed about the Crown, that sentiment scarcely scratches the surface of the much more complex topic at issue here – the Crown and the Constitution. A number of examples might be offered to support that generalization. Prorogation is one of them. Much has been said since 2008 about the governor general's acceding (twice) to the prime minister's advice to prorogue Parliament. It is not the intent here to discuss the details of those actions or to assess their constitutional correctness from the perspective of either party to that discussion. Among the topics that do deserve attention, however, are the remedies critics of the prime minister's actions have proposed.

Take, for example, the suggestion made by Professor Andrew Heard that in future the House of Commons be dissolved or prorogued only after a vote by the *chamber* (Heard 2010, A11). That vote, and not the prime minister's personal advice, would then inform the governor general's decision whether to accept or reject the request. This suggestion requires close examination, for we know – after the Harper government's experiment with legislation in 2007 to establish fixed election dates – that uncertainty may arise when statute law is offered as a substitute for exercise of the prerogative. In September 2008, the prime minister advised the governor general to dissolve Parliament and set a polling day for October 14, 2008. The following year, that advice was challenged in the Federal Court by Duff Conacher and Democracy Watch as being in contravention of the fixed election date legislation (more precisely, the *Canada Elections Act*, as amended in 2007). In its decision, the Court found that "the Governor General has discretion to dissolve Parliament pursuant to Crown prerogative … Any tampering with this discretion may not be done via an ordinary statute, but requires a constitutional amendment under section

41 of the *Constitution Act, 1982"* (Federal Court 2009, para. 53; Stoltz 2010). Moreover, Professor Heard's proposal is not as modest as it may at first appear. It would give to one chamber of the legislative branch a power that has historically rested with the executive. Still, the proposal has the advantage, in light of the Federal Court's decision, that it would reduce but not remove the Crown's discretion, since the governor general would grant or deny dissolution or prorogation according to his or her interpretation of the vote of the House.

Here is a proposal, the constitutional consequences of which would take some time to examine. Nonetheless, in its barest outline it reveals the contradictions that reside in the constitution but which are normally disguised by the operation of its conventions. How to reconcile prerogative with accountability? In this context it deserves mention that following the governor general's acceptance of prime ministerial advice to prorogue Parliament in December 2009, some critics of the decision argued that the governor general should provide "a written decision," which would "force the governor to examine whether the reasons are appropriate for modern Canada" (Hicks 2009, 69; see also Martin 2008). Behind that recommendation lies a whole philosophy of mind at odds with the assumptions that support constitutional monarchy. Whether stated reasons would clarify the constitutional issues and relationships at play in this set of facts is open to doubt, or at least speculation. Here again is one more subject that deserves careful analysis.

Section 9 of the *Constitution Act,1867* states that "the Executive Government and Authority of and over Canada is hereby declared to continue and be vested in the Queen." It is difficult to overemphasize the significance of that provision. Of its manifold and important features, none is greater than this: under the Canadian constitution the executive is not a creature of legislation but independent of it. The implications of that status or placement are profound in an era, such as the early twenty-first century, concerned with enforcing executive accountability. Yet, like so much else about the Crown and the Constitution, this central feature of government is inadequately understood. As an aside, it should be said that it is the absence of "constitutionally rooted executive authority" that makes Nunavut, the Northwest Territories and Yukon "in effect federal protectorates" (Sossin 2006, 53).

In the Canadian constitutional arrangement, the government of the day is no mere executive. As a monarchy where there is a "real" executive and a "formal" executive, where the real executive is made up of members of the legislature, where that real executive exercises prerogative power inherent in the formal executive, where the formal executive in a province (the lieutenant-governor) is constitutionally empowered (s. 90) to reserve provincial legislation for the "Signification of Pleasure," that is, approval, by the federal real executive (cabinet), where the same body (the federal cabinet) may direct Parliament to make remedial laws in the matter of denominational education in a province – in such an arrangement of responsibilities the easy distinction presumed to exist between legislative and executive powers in the Canadian constitution is not immediately apparent. Arguably, this imprecision is a source of great power – usually to the executive. The unconvinced might reply that, the prerogative aside, these are archaic, moribund powers, relics of the quasi-federal system the Fathers created.

In addition to the obvious retort that there have been a number of opportunities to remove these provisions yet they remain in the Constitution (in the case of s. 90 entrenched after 1982 by a unanimity amendment provision), there is Eugene Forsey's oft-repeated pronouncement that provisions in respect of lieutenant-governors give to the central government power to preserve, in each province, the system of responsible cabinet government (Forsey 1960). He repeated this view in 1979 following the appearance of a Canadian Bar Association recommendation that the lieutenant-governor should be renamed "the Chief Executive Officer of the province [and] should not be subject to federal control." That recommendation he termed "objectionable" because it would "remove one of the few safeguards against a province playing ducks and drakes with the Constitution" (Forsey 1979).

The legal basis of responsibility of ministers lies in the Privy Council oath all cabinet ministers take on becoming members of the Council. It is the Privy Council which, according to section 11 of the *Constitution Act, 1867*, "aid[s] and advise[s] in the Government of Canada." At any particular time, the current cabinet is the active part of the Privy Council, although it speaks and acts in the name of the entire Council. "[T]he Governor General acting by and with the advice of Cabinet [is] the first emanation of executive power" (*Angus v. Canada* (1990), cited in Tardi 1992, 83). Ministerial authority for a portfolio established by departmental statute originates in a second oath ministers swear on appointment to cabinet, an Instrument of Advice and Commission under the Great Seal being a necessary formality.

Ministers are chosen by the prime minister, their appointment recommended to the governor general, and their tenure in a portfolio at the discretion of the prime minister. Ministerial dismissal or ministerial resignation occurs only on the agreement of the prime minister. Similarly, the life of a government is tied to the decision of the prime minister, since he or she is the sole adviser to the governor general. More than this, deputy ministers are appointed, and may be dismissed, by the prime minister as one of his or her special prerogatives. That power is regularized by order-in-council going back to Sir Wilfrid Laurier's time.

What has the foregoing discussion to do with the subject of this paper – the Crown and the Constitution? A one-word reply: everything. Support for that claim may be found in the proliferation of literature on the Crown and its prerogatives. See, for instance, M. Sunkin and S. Payne, *The Nature of the Crown: A Legal and Political Analysis* (1999); Philippe Lagassè, *Accountability for National Defence: Ministerial Responsibility, Military Command and Parliamentary Oversight* (2010); Paul Craig and Adam Tomkins, *The Executive and Public Law* (2006). A common theme in this literature is the contribution the Crown makes to concentrating power in the political executive in British-styled parliamentary systems. The obverse of concentrated power is what Canadian critics call the democratic deficit. In fact, it is the Crown's powers exercised on the advice of the prime minister, as in prorogation or dissolution of Parliament, or myriad appointments – to the judiciary and the Senate, for example – that have begun to focus public attention on the Crown.

This attention is neither sustained nor the criticism accompanying it always well-informed. Nonetheless, and in marked contrast to the past, the focus of comment is constitutional in nature: no longer the conventional (and limited) talk of the Crown as a unifying national symbol, although it may still play that role in different dress – honours, for instance; no longer agitation over its imperial-colonial dimension, although this was never a prominent feature of debate about the Crown in Canada. British personalities – the Queen and Prince Charles, for instance – continue to cast a shadow over discussion of the Crown in Canada, but less than formerly. Equally significant is the prominence of the individuals who have occupied the office of governor general over the last decade-and-a-half and the fragmentation of the party system in the same period, thus denying to any one party the opportunity to form a majority government and thereby linking in the public mind, to a degree rarely seen before, the governor general with the political forum. In the language Bagehot made familiar, the Crown in Canada, as represented by the office of governor general, is ceasing to be the indisputably dignified institution political science textbooks made it out to be and is emerging, for some observers at least, possibly as an efficient institution.

Can the opinion in that last sentence really have any substance? Is it too extreme to defend? The answer to the first question is "yes," and to the second "no." For almost two years a continual controversy enveloped the relationship between the governor general and the prime minister or between the governor general and the leaders of the opposition parties, whether the subject was the proposed coalition, or prorogation of Parliament, or dissolution of the House of Commons. In the discussion surrounding these issues, the constitutional crisis of 1926 has invariably been cited, as has the exhaustive analysis of that event written by Eugene Forsey (Evatt and Forsey 1990). Again, there is no need to explore in detail what happened eighty years ago, except to say that the Byng-King affair and its resolution – and unlike the events of 2007 through 2010, the 1926 controversy actually did have a conclusion – have only peripheral relevance to the current situation. While the controversy of 2008–09 may have been confined to the period of Michaëlle Jean as governor general, the autobiography written by her predecessor, Adrienne Clarkson, speaks to similar concerns on her part about Paul Martin, who led a minority government after the 2004 election, seeking an early dissolution to the 38th Parliament (Clarkson 2006, 192).

Compared to Canadian-born governors general since 1952, or to Viscount Byng in 1926 for that matter, the most recent governors general have been very much centre-stage in matters that are by any definition constitutional. The discussion that has taken place has been as national in character as it has been partisan, in the sense that while the leaders of the opposition parties have disagreed with the advice the prime minister has offered the governor general, public and media opposition have been rooted in concern for preserving democratic values and limiting prime ministerial power (*The Globe and Mail* 2010, A18). A petition signed by 170 academics accusing the prime minister of "undermining our system of democratic government" may not be conclusive evidence of popular unrest, but, in the words of *The Globe and Mail* columnist Lawrence Martin, it "shows democracy matters to Canadians" (Martin 2010; see also Dickerson 2010). Is this a pale, Canadian parallel to the Tea Party movement in the United States, at whose core, says American legal academic Sanford Levinson, lies "the lawyerhood of all citizens"? (Liptak 2010).

What exactly are these constitutional matters? There are three meanings associated with the adjective. First, there is constitution as law (and convention). As already noted, the Crown provides the legal foundation for the structure of government and the doctrine of ministerial accountability. How adequately that doctrine is realized in practice is a different matter. Second, there is constitution as composition or aggregation. Essentially, this is about federalism, and really beyond the boundaries of this paper, except that federalism in Canada is very much about the Crown. Elsewhere, I have described the Canadian federation as one of compound monarchies. From being perceived as an institution amenable to enforcing Sir John A. Macdonald's highly centralized federal ambitions, the Crown came to underwrite the autonomy of the provinces and thus lay the foundation for the federative principle in Canada. This is the explanation for the strength of executive federalism in Canada and why Canada differs so markedly from its neighbour, the United States, the first modern federation. There, federalism is about representation; indeed, that is all that it is about. Here, it is about jurisdiction. In this contrast lies the source of frustration would-be reformers of Canada's Senate experience, since the Canadian body is unrepresentative in any popular sense of the term.

The third meaning of constitution is health or condition, in other words, the subject alluded to in the sub-title of this paper. Does the Crown strengthen or weaken the constitution? Somewhere in his voluminous writings, Harold Innis remarks that "lack of unity preserves Canadian unity." Anyone familiar with Canadian history and politics will understand the logic of that aphorism. The potential for the country to fly apart – although it never does – seems not too exaggerated, whether the threat comes from annexationist sentiment, secession movements, or continental integration. Does the Crown make that potential real, or does it limit it? At Confederation, the Crown was expected to strengthen the centre, yet over time executive power in the provinces was found to be co-equal with legislative power. As a consequence, the concept of the province as an administrative unit and the lieutenant-governor as its executive officer disappeared. In its place, as the Judicial Committee of the Privy Council said (with emphasis added): "[T]he Dominion government should be vested with such ... powers, property and revenues as were necessary for the due performance of its constitutional functions, and ... *the remainder should be retained by the provinces for the purposes of the provincial government"* (*Liquidators of the Maritime Bank v. The Receiver General of New Brunswick* 1892).

In his review of *The Invisible Crown: The First Principle of Canadian Government*, J.L. Granatstein wrote that, whatever the author's intent, "his complex argument [about compound monarchies] is sure to bolster the case put forward by Canadian monarchists, though there seems no reason whatsoever that the same system could not exist even in the absence of a Canadian monarch" (Granatstein 1996). One response to that comment is that while perhaps the same "system" might exist (or be perpetuated) in the absence of monarchy, it would not have developed as it has without the monarchically based constitution given Canada in 1867 and without subsequent judicial determination that the Crown (along with its prerogatives) was divisible in conformity with federal and provincial spheres of jurisdiction. Irrespective of one's sympathies as to what might be thought the right constitution for the country, there is no question that in the evolution of Canadian federalism the Crown and its interpretation by the courts is the turning point.

Sustaining federalism is not the same thing as sustaining democracy. For that matter, the division of powers embedded in federalism presents its own challenge to democracy's goal of communicating the popular will regardless of divided jurisdictions. The juxtaposition of monarchy and democracy is stark because two millennia ago Aristotle saw them as incompatible forms of government. In modern-day Canada neither exists in pure form. Constitutional monarchy in Canada is different from its counterpart in the United Kingdom just as is the relationship of each to its own Parliament. At no time and in respect to no subject has this contrast been more sharply defined than it was in 2008–09 on the topic of prorogation. It is not necessary to undertake a comparative study of prorogation or other practices associated with the prerogative in the two countries to make the point. The principle that informs the relationship between Crown and prime minister in each is now fundamentally different. The contrast between what has occurred in 2008–09 in Canada and decades-long practice in the UK is eminently set down in the following letter (dealing with the dissolution of Parliament) written to *The Times* a quarter of a century ago:

> [I]t is often argued in Britain that because there are no precedents for a royal refusal of a request to dissolve Parliament, the power to refuse is moribund. Surely ... the fact that acute controversy concerning the role of the Crown has been consistently avoided in the United Kingdom for more than a century is evidence, not that the Sovereign has been bound by convention invariably to follow advice of a government to dissolve Parliament, instead of seeking an alternative ministry, but that ... all ministers have been particularly scrupulous to shield the Sovereign from the necessity of making any debatable use of the royal discretion (Heasman 1985).

If ever there was such a convention in Canada (or even appreciation of the issue), that is no longer the case. The greater frequency of minority governments here than in the United Kingdom may be one explanation, since the pressure of governing increases when legislative majorities disappear. That said, discussions among party leaders in the United Kingdom following the general election in May 2010 that produced no single party majority in the Commons, and which led to the country's first coalition government in over a half century, involved the Queen in no respect until the leader of the Conservative Party, who it was understood would be the new prime minister, was invited to Buckingham Palace. The aura, the experience and the independence of the Sovereign from government in London stand in contrast with the absence of these characteristics for the governor general in Ottawa. The visibility of the Sovereign is one of her strengths – just being there is enough. Arguably, the more visible the governor general the more vulnerable he or she appears. Governors general must do something – charity, sports, arts, the North – in addition to the conferring of honours, to anchor themselves in the public's mind and in public life.

It is too early to pronounce definitively, but there is reason to believe that events of 2008–09 may be interpreted as repositioning the office of governor general. It is one thing to intone, in textbook style, Bagehot's trinity of rights due the Crown; it is another for a governor general, enveloped by constitutional controversy and the focus of media attention, to make a decision that he or she knows will inevitably lead to public criticism. That said, the most significant feature of this rare constitutional "moment" lies in this: as "the crisis" mounted, the governor general seemed more and more relevant to the situation. The media and the public paid close attention to the issue as it developed, and at no time did the subject of the utility of constitutional monarchy as Canada's form of government enter the debate. Tom Flanagan, who advanced the argument that "only voters have the right to decide on the coalition," also acknowledged that it was "the Governor General, as protector of

Canada's constitutional democracy, [who] should ensure the voters get [that] chance." Significant too, no governor general's "party" emerged. (Michael Ignatieff's decision in May 2010 to press publicly for an extension to Michaëlle Jean's term as governor general suggests that qualification to that general statement may yet be required.) Throughout the prorogation controversy, the positions taken by participants were defined by where they sat in the House of Commons. Among the ranks of the public, partisan allegiance was almost as predictable an indicator of support for or opposition to the prime minister's request. In contrast, the governor general was perceived by public and politicians alike as impartial. Thus the constitutional issue at stake remained clear because the principal actors – prime minister, leaders of the opposition parties and governor general – played the roles assigned to them.

Whether or not the prime minister's initiative and the response it elicited constituted a parliamentary crisis remains an open question; it is tangential as well. Nonetheless, the fact that since late 2008 the governor general has acceded twice to the request of the first minister to prorogue Parliament is of major importance to the conduct of politics in Canada. Constitutional choices are not just events from the past; they continue at all levels and at all times. Recent precedents are no less compelling as guides to future decisions than precedents that arise out of the actions by prime ministers of a century ago.

From the perspective of the topic of this paper, and especially its subtitle, "sustaining democracy," the key element to understand is the logic of the constitutional choice that is made. To echo a theme mentioned earlier, is this best accomplished if the governor general gives reasons for his or her actions? Although the analogy with the courts may not be perfect, still it needs emphasizing that the work of the courts is not just about judging. On the contrary, the law is found, it is enunciated, it is delivered and it is debated in the press, scholarly journals and by the public. In this manner law and understanding of the law develop.

This is not the way of the Crown, but should it be? One of the features of the prorogation controversy, as indeed of all activity that might be defined as constitutional – and this is distinct from other gubernatorial work that involves ceremony, or the military, or patronage of institutions – is that it is the subject of commentary or interpretation. It was in this capacity that Bagehot made his reputation. Monarchy, he wrote, is "strong government … [because] it is intelligible government." By contrast, he said: "The nature of the constitution, the action of an assembly, the play of parties, the unseen formation of a guiding opinion, are complex facts, difficult to know, and easy to mistake" (Bagehot 1961, 89). That is, they have to be explained.

Bagehot was a journalist, and especially well-qualified for the role he assigned himself. Afterward came the scholars: among them Ivor Jennings, K.C. Wheare and Geoffrey Marshall in the United Kingdom and Eugene Forsey, J.R. Mallory and Peter Russell in Canada. The merit of their work does not require comment because it is not at issue. What deserves notice is that the part of the constitution that is the Crown's component of Parliament has long been deemed as foreign to popular understanding and deserving of specialists' treatment. There may be just cause for this tradition, popular ignorance of the constitution's provisions (for example, belief that the prime minister is elected) being one of them. Notwithstanding that explanation, the consequence of this interpretive tradition is to establish in matters constitutional a division between those who are insiders and those who are outsiders.

It is the specialist who answers not the most arcane but rather the most basic of constitutional questions: What constitutes a defeat of a government? When there is a defeat, what options does a government have? Where no party secures a majority of seats at a general election, which party forms a government? What constitutes sufficient grounds for a prime minister to secure assent from the governor general to a request for a dissolution or prorogation of parliament? The answers are based less on knowledge of rules than they are on understandings of courses of action suitable to a particular constellation of facts. How else to explain why the political party with the largest number (but not a majority) of legislative seats may form a government but sometimes it does not?

The concept of democracy does not fit well with the conventions of constitutional monarchy because whatever else it may be, the former concerns numbers. Democracy is about counting while constitutional monarchy is about weighing. The exercise of discretion is the foundation of the latter: when and whether the first minister advises dissolution (or prorogation) of Parliament; when and whether the governor general decides to accept that advice. Judgment on the part of all participants is required to make responsible government operate effectively. The system also requires a governor general who is perceived by the public to be impartial. Unlike the monarch in the United Kingdom, who can assume an authority that derives from tradition and public loyalty, the governor general requires approval (or acceptance) of the elected and the electors. These dual "constituencies," so to speak, have always existed. It is their comparative standing, vis à vis one another, that has changed, and changed relatively quickly.

The symbolic role of the governor general, that is, representing Canadians to themselves as well as to non-Canadians, remains a highly visible activity. One might say that it always has been visible. Still, a qualitative change has accompanied the transformation of communication in the last couple of decades. The protests about prorogation and the rallies organized across the country to communicate that opposition owed much of their rapid organization to the democratizing power of new technologies. Of course, this development is not unique to matters touching the Crown in Canada; it is the fact that the development now extends to the

Crown that is significant. From this perspective, it is arguably deceptive in the prorogation controversy to focus attention on the persons, or even offices, of the governor general and prime minister. The deception lies in this: limiting discussion to those "parties" omits the innovative feature of what has been happening with regard to the governor general, which is the emergence, outside of the walls of Parliament and the traditional organs of communication, like the print media, of the public as an engaged participant in the debate. To the degree that this is the case, then arguments that making and unmaking of governments are prerogatives of the House of Commons and dissolution and prorogation of Parliament are prerogatives of the prime minister as sole adviser to the governor general do not accord with public sentiment.

There is a paradox about democratic government in the early twenty-first century, one that is not limited to Canada. American scholars have discovered that people in the United States "desire to increase the influence of ordinary people" and are willing to achieve this end "by increasing the influence of ... unelected experts" (Hibbing and Theiss-Morse 2002, 140). This is the same rationale that explains Ipsos Reid's finding in 2004 that the current auditor general was "immensely trusted" by Canadians because "she has no vested interest and is viewed as being above politics" (Ipsos Reid 2004). Admittedly, it would be rash to apply these findings directly to the governor general without further study, which is not possible here. Yet, as the pre-eminent office under the constitution that lacks a "vested interest" and, moreover, is perceived to be "above politics," the office of governor general may be a candidate for inclusion in the category of non-partisan institutions that people disaffected with the conduct of electoral politics find attractive. (Analogously, Sir Michael Peat, the private secretary to Prince Charles, has defended the Prince's long-standing criticism of contemporary architecture on comparable grounds: "It is part of the Prince of Wales's role and duty to make sure the views of ordinary people that might not otherwise be heard receive some exposure" (Peat 2010, C2). At best a surmise, still this interpretation helps to explain the increased attention the office has received in the last decade. Canadian journalist Susan Riley said much the same thing about the "personal style" of Michaëlle Jean: "[It] endeared her to ordinary people; she gave them, if not a political voice, momentary visibility" (Riley 2010). To be more specific, controversy surrounding prorogation has augmented rather than initiated interest in the governor general who, in the person of either Michaëlle Jean or Adrienne Clarkson, has generated far greater publicity and in turn public awareness of the position than their predecessors ever did.

There is another paradox in the offing: if the governor general were to be perceived as sustaining democracy in a popular sense because he or she had become less identified with the operation of Parliament only, then the three parts of Parliament, once so close-knit, would become less so. The movement over time that has seen cabinet separate from the Commons and prime minister from cabinet would be followed, in this scenario, by a growing space between prime minister and governor general. With apologies to William Wordsworth, one can only say: "Bagehot! Thou shouldst be living at this hour: Canada hath need of thee." Or perhaps not: one of the few Canadians from the Confederation period to refer to Bagehot was Alexander Campbell, himself a Father of Confederation, who, in a letter to Sir John A. Macdonald, succinctly summarized his opinion of *The English Constitution*: "You must have experience in a colony to enable you fully to appreciate the inapplicability of much of the book" (rs, 83495-8).

Nonetheless, Bagehot perceived where others had not that the constitution was a construct. Each piece (in Canadian nomenclature – Crown, Senate and Commons) interlocks in myriad patterns over time producing a shifting set of relationships, although in Canada the political executive has always been dominant. The image that Bagehot painted of the constitution was one of hierarchy. A century and a half later, when the country is much more a mass political culture, that depiction is under scrutiny. Where do the people enter this arrangement? Reform of the Senate and reform of the plurality electoral system of the Commons are now promoted as means of aggressively injecting popular opinion into institutions of government. Participation of the public along with members of Parliament in the selection of members of the Supreme Court of Canada has also been proposed. Is it any wonder then that the office of governor general should attract the same popular desire when the issue is selecting its occupant (public consultations or Internet straw polls (Chase 2010)) or assessing the performance of his or her duties once selected?

How can the Crown, in the words of the subtitle of this paper, "sustain democracy" when the people have no direct role to play in its composition and activities? Then again, how can they have more of a role when popular politics in Canada is partisan politics, and for the Crown neutrality is everything? No one serves the Crown by exposing it to suspicion or criticism. In Canada, its reservoir of legitimacy is constrained by virtue of the relatively short terms of its appointees (as another paper in this conference notes, that term is shorter than for any officer of Parliament) and thus their frequent turnover, by the demanding set of criteria prospective appointees must meet, and by a political culture that seems ever more ready to exploit the Crown's powers for partisan advantage or, alternatively, to weaken them.

Does the Crown sustain Canadian democracy? The answer is a qualified "yes," if democracy is understood to mean constitutional government, such as, for instance, the rights of Parliament, and if it is understood that the Crown is not involved in a form of gladiatorial combat with the political executive. The Crown does not triumph over the executive by vanquishing it so much as it stands in the breach, so to speak, and bears the brunt of the attack on behalf of the people. It is in that respect that the relationship between the Crown and the Canadian constitution has become manifest in recent years in a manner hitherto unacknowledged and the implication of whose development remains still uncertain.

When Stephen Harper sought a candidate to replace Michaëlle Jean as governor general, he was reported to have established a "secret committee to search for candidates" who would possess constitutional knowledge and be non-partisan (Curry 2010). Ned Franks, a constitutional authority, praised the "new" process and "recommended that it be made permanent in law." How that object might be accomplished, he did not specify. Still, there was the sense that a precedent had occurred and that henceforth the nomination of individuals with close partisan attachments to the government-of-the-day – as had on occasion happened in the past – would not in future be tolerated. From this perspective, the relationship between formal and political executives had to a degree altered, and in a manner quite different from countries where that relationship is in fact regulated by statute law. At the same time that Canada's new governor general was being designated, Germany was choosing a new president through a "secret" election by a college of electors composed of members of the federal Parliament and of state representatives. Despite the institutional separation intended to discourage partisan influence, the presidential vote, according to *The New York Times*, was a "Test [for] Merkel's Ailing Coalition," one that the coalition survived. No one in Germany appears to find this manner of selection of the president problematic for the intrusion of partisan politics it permits, but then German presidents possess few of the prerogative powers that rest in the hands of Canada's governors general.

References

Angus v. Canada, [1990] 72 DLR (4th), 684 (FCA).
Bagehot, W. (1867) 1961. *The English Constitution*. Garden City, N.Y.: Doubleday.
Chase, S. 2010. "Ignatieff calls for Jean's term to be extended." *The Globe and Mail*. 3 May, A6.
Clarkson, A. 2006. *Heart Matters*. Toronto: Viking Canada.
Craig, P. and A. Tomkins. 2006. *The Executive and Public Law: Power and Accountability in Comparative Perspective*. New York: Oxford University Press.
Curry, B. 2010. "Harper's quest for a new G-G: Partisans need not apply." *The Globe and Mail*. 12 July, A4.
Curtis, L.J. 1983. "Freedom of Information in Australia." *Federal Law Review* 14: 5–27.
Dickerson, K. 2010. "Prorogation Protest Primer: Highlights and Must-Reads." Centre for Constitutional Studies. http:www.law.ualberta.ca/centres/ccs/issues/prorogation_Protest_Primer.php.

Evatt, H.V. and E.A. Forsey. 1990. *Evatt and Forsey on the Reserve Power*. A complete and unabridged reprint of H.V. Evatt, *The King and his Dominion Governors* (2nd ed., 1967) and E.A. Forsey, *The Royal Power of Dissolution of Parliament in the British Commonwealth*, 1968 reprint together with a new introduction by Dr. Forsey. Sydney: Legal Books.

Duff Conacher and Democracy Watch and the Prime Minister of Canada, the Governor in Council of Canada, the Governor General of Canada, and the Attorney General of Canada. [2009] FC 920.

Flanagan, T. 2009. "Only voters have the right to decide on the coalition." *The Globe and Mail*. 9 January, A13.

Forsey, E. 1960. "Extension of the Life of Legislatures." *Canadian Journal of Economics and Political Science* 26(4): 604–16.

Granatstein, J.L. 1996. Review of *The Invisible Crown: The First Principle of Canadian Government*, by David E. Smith. *Canadian Book Review Annual*. http://www.cbraonline.com/member/search/?action=details&page=0&sort_col=TITLE&so…

Heard, A. 2010. "Give the House the authority." *The Globe and Mail*. 11 January, A11.

Heasman, D.J. 1985. "Queen's prerogative." *The Times*. 24 October.

Hibbing, J.R. and E. Theiss-Morse. 2002. *Stealth Democracy: Americans' Beliefs about How Government Should Work*. New York: Cambridge University Press.

Hicks, B. 2009. "Lies My Fathers of Confederation Told Me: Are the Governor General's Reserve Powers a Safeguard of Democracy?" *Inroads* 25 (Summer/Fall): 60–70.

Ipsos Reid. 2004. "Straight talking Fraser strikes fear on the hill." *The Globe and Mail*. 12 February, A4.

— 2010. "In the Wake of Constitutional Crisis: New Survey Demonstrates that Canadians Lack Basic Understanding of Our Country's Parliamentary System." Survey. 15 December 2008. http://www.dominion.ca/DominionInstitute December15Factum.pdf.

Kempton. 2010. "The Professors' Letter Against the Prorogation of Parliament." *Ideas Revolution* (blog). http://kempton.wordpress.com/2010/01/11/the-professors-letter-against-the-prorogation-of-parliament.

Kulish, N. 2010. "Presidential vote tests Merkel's ailing coalition in Germany." *The New York Times*. 26 June, A5

Lagassè, P. 2010. "Accountability for National Defence: Ministerial Responsibility, Military Command and Parliamentary Oversight." IRPP Study no. 4, March. Montreal: Institute for Research on Public Policy.

Library Archives Canada, MG 26A, John A. Macdonald Papers. Alexander Campbell to Macdonald, 7 March 1888, 83495-8.

— MG 31, E 46, Escott Reid papers, vol. 28 (Constitutional Issues and Royal title, 1942-1960).

— MG 30, A 25, Eugene Forsey Papers (file 57/17 Corrections to "Canadians and their Government: Towards a New Canada," CBA report, n.d. [1979])

Liptak, A. 2010. "Tea-ing up the constitution." *The New York Times*. 14 March, WR5/6.

Liquidators of the Maritime Bank v. Receiver General of New Brunswick (1892) AC 437.

Martin, L. 2008. "The G-G needs to Break Her Queenly Silence and Explain Herself." *The Globe and Mail*. 22 December, A13.

— 2010. "Snowballing protest shows democracy matters to Canadians." *The Globe and Mail.* 14 January.

"Merkel's pick wins German presidency." 2010. *USA Today.* 1 July, 7A.

Potter, A. 2009. "Unbalanced Thoughts: Essays About Last Fall's Ottawa Show-down Highlight Only the Values of Parliamentary Tradition." *Literary Review of Canada* 17 (July/August): 3–4.

"Prince Charles defended for criticizing buildings." 2010. *The New York Times.* 2 July, C2.

Riley, S. 2010. "Harper's GG: The brand is bland." *Leader-Post* (Regina). 12 July, B9.

Russell, P.H. and L. Sossin, eds. 2009. *Parliamentary Democracy in Crisis.* Toronto: University of Toronto Press.

Sossin, L. 2006."The Ambivalence of Executive Power in Canada." In *The Executive and Public Law: Power and Accountability in Comparative Perspective*, eds. P. Craig and A. Tomkins. New York: Oxford University Press.

Sunkin, M. and S. Payne. 1999. *The Nature of the Crown: A Legal and Political Analysis.* New York: Oxford University Press.

Tardi, G. 1992. *The Legal Framework of Government: A Canadian Guide.* Aurora: Canada Law Book.

"Time to stand up for Parliament: The problem of excessive prime ministerial powers." 2010. *The Globe and Mail.* 23 January, A18.

5

THE CONSTITUTIONAL ROLE OF
THE GOVERNOR GENERAL

PATRICK J. MONAHAN

Ce chapitre examine dans quelles circonstances le gouverneur général peut refuser ou accepter l'avis du premier ministre. Tout en insistant sur l'extrême rareté de telles circonstances, l'auteur observe que le gouverneur général peut se voir obligé d'exercer son pouvoir discrétionnaire lorsque le premier ministre semble avoir perdu la confiance de la Chambre des communes. Mais y compris en pareille situation, il lui faut dans toute la mesure du possible s'en remettre au processus politique. À l'examen du précédent de décembre 2008, il estime que la gouverneure générale Michaëlle Jean a été bien avisée d'accepter la demande du premier ministre Stephen Harper de proroger le Parlement. En conclusion, il recense les avantages d'un « Manuel du Cabinet » qui établirait les conventions et principes constitutionnels en la matière.

INTRODUCTION

Until recently, most Canadians would have been entitled to assume that the constitutional role of the governor general was largely ceremonial, with little real opportunity to affect political outcomes. But the dramatic events of the first week of December 2008, in which Governor General Michaëlle Jean met for more than two hours with Prime Minister Harper before accepting his request to prorogue Parliament, have sparked renewed popular interest and considerable academic debate over the role of the governor general. Of particular interest is the question whether the governor general has a right or even a responsibility to refuse to accept the advice of a prime minister who has not been defeated on a motion of non-confidence.

In light of those events and the controversy they have engendered, this paper will focus on three questions relating to the constitutional role of the governor general. First, in what circumstances might it be appropriate for the governor general to refuse to act on the advice she receives from the prime minister? Second, was Governor General Jean's acceptance of Prime Minister Harper's 2008 request to prorogue Parliament consistent with established constitutional principles? Third, should there be additional or new legal restrictions imposed on the ability of the prime minister to request or obtain a prorogation of Parliament in the future?

THE GOVERNOR GENERAL'S RESERVE POWERS

Under the *Constitution Acts* as well as by statute, the governor general possesses extensive and far-reaching legal powers. These include the power to appoint or dismiss a prime minister, the power to appoint senators, superior court judges and lieutenant governors of the provinces, the power to summon and dissolve the House of Commons, and the power to assent to legislation (Monahan 2007, 58–61). But because the governor general is an appointed official who is not democratically accountable, it would generally be intolerable in a democratic country such as Canada for such broad powers to be exercised in accordance with the governor general's personal judgment or discretion. Therefore, it is a firmly established constitutional convention that the governor general must exercise her powers based on the advice of a prime minister who enjoys the confidence of (or who commands a majority in) the elected House of Commons. In this way, the governor general's considerable legal powers are actually controlled by the prime minister (or by ministers whom he has selected), which does accord with democratic principles.

Are there circumstances in which it can be said that a governor general is justified in refusing to act on the advice of the prime minister? Despite the principle of democratic accountability described above, the answer to this question must be "yes." This can be illustrated by considering the situation of a prime minister who has clearly lost the confidence of the House. It is widely understood that a prime minister in such a situation is constitutionally required to either resign or to request that the governor general dissolve Parliament and call a general election. But because this is an obligation that arises from constitutional convention rather than any legal requirement, it is theoretically possible (although in practical terms extremely unlikely) that a prime minister who has lost confidence would refuse to resign. In such an event, the governor general would be justified in refusing to accept advice from the prime minister and could, instead, dismiss him or her and appoint a new first minister, or else dissolve Parliament and call an election on her own motion.

Given the bedrock nature of the conventions of responsible government in the Canadian parliamentary system, a prime minister who has clearly lost the confidence of the House is certain to resign. The situations that will prove difficult in practice are those in which it is not entirely clear whether the prime minister does or does not enjoy the confidence of the

House. In situations where the political dynamic is ambiguous or uncertain, a prime minister may attempt to cling to office and refuse either to face the House of Commons on a clear question of confidence or agree to a dissolution and a general election. In such circumstances, it is possible that the governor general may be called upon to evaluate whether, in fact, the prime minister continues to enjoy the confidence of the House. How is the governor general to approach that task and, more particularly, when would it be appropriate for her to take the momentous step of refusing the advice of a prime minister who has not yet been defeated on a clear motion of non-confidence in the House?[1]

In my view, there are three key principles that should guide and inform the governor general in such special situations. The first is simply that there are, indeed, circumstances in which the governor general is entitled to come to a different view than that of the prime minister on the question of confidence, even though the government has not yet been defeated on a clear confidence measure. The reason is simply that otherwise, a government that had almost certainly lost the confidence of the House but had not yet been actually defeated could continue to cling to office by refusing to face the House for a period of up to one year.[2] It would seem to be wrong for the governor general to abdicate any role or judgment in the matter, simply because the government had not yet been formally defeated on a motion of non-confidence.

I should emphasize that this first principle is a narrow one. It does not seek to identify the precise circumstances in which the governor general should exercise independent judgment on the issue of confidence. It simply asserts that such circumstances must in fact exist.

The second principle is that, even if the governor general were to conclude that she should undertake an independent assessment of the issue of confidence, she should be extremely cautious before coming to a different conclusion from that of the prime minister on the question. As noted above, were the governor general to come to a different conclusion on the question of confidence from that held by the prime minister, thereby placing the governor general into direct conflict with her first minister, a major constitutional crisis would immediately ensue. It is impossible to predict how such a crisis would unfold, or what its long-term impact would be on the legitimacy and/or proper functioning of the office of

---

[1] The fact that such a course of action would be momentous is reflected in the fact that the last time a governor general refused to act on the advice of a Canadian prime minister who had not been defeated in the House was in 1926, at the time of the so-called King-Byng incident. That decision provoked a serious constitutional controversy, and any such action by a governor general in the contemporary context would certainly give rise to a constitutional crisis, since we would be faced with open conflict between the governor general and the prime minister.

[2] Section 5 of the *Constitution Act, 1982* requires a sitting of Parliament at least once every 12 months.

governor general. One of the imperatives for a governor general is to ensure continuity and legitimacy in the office of governor general itself. Thus before a governor general could come to a different view on the issue of confidence from that of her prime minister, and act on that view, truly exceptional circumstances would need to be present.

The third point, which grows out of the second, is that, where there is a potential for conflicting views on the question of confidence, the governor general should favour processes that will enable the democratically accountable political actors or processes to resolve authoritatively such ambiguity or uncertainty. In other words, the governor general should avoid, to the greatest extent possible, being placed in a position where she is required to make her own independent determination of who should hold the office of prime minister, or whether or when to hold an election. In practical terms, this suggests that the governor general should favour processes that force the leading political actors to clarify or firmly resolve amongst themselves, utilizing legitimate political processes, any ambiguity over the question of confidence. Once such a political resolution is achieved, the governor general can then revert to her normal and accepted role of acting on the advice of the prime minister. The governor general's role in such situations is not unlike that of a referee in an athletic contest, who should strive to ensure that the players determine the outcome of the contest themselves, in accordance with the fair rules agreed in advance, rather than have the outcome determined by the actions of the referee.[3]

Of course, these are not the only considerations relevant to situations where the matter of confidence is unclear. It will also be appropriate to consider a range of other factors, including the nature of the advice or request from the prime minister, as well as whether there is an alternative political leader who could reasonably be expected to command confidence and form a stable government. But in my view the three principles outlined above are fundamental considerations that will prove critical for a governor general in navigating the shoals of any potential constitutional crisis or deadlock in circumstances where it is unclear whether the prime minister retains the confidence of the House.

THE DECEMBER 2008 PROROGATION

With these background principles in mind, I turn to a consideration of the December 2008 precedent, in which Governor General Jean accepted

---

[3] This principle is reflected in the Government of New Zealand *Cabinet Manual 2008* (Cabinet Office, Department of the Prime Minister and Cabinet, Wellington, 2008) at paragraph 6.37: "The process of forming a government is political, and the decision to form a government must be arrived at by politicians." The New Zealand Cabinet Manual is discussed in more detail below.

Prime Minister Harper's request to prorogue the House until late January 2009.[4]

In the federal general election held on October 14, 2008, the Conservative Party led by Prime Minister Harper had been returned with an increased number of seats but remained in a minority position.[5] Parliament was called into session on November 18, 2008, and the Speech from the Throne was delivered on November 19. The Liberals indicated that they would not oppose the Speech from the Throne and, on November 27, the House of Commons approved the Speech in an unrecorded vote, thereby affirming confidence in the government (Valpy 2009, 3).

However on the same day (November 27), the finance minister delivered a fiscal and economic update. In addition to the normal projections regarding government revenues and expenditures, the update contained a number of highly controversial measures, including a proposal to eliminate the existing subsidies to political parties based on the number of votes received in the most recent general election. Finance Minister Flaherty indicated that elimination of the vote subsidy was part of the government's fiscal framework and would be regarded by the government as a confidence measure.

This provoked vehement opposition from the opposition parties, who immediately entered into negotiations with a view to defeating the government and, rather than provoking another election, forming a coalition government. On December 1, the leaders of the three opposition parties in the House announced that they had lost confidence in the Harper government and indicated their intention to introduce a non-confidence motion in one week's time (which was the earliest opportunity for such a motion to be debated and voted upon). They also announced that they had reached agreement on the terms under which a coalition government led by Liberal Leader Stéphane Dion and including members of the Liberal and New Democratic parties would take office. The Accord between the two partners to the coalition indicated that it would continue in effect until June 30, 2011, with Bloc Québécois leader Gilles Duceppe indicating that his party would refrain from voting non-confidence in the coalition government prior to June 30, 2010.

On December 4, the prime minister and the clerk of the privy council met at Rideau Hall with Governor General Jean and her secretary, Sheila-Marie Cook, and requested that Parliament be prorogued until January 26,

---

[4] I disclose that during this period I served as legal advisor to then-clerk of the privy council, Mr. Kevin Lynch. However, my discussion and analysis are based upon factual information in the public domain and do not disclose any advice I may have provided or confidential discussions that took place at that time.

[5] The party standings in the House of Commons after the 2008 election were as follows: Conservative Party 143; Liberal Party 77; New Democratic Party 37; Bloc Quebecois 49; Independent 2.

2009. The prime minister also indicated that on January 27 the government would introduce a budget, which would be a confidence measure. The meeting with the governor general lasted for over two hours, during which time Madame Jean met separately with her principal legal advisor, Osgoode Hall Law School Professor Peter Hogg.[6] At the conclusion of the meeting, the governor general accepted the prime minister's advice and Parliament was prorogued until January 26, 2009.

By the time Parliament reconvened on January 26, 2009, Michael Ignatieff had replaced Stéphane Dion as leader of the Liberal Party. Under Mr. Ignatieff's leadership, the Liberals supported the Speech from the Throne opening the new session as well as the budget introduced on January 27, thereby affirming the confidence of the House in the government and averting any potential political or constitutional crisis.

It is evident from this account that the governor general made her own independent assessment of whether to accept the prime minister's request for prorogation. This is reflected in the fact that, rather than automatically act on the prime minister's request (which would have been the normal and expected response if there had been no issue regarding confidence), the governor general sought her own independent advice and took over two hours to make a decision. Thus the first question to be asked is whether it was proper from a constitutional perspective for her to have undertaken this independent assessment.

The answer to this question is affirmative. Although the government had not yet been defeated on a clear motion of non-confidence, it was a certainty that it would have been defeated had the House met on December 8. As suggested by the first principle set out in the previous section, a prime minister who is about to lose a vote of confidence cannot be allowed to cling to office by depriving the House of Commons of the reasonable opportunity to vote on the matter. This is consistent with the 1926 King-Byng precedent[7] and with the views of respected commentators (Hogg

---

[6] One question that arises is the appropriateness of the governor general retaining independent constitutional advisors in these kinds of difficult situations, or whether the governor general ought to seek legal advice exclusively from the government's legal advisors. It is possible, if this practice were to continue, that the governor general's decision to seek independent legal advice could attract some controversy. Assuming that the governor general also receives advice from the government's own legal advisors, provided through the clerk, and the separate advisor is genuinely independent and impartial, and has impeccable legal credentials (such as Professor Hogg), there would seem no concern in principle over the governor general seeking outside legal advice in this manner.

[7] In 1926, Lord Byng refused to accept the prime minister's request to dissolve the Parliament and call a general election in circumstances where there had been an election eight months earlier, and where it was clear the government was about to be defeated on a motion of non-confidence. While this precedent continues to provoke debate amongst commentators, the principal issue that provokes controversy is whether the governor general was correct in calling upon Arthur Meighen to form a government, given that Mr. Meighen was defeated a week after taking office; the predominant view is that Lord Byng had the right

2009; Franks 2009, 33). Thus it can safely be concluded that Governor General Jean was correct in her decision to independently determine whether to grant the prime minister's request.

Given that the governor general had an independent assessment to make, the second, more difficult question is whether she was correct in granting the prime minister's request. Given subsequent events, particularly the ousting of Mr. Dion as Liberal leader and the decision of new Liberal leader Ignatieff to abandon the coalition and support the government, most commentators now take the view that the governor general made the correct decision.[8] But the appropriateness of the governor general's decision must be assessed based on the circumstances that were known at the time, and without the benefit of hindsight or knowledge of how subsequent events would unfold.

In considering this issue, it is important to begin by considering the precise nature of the prime minister's request, as well as the consequences that would flow as a result of the governor general's acceptance of it. The request for prorogation was certainly significant in that it had the effect of postponing for a period of approximately seven weeks an impending vote of confidence that was scheduled to take place in four days' time. But it is also important to note that the request was limited and bounded. The prime minister was seeking a prorogation only until January 26, 2009, at which time a new Speech from the Throne would be delivered and a budget tabled. Both these matters were questions of confidence which would permit the House to express its view authoritatively on the matter of confidence at that time.

It is also relevant that, although a delay of seven weeks is certainly not trivial, the House had already been scheduled to adjourn on December 12, 2008, for the holiday break and was not expected to resume sitting until January 26, 2009. In short, granting the request would only involve the sacrifice of seven days of scheduled sitting time.

Turning now to examine the other side of the coin, what would have been the result had the governor general refused the prime minister's request for prorogation on December 4, 2008? First, as discussed above, the governor general's refusal would very likely have provoked an unprecedented political and constitutional crisis. The prime minister had already indicated that he did not regard the proposed coalition government as legitimate and thus it was unlikely that he would have simply stepped aside and advised the governor general to call upon Mr. Dion to form a government. In fact, there is every indication that the prime

---

to independently assess the propriety of the prime minister's request, given the imminent defeat of the government (Hogg 2007, sec. 9.7(d)).

[8] Of the essays in Russell and Sossin, only Andrew Heard takes the position that the governor general should have refused to accept the request for dissolution (Heard 2009); see also his chapter in the present volume.

minister would have immediately sought dissolution of the House and a general election.

In the circumstances that existed at that time, it is difficult to see how the governor general could have granted such a dissolution request. Mr. Harper had previously been granted dissolution less than three months prior, and thus would have been in the position of asking for a second dissolution close on the heels of the first. Most commentators are of the view that a prime minister seeking two dissolutions within a space of less than six months is not automatically entitled to a second dissolution. Moreover, there was a viable alternative government that at the time appeared in a position to provide stable government. The two parties to the coalition, the Liberals and the NDP, had committed themselves in writing to a set of policy proposals, and they had the clearly expressed written support of the Bloc Québécois; thus they appeared to be in a position to command the confidence of the House of Commons for a period of at least 18 months. (The fact that the coalition collapsed when the House was prorogued should not lead us to conclude that the same fate would have befallen the coalition partners had they been given an opportunity to form the government. The grant of political power would have surely disciplined and solidified the coalition partnership.) Thus, unlike the situation in 1926 when the governor general called upon the leader of the opposition to form a government only to see that government defeated a week later, there was at the time every reason to believe that the coalition government (whether it was led by Stéphane Dion or, following an expected leadership campaign, some other Liberal leader) would have been able to govern effectively for an extended period of time.

It is impossible to predict the precise course of political events had the governor general refused the prime minister's request for dissolution and, in particular, whether the vote of non-confidence would have taken place in the precise manner that was anticipated at the time of the prime minister's visit to Rideau Hall on December 4. But however events would have unfolded, the most likely ultimate outcome was that the governor general would have been required to dismiss Mr. Harper as prime minister, over the latter's objections, and call upon Mr. Dion to form a government. This is because the governor general could not have properly granted Mr. Harper's request for a dissolution and it was unlikely, for the reasons discussed above, that Mr. Harper would have voluntarily resigned in order to permit Mr. Dion to form a government.

It is my view that, faced with these alternatives, and in light of the principles I have outlined above, granting the prime minister's request was far preferable to refusing it. As I have suggested, granting the request involved a significant but bounded delay in the scheduled vote of confidence. In other words, it did not involve the governor general dictating political outcomes, but merely postponing for a limited period an eventual resolution of the confidence issue by the political actors themselves. Moreover, the delay would provide an opportunity to gain a clearer understanding of the likely stability of the proposed coalition government. If the parties to the coalition were able to maintain their commitment to it during the period of prorogation, that would strengthen its legitimacy and right to form the government if Mr. Harper's government was defeated at the end of January. On the other hand if, as later events demonstrated, the coalition fragmented, that too would provide the governor general with important evidence to inform any decision she might have been called upon to make at the end of the January 2009.

The alternative scenario, involving the governor general's refusal to prorogue, followed by the likely dismissal of the prime minister and a request to Mr. Dion to form a government, would have been unprecedented in Canadian political history. Unlike in the first scenario (i.e. granting the request), the refusal to grant prorogation would have meant that the governor general was in effect deciding that a new government would take office. This involved the governor general determining political outcomes to a much greater extent than strictly necessary, which is inconsistent with the second and third of the foundational principles identified above. Moreover, this course of action involved considerable risks and dangers to the office of governor general itself, since it is likely that in any subsequent election campaign, the actions of the governor general would have featured as a significant political issue in the campaign. The outcome and long-term impacts on our political institutions generally and on the office of the governor general in particular were impossible to confidently assess at that time.

Thus, on balance, the governor general's decision to accept the prorogation request was the correct one. Although it involved a postponement of the confidence vote, the period of delay was limited and publicly known, and the fate of the government would be determined by the political actors rather than the governor general.[9] The considerable risks and uncertainties associated with the alternative option, combined with the much more prominent political role it would have involved for the governor general, indicate that it would have been both unwise and imprudent for the governor general to have refused Mr. Harper's request.

Limiting the Power to Seek Prorogation

Changes to the office of the governor general, including the power of the governor to prorogue Parliament, require a constitutional amendment

---

[9] The time-limited nature of the prorogation request was significant. Had the prime minister sought a longer prorogation, without adequate or proper explanation of the need for the additional grant of time, in my view the governor general would have been entitled to indicate that such a request would not be acceptable.

supported by both Houses of Parliament as well as all ten provincial legislatures.[10] Such agreement is highly unlikely, which rules out for all practical purposes any attempt to directly limit the power of the governor general to prorogue Parliament. However, the events of December 2008, as well as a subsequent prorogation request from Mr. Harper on December 30, 2009, which was also granted,[11] have prompted various proposals for limiting the power of the prime minister to request a prorogation. In particular, in March of 2010, the House of Commons adopted a resolution that would have required the prime minister to obtain the consent of the House prior to seeking a prorogation of more than seven days' duration.[12]

Would such a limitation on the power to request prorogation be desirable as a matter of constitutional principle? While there are persuasive considerations on both sides of this question, in my view on balance such a reform would not be desirable. The first consideration to keep in mind is that, as the precedent of 2008 indicates, the current constitutional principles and conventions governing prorogation can and do function properly (Cameron 2009, 189). As has been discussed, the prime minister does not have an untrammeled or absolute right to obtain a prorogation from the governor general. Rather, in circumstances where there is doubt regarding whether the prime minister continues to enjoy the confidence of the House, the governor general is entitled to make an independent assessment of the propriety of the request. That assessment is based on the kinds of principled considerations that have been described above.

If the prime minister were required to obtain the consent of the opposition parties prior to seeking prorogation, the power to assess the appropriateness of the request would be transferred from the governor general to the leaders of the opposition parties in the House. There is no

---

[10] The power to prorogue Parliament is one of the powers attached to the office of governor general of Canada. See *Letters Patent Constituting the Office of Governor General of Canada*, 1 October 1947, clause VI. Thus any proposed limitation of the power to prorogue Parliament would require a resolution supported by both federal Houses as well as the ten provincial legislatures, in accordance with the *Constitution Act, 1982*, s. 41.

[11] In December 2009, there was no doubt that the prime minister enjoyed the confidence of the House and thus the governor general automatically granted the request, in accordance with established principles of responsible government. However, the prorogation was criticized on grounds that it was motivated by a desire to avoid hearings into the treatment of Afghan detainees by the Canadian military. This prompted widespread political protests across the country and calls to limit the power of the prime minister to seek prorogation.

[12] By convention, the governor general's power to prorogue Parliament is exercised on the advice of the prime minister. Thus any attempt to legally limit the ability of the prime minister to seek prorogation would likely constitute an indirect attempt to amend the powers of the office of governor general and, as noted above, would require a formal constitutional amendment pursuant to section 41(a) of the *Constitution Act, 1982*. Since the House resolution passed in March 2010 was not intended to have legal effect, no constitutional issue arose. I leave the constitutional issue to one side for the moment, as I wish to consider the question of whether such a limitation would be desirable as a matter of principle.

guarantee that their assessment would be superior to that of the governor general. Indeed, it can fairly be expected that the dominant considerations for the leadership of the opposition parties would turn on short-term considerations of partisan political advantage. It is difficult to see why these political considerations and decision-makers ought to be preferred to the independent and principled analysis of a properly advised governor general, guided by the foundational principles I have earlier described (Tremblay 2010, 16).

At the same time, it is clearly desirable to attempt to further clarify the relevant constitutional principles, so that the circumstances in which an unelected governor general may be called upon to exercise independent judgment are reduced or eliminated. In this regard, the approach that has been taken in New Zealand, where the Cabinet Office has created an authoritative *Cabinet Manual* setting forth the relevant constitutional principles,[13] seems to hold considerable promise for Canada. The *Cabinet Manual* is not legally binding, but merely attempts to record current constitutional arrangements; however, the *Manual* is updated and revised as required and, upon taking office, each new government endorses it as an authoritative statement of government operations. This adds to its legitimacy and authority, with the prime minister noting in the most recent edition that "[s]uccessive governments have endorsed the Cabinet Manual as a sound, transparent, and proven basis on which to operate."[14] The New Zealand *Cabinet Manual* has a chapter describing the role of the governor general in the formation of a government, stressing the fact that the governor's role is simply to ascertain "where the confidence of the House lies, based on the parties' public statements" and not to "form the government or to participate in any negotiations …"[15]

The idea of creating an authoritative source document that could guide political actors in the exercise of their responsibilities has recently been adopted in the United Kingdom. In February 2010, then-Prime Minister Brown asked the cabinet secretary to consolidate the existing constitutional conventions applicable to government operations into a single written document.[16] The purpose of the resulting Cabinet Manual is "to guide and not to direct", and the document is to have no formal legal status and is not meant to be legally binding. A draft chapter on elections and government formation was published in early 2010, and that document is thought to have clarified the conventions that apply in a minority parliament situation. It has also been suggested that the draft

---

[13] See the *Cabinet Manual*, note 3 above.

[14] See the Foreword to the 2008 Edition by then-Prime Minister Clark at p. xv.

[15] Ibid., paragraph 6.39.

[16] See Cabinet Secretary Gus O'Donnell, "Speech on the Draft Cabinet Manual," 24 February 2011 at http://www.cabinetoffice.gov.uk/sites/default/files/resources/speech-cabinet-manual-24feb2011.pdf.

chapter helped to guide the political actors in the discussions that took place immediately following the May 2010 election and that led to the formation of a coalition government.[17] A full draft of the Manual was published in December 2010 and, following a period of public comment, it will be approved by the government as well as by the House Home Affairs Committee.

In my view, there would be considerable value in developing an authoritative source document of this kind in Canada. A Canadian version of a cabinet manual would not be legally binding, but would merely restate the existing constitutional rules and principles, which means it would not involve a constitutional amendment and not engage the constitutional amending formula (Russell and Milne 2011, paras 2.14–2.17).

At the same time, it would clarify the roles and responsibilities of all the political actors in situations where there is some question as to whether the government continues to enjoy the confidence of the House of Commons.[18] This kind of clarity on the fundamental ground rules that apply in these kinds of situations will assist the political actors in assessing how best to approach their constitutional responsibilities. It would also reiterate the desirability of resolving matters of confidence through appropriate and timely political processes and not by the exercise of personal discretion by the governor general. Further, it would advance transparency, democratic accountability and public understanding, and reinforce the legitimacy of our existing political institutions, including the office of the governor general of Canada.

REFERENCES

Cameron, D. 2009. "Ultimately the System Worked." In *Parliamentary Democracy in Crisis*, eds. P. Russell and L. Sossin. Toronto: University of Toronto Press.

Franks, C.E.S. 2009. "To Prorogue or not to Prorogue: Did the Governor General Make the Right Decision?" In *Parliamentary Democracy in Crisis*, eds. P. Russell and L. Sossin. Toronto: University of Toronto Press.

Heard, A. 2009. "The Governor General's Suspension of Parliament: Duty Done or a Perilous Precedent?" In *Parliamentary Democracy in Crisis*, eds. P. Russell and L. Sossin. Toronto: University of Toronto Press.

Hogg, P. 2007. *Constitutional Law of Canada.* 5th ed. Toronto: Carswell.

— 2009. "Prorogation and the Power of the Governor General." *National Journal of Constitutional Law* 27: 193–203.

Monahan, P. 2007. *Constitutional Law.* 3rd ed. Toronto: University of Toronto Press.

---

[17] See Ibid., p. 3.

[18] The issue of government formation is only one small part of the cabinet manuals in New Zealand and the United Kingdom, which deal with the full range of existing government practices, obligations and expectations. Presumably a Canadian manual would be similarly ambitious in its scope.

Russell, P. and C. Milne. 2011. "Adjusting to a New Era of Parliamentary Government: Report of a Workshop on Constitutional Conventions." David Asper Centre for Constitutional Rights, University of Toronto, February.

Tremblay, G. 2010. "Limiting the Government's Power to Prorogue Parliament." *Canadian Parliamentary Review* 33(2) (summer):16.

Valpy, M. 2009. "The 'Crisis': A Narrative." In *Parliamentary Democracy in Crisis*, eds. P. Russell and L. Sossin. Toronto: University of Toronto Press.

6

The Reserve Powers of the Crown: The 2008 Prorogation in Hindsight

Andrew Heard

À l'examen des pouvoirs de réserve de la Couronne, l'auteur de ce chapitre soutient que les gouverneurs généraux du pays ont en de rares occasions le droit légitime de refuser l'avis du premier ministre. Un survol des 40 dernières années montre d'ailleurs que le gouverneur général ou un lieutenant-gouverneur ont à quelques reprises refusé l'avis de leur cabinet, certains ayant révélé après avoir quitté leurs fonctions qu'ils avaient parfois songé à le faire. L'analyse des points de vue spécialisés fait ressortir des divergences d'opinion sur la légitimité d'un tel refus, mais la plupart des experts constitutionnels ayant étudié la question en profondeur plaident pour un droit de refus limité. À la lumière de ce débat sont examinées les circonstances de 2008 en vue de déterminer si la gouverneure générale aurait légitimement pu refuser la demande de prorogation du Parlement.

The events of late 2008 shone a rare spotlight on the reserve powers of the Crown in Canada and serve to remind constitutional scholars and political actors alike that considerable controversy remains over the extent of those powers and the ways in which they may be properly exercised. While a majority of analysis published since then has supported Governor General Michaëlle Jean's decision to grant prorogation, serious questions remain about the lessons to be learned from those events. The first question to consider is whether there still remains any discretion for Canadian governors to refuse to act on the advice of their first ministers and cabinets. A second issue involves the necessity of gauging whether a viable alternative government is available, in the event that the government resigns or loses a vote of confidence as a result of the rejected advice. The ultimate collapse of the opposition coalition following the 2008 prorogation, however, highlights the difficulties in assessing that viability. An analysis of these issues can help demonstrate that the reserve powers are indeed alive and well in Canada, and that there still remains a legitimate discretion for a governor to refuse advice in circumstances such as those found in 2008.

The basic requirements of responsible government mean that Canadian governors general are normally obligated to act on the advice put to them by their first ministers and cabinets. Modern norms of democratic governance do not easily countenance an appointed official substituting personal judgment in place of the decisions made by elected politicians. And yet, there may still be occasions when a governor may properly have a right, or even have a duty, to refuse the advice of his or her ministers.

Canadian scholarly opinion on the reserve power to refuse advice may be grouped into at least three general categories. A minority of Canadian constitutional scholars argues that modern governors general have absolutely no discretion at all to refuse the advice of a prime minister who enjoys the confidence of the House of Commons. They say that only when a government has clearly lost the confidence of the House, can the governor general refuse to act on cabinet advice. Henri Brun put forward this position to the French press during the 2008 constitutional crisis (Brun 2008). By contrast, other scholars concede a power to refuse unconstitutional advice in a narrow range of other circumstances. Patrick Monahan exemplifies this group when he says:

> As a general rule, the governor general should continue to act on the advice of the prime minister, assuming that he/she continued to enjoy the confidence of the House and should leave issues of legality or constitutionality to be adjudicated before the courts. ... There may be one exception to this rule arising where a government was persisting with a course of action that had been declared unconstitutional or illegal by the courts. In the event that the government sought the governor general's participation in a decision or action that had previously been declared unconstitutional, it might well be appropriate for the governor general to refuse to approve or participate in the illegal or unconstitutional conduct (Monahan 2006, 75–76).

Such a position, however, assumes that any unconstitutional advice tendered by a prime minister would in fact be unconstitutional in a judiciable sense. Unfortunately, this presumption does not stand up to scrutiny. Only some constitutional dilemmas involve questions of law that the courts are most suited to resolve. So much of our constitution – certainly the parts that most concern a governor general – is governed not by law but by constitutional convention. Given the reluctance and generally limited abilities of Canadian courts to deal with political rules like conventions, a judicial resolution of the full range of potentially unconstitutional advice seems impractical. The unworkable nature of Monahan's solution is further compounded by the drawn-out time frame involved in most court cases; the wheels of justice can turn very slowly through various stages of hearings and appeal. For example, Duff Conacher's challenge of the early federal election held in October 2008 resulted in a ruling from the Federal Court in October 2009 and a decision from the Federal Appeal Court, in May 2010 – fully 19 months after the election was held. Had this case been appealed to the Supreme Court of Canada many more months would have been added to the process.[1] Some constitutional crises simply cannot wait that long and need to be definitively settled in a matter of days, or even hours. Furthermore, the courts can usually only bolt the proverbial door after the horse has left.

Most scholars who have explicitly analyzed the reserve powers of the Crown argue for a broader power to refuse advice. Peter Hogg holds that the logic of allowing a governor to reject advice offered by a government that has lost the confidence of the House must extend to rejecting the advice of a government which is seeking to escape defeat in that chamber:

> Since an actual loss of confidence in the government would open up the Governor General's personal discretion, it should also be the case that an imminent loss of confidence opens up the same personal discretion. If that were not so, a Prime Minister could always avoid (or at least postpone) a pending vote of no-confidence simply by advising the prorogation (or dissolution) of the pesky Parliament (Hogg 2010, 198).

The most frequently cited example of permissible rejection of advice is the refusal to authorize a second general election within a few months of the first polling day if another viable government might be formed; but there are a range of other contexts in which the reserve powers might be exercised (Cheffins and Tucker 1976; Forsey 1943, 262; Heard 1991, ch. 2; Hogg 2009, 209–11; Mallory 1984, 51–57; Marshall 1984, 36–42; Massicotte 2010, 51; Saywell 1986, 154).

Political practice reveals a very clear willingness on the part of modern Canadian governors general to exercise their reserve powers, either by refusing advice or contemplating a forced election. There are at least four instances of Canadian governors refusing advice in recent decades. A lieutenant governor of Newfoundland, John Harnum, refused Premier Frank Moores' request for dissolution in 1972 (Roberts 2009, 16). Alberta's Lieutenant Governor Gordon Towers refused to sign an order in council in 1993 to provide a grant he believed to be inappropriate.[2] Governor General Adrienne Clarkson refused Paul Martin's request in 2003 that his swearing-in ceremony be held on Parliament Hill instead

---

[1] The deficiencies of the judicial handling of constitutional conventions in this example are analyzed in Heard 2010.

[2] While the details are not clear, it would appear to have been a concern about a particular grant recipient. The order in council was rewritten to provide greater control over the use of the funds (Crokatt 1994, A.1).

of the traditional venue at Rideau Hall.[3] And in 2010, Quebec Lieutenant Governor Pierre Duchesne refused Premier Charest's advice to appear before a National Assembly committee to discuss the expenditures in his office. Duschesne relied on the royal prerogative to argue that the monarch or the monarch's representative cannot be required to appear before the legislature for questioning and that ministers should answer on behalf of the institution instead (Rhéal Séguin 2010, Radio Canada 2010). To these precedents one can add a possible fifth: Michaëlle Jean's decision to act on her own personal initiative to return to Ottawa to deal with the constitutional crisis in 2008 (Radio Canada 2008). This was an implicit refusal to follow Prime Minister Harper's advice to travel to Eastern Europe despite the growing constitutional impasse.

In addition, there are the cases of "might-have-beens." Former Governor General Edward Schreyer is widely known to have contemplated forcing an election if the Trudeau government had proceeded unilaterally with the constitutional patriation package. Ontario Lieutenant Governor John Aird reportedly informed Premier Frank Miller that he would refuse a request for dissolution if the government was defeated when the legislature resumed after the general election in 1985 (Brazier 1999, 29). A former lieutenant governor of British Columbia, David Lam, revealed that he was prepared to remove Premier Vander Zalm from office if he had not resigned in 1991 (Cheffins 2000, 17). And Adrienne Clarkson was prepared to refuse an early dissolution following the election of a minority government in 2004 (Clarkson 2006, 192).

The events of 2008 provided a rare opportunity for a wide range of Canadian scholars to express their views on the reserve powers. The majority of published opinion supports the belief that the governor general indeed enjoyed a legitimate right to refuse the prime minister's improper advice to prorogue Parliament, but that for various reasons she chose the wisest course of action in acceding to it.[4] It is worth briefly reviewing some of the key arguments to see whether she was right.

Many writers have hinged their conclusion that Michaëlle Jean acted appropriately on two key considerations of the context she faced in 2008. The first is an argument that the period of prorogation was not unduly long. For example, Peter Hogg has written that the prorogation lasting from December 4 until January 26 "… only spared the government a confidence vote for a short period of time" (Hogg 2010, 200). By implication, this argument presumes that a lengthy delay would be unacceptable. Just

---

[3] She rejected this on the grounds that it brought an unwarranted note of presidentialism to our parliamentary traditions, which had seen swearing ceremonies held at Rideau Hall for over a century. It should be noted that this advice does not appear to have been based on a formal instrument of advice (Clarkson 2006, 195).

[4] For a range of views see various authors in Russell and Sossin 2009; Desserud 2009, 40; and Hogg 2010, 193.

what length of delay is unacceptable, however, remains a matter of relative perspective. Prior to the events of 2008, it was generally established that any serious doubt about whether a government continues to enjoy the confidence of the House needs to be settled within a very short order; this was a matter of just nine days for both Pearson in 1968 and Martin in 2005. When one considers that the Conservative government had already delayed the 2008 confidence motion by a week, using its procedural prerogative under the Standing Orders of the House, an additional six weeks of delay seems not just unprecedented but excessive. The justification for a delay has been understood to allow all available members to return to Ottawa, and for there to be some opportunity for full reflection and negotiation before voting. Neither of those reasons justified a seven-week delay in 2008, especially since a majority of members of the House had signed statements saying they were ready to support Dion's proposed motion of no-confidence on December 8.

Ultimately, there appears to be a logical disconnect when many writers either implicitly or explicitly maintain it is wrong for a prime minister to try to avoid certain defeat on a confidence motion but then go on to suggest that if he or she nevertheless manages to convince the governor general to suspend Parliament, then a seven-week delay is acceptable. When a serious doubt arises about whether the government has lost, or is about to lose, the confidence of the House, that doubt must be settled expeditiously. At stake is the very legitimacy of the government's claim to govern.

The second concern for many observers is that the governor general could not refuse the prime minister's advice if there was no viable alternative government available. By tradition, but not necessity, it is sometimes believed that the refusal of advice should result in the prime minister's resignation as it did in 1926. But, the examples of refused advice discussed above do not indicate that this has been widely believed to be a rule by modern incumbents, as none of the political leaders involved appeared to have considered resigning after their advice was refused. The requirement for a viable alternative was a necessary consideration in 2008, however, given the almost certain defeat of the government on the motion that would have been held on December 8 had Parliament not been prorogued. The subsequent collapse of the proposed coalition has been held up by many writers as key evidence that the governor general made the right choice in granting prorogation. However, this conclusion is questionable on several grounds.

The *ex post facto* assessment of the coalition's demise is of limited use to determine what the governor general could have known when making her decision on December 4. Any future governor general facing a similar dilemma needs guidance about what can be adduced at the time a decision must be made. The facts known at the time of the decision were strongly indicative of the coalition's viability. The probability that a workable government could be formed from the opposition parties was clearly indicated when a majority of MPs signed petitions sent to the governor general on December 4, stating that they would be voting in favour of Dion's motion that "… this House has lost confidence in this government, and is of the opinion that a viable alternative government can be formed within the present House of Commons." Most importantly, there was a written agreement signed by the leaders of all three opposition parties. The Liberals and NDP were committed to a minimum of 30 months as coalition cabinet partners, and the Bloc Québécois was committed to support that government on all confidence votes for a minimum of 18 months. Together these parties commanded 163 seats out of 308, enough for a clear majority. Based on these signed petitions and agreements alone, there was demonstrable evidence that a viable government could be formed to replace the Conservatives. As former governor general Ed Schreyer commented at the time, "If it's solemn, formal and written, I could only speak for myself, I'd certainly feel obliged to proceed accordingly" (CBC News, 2008). Indeed, it is hard to think of more concrete evidence that any governor could wish to have to settle doubts about the viability of an alternative government.

The NDP and Bloc committed themselves to this arrangement, knowing full well that the Liberal Party would hold a leadership contest in the new year. That Dion would be an interim prime minister was fully appreciated by all concerned. It was not likely at the time, nor has it proved so since, that any new leader would take the Liberal Party in a fundamentally different direction. The prospect of a leadership change in the Liberal Party was far from a fatal flaw for the coalition.

Some have commented that the coalition was inherently dubious, given the speed with which it was negotiated and the lack of substantive stipulations on a shared policy program in the agreements.[5] But this concern about speed seems to be something of a red herring, with little constitutional significance. The negotiations were spread over four days, while the agreement that formed the current coalition government in Britain was negotiated in five days. Perhaps of more concern is the suggestion that the coalition had reached no agreement on any substantive policies, and would risk falling apart over the first major policy difference. However, Brian Topp's book on the coalition reveals parallel negotiations on a range of policy issues (Topp 2010). The Liberals and NDP reached a separate framework agreement on principles to be followed in creating an economic stimulus package, which was the single most pressing policy item on the government's agenda at that time.[6]

---

[5] Hogg argued that the coalition "had been negotiated in haste and in anger" (Hogg 2010, 200).

[6] The text of the agreement is available at "A Policy Accord to Address the Present Economic Crisis," http://www.cbc.ca/news/pdf/081201_Policy%20Frame_en.pdf.

Any governor facing the prospect of a new coalition government can only seek to be assured that the partners commit themselves to make the arrangement work and that they have enough votes in the legislature to support it. All three party leaders had committed themselves in writing, as had their caucuses. Quite simply put, no governor can – or should – ask for anything more.[7] Just how long any potential government will last, whether minority or coalition, cannot be known in advance. In early November 2008, for example, it appeared that the Conservative minority government would be safe for some time to come, but by the end of the month its very existence hung in the balance.

The ultimate collapse of the coalition is widely offered as proof that the governor general did the right thing. That logic is seriously flawed, however, because it applies hindsight to a completely new set of events brought about by prorogation that have very little to do with the reality which would have ensued if prorogation had been refused. Had Jean rejected Harper's request, Stéphane Dion would not have resigned from the leadership until Michael Ignatieff took up the Liberal helm on December 8. The no-confidence motion would have passed on December 6, and Harper would have been replaced as prime minister by Dion. Harper might have tried to advise fresh elections but that gambit would most likely have been unsuccessful.[8] Ignatieff would most probably have won the eventual Liberal leadership contest, but he would have succeeded Dion as prime minister, not as leader of the opposition in charge of a disintegrating strategy. Whatever doubts Ignatieff harboured about the coalition government in late 2008, he would have taken office in a different reality, as head of a coalition government of some months' duration.

It is curious that some commentators have suggested that it was not only acceptable but wise to put the aspiring coalition to the test of a seven-week delay. There is some deep irony in saying that a potential alternative government should be put to a test of time rather than the incumbent government being put to a test of confidence in the House. The first notion is profoundly paternalistic, while the other is undeniably democratic. Our

---

[7] The text of the Liberal NDP coalition agreement is available at "An Accord on a Cooperative Government to Address the Present Economic Crisis," http://www.cbc.ca/news/pdf/081201_Accord_en.pdf.

[8] Most published analyses clearly assert that the governor general would have had the right to refuse a request for dissolution if the Harper government had been defeated on the confidence vote to be held on December 8. Former governor general Ed Schreyer even told the press in 2008 that he believed that the legitimacy of the proposed coalition was "unquestionable" and that it would have to be given the opportunity to govern if the government lost the vote of confidence; see CBC News, "Former GG Says He Would Support coalition," 3 December 2008, available at http://www.cbc.ca/mobile/text/story_news-canada.html?/ept/html/story/2008/12/03/parl-schreyer.html. For examples of academic opinion on the issue of refusing dissolution in 2008, see Desserud 2009, 45; Hogg 2010, 199; Massicotte 2010, 51. For a contrary view see Schwartz 2010, 37.

elected politicians should not be treated like naughty school children who need a seven-week time out. If three political parties that together hold a clear majority in the House sign a collection of documents pledging themselves to making a coalition government work, then they must be taken at face value by the governor general. Any subsequent judgment on the wisdom of forming that coalition, or on the later successes or failures of that coalition, should be made by electors at the ballot box.

It is important, as well, to bear in mind that these events unfolded within the first three weeks of Parliament resuming after the general election. The normal standard in a minority situation is that the incumbent government has a right to meet Parliament to try to win its confidence. If it fails to win that confidence or loses it within a very short period of time, the governor is bound to allow another party leader to try to form a government. It is crucial to appreciate that the standard usually referred to is that this leader has the opportunity to *try* to form a government. The likelihood of success must be high to appoint another prime minister, but the governor general has never been expected to insist on a guarantee that a new government will survive for one or more years. In the immediate period following an election, the newly elected members must sort out which party or combination of parties has their confidence.

But if other writers can draw from the partisan political context of 2008 to cast doubt on the viability of the coalition, it is only fair to pause and question the significance of the vote of confidence won by the government just as the 2008 crisis erupted. The very first vote of confidence held after the election came on the speech from the throne, to which none in the opposition objected strenuously. The opposition House leaders had met and agreed with the government that this vote would be held on Thursday September 27, after the minister of finance delivered an economic update to the House. That speech proved to be a disaster, and leaders of each of the opposition parties immediately announced that they would defeat the government on that matter when it came up for a vote. However, in a case of phenomenal misjudgement, they then trooped back into the House for the vote on the speech from the throne, which passed without a recorded vote – as previously agreed to by the House leaders. This was theatre of the absurd at its most absurd. Having announced their intention to defeat the government, all the opposition parties then immediately allowed the government to win a vote of confidence! The sequence of events on November 27 clearly undermines the political significance of that *pro forma* vote of confidence. Without that vote, the government would have had little constitutional basis to insist on prorogation. The Liberal Party committed the procedural gaffe of the century in failing to force a formal division on the motion, at which point the Liberal whip could have relied on Standing Order 45 to defer the vote until the following Monday. That delay would have permitted the opposition to negotiate the coalition and deprive the government of the constitutional legitimacy which flowed from securing the confidence of the House.

In 2008, the governor general was faced with a government insisting on an unprecedented six-week suspension of Parliament only three weeks into its life, purely to avoid certain defeat. Such a request was considered by the vast majority of observers to be a fundamental breach of constitutional understandings that a government must not try to avoid defeat by suspending parliament. Such a move was unprecedented in the past century in any well established parliamentary democracy. Prorogation was nevertheless granted, despite a majority of MPs having signed statements declaring both that they would support an impending vote of no-confidence in the current government and that there was a viable alternative government. Although a number of scholars suggest that prorogation wisely tested the fortitude of the proposed coalition, no governor can seek guarantees about an alternative government's long-term viability as no one can foretell the future. A strong probability of survival into the intermediate future is the most one can hope for. The signed agreements provided as conclusive evidence as one could expect in any circumstance, and they should have provided the governor general with grounds to refuse to interfere in Parliament's most important business. The subsequent collapse of the coalition is not proof that it would have failed as a government. An entirely new set of events was put in train when the governor general decided to prevent Parliament from continuing to sit. Quite an alternative reality would have unfolded if the House of Commons had been allowed to vote no confidence in the current government.

The lessons to be learned from the events of 2008 underline the very real nature of the reserve powers of the Crown. A Canadian governor general or lieutenant governor retains material authority, in exceptional circumstances, to form an independent judgment on whether he or she should follow unconstitutional advice offered by the first minister or cabinet. These reserve powers are essential to the proper functioning of our parliamentary system, in which the government's legitimacy flows from the support of the elected members of the legislature. Governors have a right to protect parliamentary democracy by insisting that the legislature be allowed to function. And there is no more important function for any parliament than the process of testing the members' confidence in the government of the day. However, any independent action by a governor will be the subject of controversy in a crisis such as in 2008. Not only will the slighted government actors object strenuously, perhaps even viciously, but scholarly opinion is also sufficiently fragmented that some commentators will cast doubt on the propriety of the governor's actions. Such is the inherent nature of constitutional crisis, however, as without controversy there is no crisis.

References

Brazier, R. 1999. *Constitutional Practice: The Foundations of British Government*. 3rd ed. New York: Oxford University Press.
Brunet, H. 2008. "Michaëlle Jean n'a Pas le Choix." *Cyberpress*. 4 December 2008. Accessed online at http://www.cyberpresse.ca/opinions/forums/la-presse/200812/04/01-807213-michaelle-jean-na-pas-le-choix.php
CBC News. 2008. "Former GG Says He Would Support Coalition." 3 December. Accessed 28 January 2009 at http://www.cbc.ca/mobile/text/story_newscanada.html?/ept/html/story/2008/12/03/parl-schreyer.html
Cheffin, R. and R. Tucker. 1976. *The Constitutional Process in Canada*. 2nd ed. Toronto: McGraw-Hill Ryerson.
— 2000. "The Royal Prerogative and the Lieutenant Governors." *Canadian Parliamentary Review* 1.
Clarkson, A. 2006. *Heart Matters*. Toronto: Viking Canada.
Crokatt, J. 1994. "Lt-Gov. Won't OK Grant from Kowalski." *Edmonton Journal*. 23 December, A1.
Desserud, D.A. 2009. "The Governor General, The Prime Minister and the Request to Prorogue." *Canadian Political Science Review* 3(3): 40–54.
Forsey, E. 1943. *The Royal Power of Dissolution in the British Commonwealth*. Toronto: Oxford University Press.
Heard, A. 1991. *Canadian Constitutional Conventions*. Toronto: Oxford University Press.
— 2010. "Conacher Missed the Mark on Constitutional Conventions and Fixed Election Dates." *Constitutional Forum* 19(1).
Hogg, P. 2009. *Constitutional Law of Canada. 2009 Student Edition*. Toronto: Carswell.
— 2010. "Prorogation and the Power of the Governor General." *National Journal of Constitutional Law* 27.
Mallory, J.R. 1984. *The Structure of Government*. Rev. ed. Toronto: Gage.
Marshall, G. 1984. *Constitutional Conventions: The Rules and Forms of Political Accountability*. Oxford: Oxford University Press.
Massicotte, L. 2010. "Can a Change of Government Occur Without a General Election?" *Journal of Parliamentary and Political Law* 4.
Monahan, P.J. 2006. *Constitutional Law*. 3rd ed. Toronto: Irwin Law.
Radio Canada. 2008. "Les Conservateurs Contre-Attaquent." Available at http://www.radio-canada.ca/nouvelles/Politique/2008/12/02/001-coalition-mardi.shtml
— 2010. "Le Lieutenant-Gouverneur Refuse de Témoigner." Available at http://www.radio-canada.ca/nouvelles/Politique/2010/02/04/002-duchesne_depenses.shtml
Roberts, E. 2009. "Ensuring Constitutional Wisdom During Unconventional Times." *Canadian Parliamentary Review* 32(1).
Russell, P. H. and L. Sossin, eds. 2009. *Parliamentary Democracy in Crisis*. Toronto: University of Toronto Press.
Salvet, J.-M. 2010. "Le Lieutenant-Gouverneur Délègue son Adjoint." *Le Soleil*. 29 January. Available at http://www.cyberpresse.ca/le-soleil/actualites/politique/201001/29/01-944133-le-lieutenant-gouverneur-delegue-son-adjoint.php
Saywell, J. 1986. *The Office of Lieutenant Governor*. Toronto: Copp Clark Pitman.

Schwartz, B. 2010. "Constitutional Conventions Concerning the Dissolution of Parliament and the Parliamentary Crisis of December 2008." *Journal of Parliamentary and Political Law* 4.

Séguin, R. 2010. "Quebeckers Feel Short-Changed by Lieutenant-Governor's Coin." *The Globe and Mail*. 5 February, A4.

Topp, B. 2010. *How We Almost Gave the Tories the Boot: The Inside Story Behind the Coalition*. Toronto: Lorimer.

7

WRITTEN REASONS AND CODIFIED CONVENTIONS IN MATTERS OF PROROGATION AND DISSOLUTION

ROBERT E. HAWKINS[*]

Une vive controverse a accueilli la décision de la gouverneure générale d'agréer à la demande du premier ministre de proroger la première session du 40ᵉ Parlement, alors que celle-ci était amorcée depuis seulement 16 jours et que le gouvernement était vraisemblablement menacé par un vote de censure. À l'examen des conventions en la matière, l'auteur réfute l'argumentation voulant qu'elles doivent être codifiées ou que le gouverneur général doive étayer les motifs de sa décision. Toute tentative de codification provoquerait en effet de multiples conséquences imprévisibles. Et toute exigence d'exposition des motifs viendrait politiser la charge vice-royale, mettant en cause sa neutralité et sapant la légitimité de l'exercice par le gouverneur général d'un pouvoir non démocratique. Cette exigence entraînerait aussi une judiciarisation de la fonction propre à inciter des politiciens déçus à invoquer les motifs avancés par le gouverneur général pour faire annuler sa décision par les tribunaux. L'auteur conclut à la nécessité du silence vice-royal pour préserver le rôle d'arbitre final de la Constitution du gouverneur général.

PATHOLOGICAL CASES

On October 14, 2008, Canadians elected their 40th Parliament. As in the 39th Parliament, Prime Minister Harper led a minority government, although this time the number of Conservative Party members, 143, was considerably greater than the 127 members at dissolution. The Liberal Party suffered its worst popular vote result in history and fell to 77 members,

*I am grateful for helpful comments from Dr. Peter Neary, Professor Emeritus, University of Western Ontario.

down from 95 at dissolution. The Bloc Québécois and the NDP elected 49 and 37 members, respectively.

The initial session of the 40th Parliament opened on November 18, 2008. It was prorogued two-and-a-half weeks later on December 4, 2008. Shortly after the session opened, Finance Minister Flaherty indicated that he would present an economic update, a kind of state-of-the-economy report, in the House of Commons on November 27. On the morning of the 27th, in response to rumors that Flaherty was not planning to stimulate the economy and was planning to eliminate public funding to political parties for election expenses, the opposition parties began discussions on voting no-confidence in the government and on forming a coalition that could serve as a government if invited to do so. Later that day, immediately following the economic update, the Liberals joined with the government to approve a motion, as amended, for an address in reply to the speech from the throne. For the first time in the 40th Parliament, as the government House leader, Jay Hill, noted immediately, the Commons had voted confidence in the government[1] (Neary 2009, 46). This milestone was shortly to prove enormously significant. Given the opposition's intention to defeat the government several days later over the just-presented economic update, the vote of confidence represents the greatest tactical blunder in the House since Prime Minister Clark failed to see that his Conservative government would be defeated on a confidence matter on December 13, 1979.

Opposition party talks culminated on December 1, 2008, with the three leaders publicly signing an accord which was to last until June 30, 2011. The Liberals and NDP agreed to form a coalition government, at the governor general's request, upon defeat of the Harper government. The Bloc Québécois agreed to support the coalition government on all confidence matters until June 30, 2010. The leader of the official opposition wrote a letter to the governor general in which he "respectfully advised" that he had the confidence of the Commons to form a coalition government if called upon. Aware of the very real possibility of a successful no-confidence vote if an opposition day scheduled for December 8 was allowed to proceed, the prime minister visited the governor general on December 4 in order to advise that Parliament be prorogued. After an interview of over two hours with Her Excellency, the prime minister appeared in the snow on the steps of Rideau Hall to announce that his request had been granted

---

[1] The next day, Hill made the following statement in a government press release: "Acceptance by the House of Commons of a Speech from the Throne is an expression of confidence in the government. I am pleased that the House endorsed our government's general program, particularly with full knowledge of the content of the Economic and Fiscal update. Yesterday's vote and today's motion to communicate with the Governor General accepting her Speech are critical demonstrations of Parliament's affirmation of our newly re-elected government" (Canada 28 November 2008).

and that Parliament would be summoned for a new session on January 26, 2009. Harper indicated that he would work in the interim to build a consensus on an economic package.

The story ends with the Liberal party changing its leader on December 10, the coalition subsequently falling apart amid recriminations, and the Conservative government abruptly reversing its budgetary course. The 2nd session of the 40th Parliament opened on January 26, 2009. A new speech from the throne was read and passed quickly. Finance Minister Flaherty presented a budget which contained considerable deficit spending in response to the deepening economic recession but no talk of plans to legislate an end to public election financing for political parties. The budget passed on February 3, 2009, with Liberal support, after the government agreed to give regular economic reports on the progress of stimulus spending (Valpy 2009, 3). The threat to the government was over.[2]

Prior to the 2008 prorogation, there were only two other instances in national parliamentary history in which the government's attempt to shut down parliament raised constitutional controversy. One involved prorogation; the other dissolution. In 1873, the Pacific Scandal erupted. Allegations were made that Prime Minister Macdonald and other Conservative ministers had accepted money from Sir Hugh Allan to help the Conservative party fight the 1872 election. Allan hoped to be awarded the upcoming contract to build the promised railway to British Columbia. In order to avoid an ongoing investigation into the matter by a parliamentary committee and a non-confidence vote in the House, Macdonald requested that Governor General Lord Dufferin grant prorogation. A number of Conservative MPs joined with the Liberal opposition in signing a memorandum to the governor general pledging support for the formation of a new Liberal government. The Liberal press argued that the Crown would be brought into disrepute should the governor general shield the Conservative ministry from a confidence vote by agreeing to prorogation. In the end, Lord Dufferin reluctantly assented to the prorogation, but required that the House meet within ten weeks and that a committee be appointed in the interim to report on the allegations. The House was summoned back into session in October, 1873, and the Royal Commission Relating

---

[2] Harper's second request for prorogation, made on December 30, 2009, was also controversial, but not unusual. On December 30, 2009 the governor general accepted his advice and ended the 2nd session of the 40th Parliament. At the time, there was no question but that the government enjoyed the confidence of the House. It maintained that the prorogation was a "quite routine" matter, designed to permit it to consult with Canadians on the next phase of the "Economic Action Plan" in light of signs of economic recovery. Of note was the pending Vancouver Olympics in February, 2009. The opposition charged that the prorogation was designed to shut down the parliamentary committee which was examining allegations that the government ignored warnings about the torture of Afghan prisoners which Canadian forces were transferring to Afghan authorities. See http://www.cbc.ca/politics/story/2009/12/30/parliament-prorogationharper.html

to Canadian Pacific Railway reported. Pressure mounted on Macdonald and he resigned on November 5, 1873. Mackenzie formed a government two days later, which then won an election called for January 22, 1874.

The other instance trips easily off the tongue of every beginning student of Canadian government, perhaps because the names of the protagonists rhyme so memorably. The King-Byng affair concerned the use of the governor general's discretionary power to dissolve the House. A federal election in October, 1925, gave Prime Minister William Lyon Mackenzie King 101 seats, Opposition Leader Arthur Meighen 116 seats, and the third party, the Progressives, 28 seats. Rather than resign, Mackenzie King continued to govern with the support of the Progressives. Following a report on corruption indicating widespread fraud in the Department of Customs and Excise, it appeared that King's government would lose a vote of non-confidence in the House. In order to avoid this result, King, in June 1926, asked Governor-General Lord Byng to dissolve the House and call an election. Over the course of the next two days, Byng steadfastly refused several further requests for dissolution, finally prompting King to resign. Byng then called on Arthur Meighen to form a minority government. The new government was shortly defeated in the House on a motion of confidence. The governor general then granted Meighen the dissolution that he had recently refused King. King campaigned against the governor general, arguing for Canadian independence from imperial interference. Despite losing the popular vote, King was returned at the September 14, 1926, election with a majority of seats in the House.

THE CONVENTIONS GOVERNING PROROGATION AND DISSOLUTION

Normally, the exercise of the reserve powers of dissolution and prorogation passes with little comment. These powers, originally a matter of common law, are now codified by section 38 of the *Constitution Act, 1867*,[3] and by Letters Patent Constituting the Office of the Governor General of Canada (1 October 1947).[4] They give the governor general an absolute discretion to summon, prorogue and dissolve Parliament.

By convention, the governor general must accept the advice of the prime minister in matters of prorogation and dissolution once his government has successfully won a confidence vote in the House. Having

---

[3] "The Governor General shall from Time to Time, in the Queen's Name, by Instrument under the Great Seal of Canada, summon and call together the House of Commons." The power to "from Time to Time … summon and call together" includes the powers to prorogue and dismiss [Tremblay 2010, p. 16].

[4] "Summoning, proroguing, VI. And We do further authorize and empower Our Governor General to exercise all powers lawfully belonging to Us in respect of summoning, proroguing or dissolving the Parliament of Canada" [Desserud 2009, fn. 38 and citations there].

demonstrated confidence, the prime minister is in charge. Should he subsequently be defeated in the House, he has two options. He may advise the governor general to dissolve the House and hold a general election, advice which is binding once confidence has been established. During the electoral period, the prime minister continues in office. Alternately, the prime minister might resign and, if asked by the governor general, might recommend someone who could possibly gain the confidence of the House. In discharge of her duty to ensure continuity of administration, the governor general will exercise her reserve powers to appoint a new prime minister. He will either win the confidence of the House or himself face the two choices outlined above. These conventions guarantee democracy in the Westminster system of responsible government. If cabinet is to act, in David Smith's memorable phrase, as the "hinge of the Constitution," ministers must enjoy the confidence of the House and the governor general must respect that confidence by accepting advice offered by the cabinet[5] (Smith 2006, 104).

These conventions govern with one exception. In "extraordinary circumstances," the governor general may exercise her reserve powers and reject the advice of her prime minister, even after he has established confidence. The only point of contention in this entire scheme is determining what constitutes "extraordinary circumstances."

On the one hand, there are those who suggest that these circumstances are narrow (Neary 2009; Brun 2008). One senior constitutional lawyer, Neil Finkelstein, has put it this way: "The governor general is supposed to look at votes in the House, not letters sent to her by opposition MPs ..." (*Lawyer's Weekly* 2009). As a consequence, the role of the governor general, while critical, is limited. She is there, *in extremis*, to ensure that no deadlock threatens the operation of responsible government as, for example, where the prime minister refuses to meet a newly elected House desperately hoping, through repeated dissolutions, to better his electoral fortunes. The merit of this approach is two-fold. First, the confidence rule is a clear and easy one to operate. Second, because it is based on a vote of the representatives of the people, it embodies the democratic principle.

On the other hand, there are those who would have the governor general adopt a more activist role, one which would require her to weigh and

---

[5] The position of opposition parties vis-à-vis the Governor General is equally clear: "The opposition does not have any standing with the Governor General when she is considering dissolution or, for that matter a proroguing request; she only takes advice from her prime minister, and only the most extraordinary circumstances would convince her not to accept that advice" [Desserud 2009, 44]. See also: "If it is conceded that a contemporary governor [general] is required to accede to a prime ministerial request for a dissolution in the event of a ruling party losing supply or a key confidence vote, ..., it is also emerging that opposition parties enjoy the right to seize the initiative in informing the governor of their willingness to try to form a government. Obviously, such communication can never constitute formal advice" [Boyce 2008, 58].

balance a variety of factors in order to determine whether circumstances are sufficiently extraordinary as to warrant rejecting the advice of a prime minister who has won the confidence of the House (Heard 2009). There is no agreement on what those factors might be. Some would limit them to such constitutional considerations as the length of time from the last general election, the possibility of success of a pending non-confidence vote, the degree of likelihood that a potential new government could gain the confidence of the House, and whether the request is for prorogation or dissolution. Specifics are also a problem. How long a period must have elapsed since the most recent election?[6] How likely must it be that a pending confidence vote will succeed? How stable must an alternative government appear to be? Others would go even further by including in the list of extraordinary circumstances such overtly political factors as the state of the economy, federal-provincial relations, the mood of Parliament, the results of public opinion polls, public and media agitation, national unity considerations, the need for a "cool down" period, and so on (Franks 2009).

Like those advocating a narrow approach, those seeking a greater role for the governor general, even when the prime minister has established confidence, use democratic arguments to justify their position. With respect to the date of the most recent election, they argue that a freshly mandated House should have an opportunity to do its work so long as there exists another party capable of forming a government. With respect to the likely success of a pending confidence motion, they argue that the governor general must not exercise her discretion in a way that would permit a prime minister to subvert the will of the House by avoiding a vote.[7] With respect to the stability of an alternative government, they argue that a government of opposition members must at least be given a chance to demonstrate that it can command confidence. Finally, with respect to denying prorogation, they argue that this is less of an affront to

---

[6] Former Governor General Adrienne Clarkson, in her autobiography, wrote the following after leaving office: "The question arose during Paul Martin's minority government of whether or not I as governor-general would grant dissolution and allow an election to be called if the prime minister requested it. After considering the opinions of the constitutional experts whom I consulted regularly, I decided that, if the government lasted six months, I would allow dissolution. To put the Canadian people through election before six months would have been irresponsible" (Clarkson 2006, 192).

[7] Peter Hogg reflects this view when he states: "… the same discretion must surely be available when the Prime Minister is *about to lose* a vote of no-confidence" (Hogg 2010, 9–35). Those who feel that a prime minister has confidence until it is denied by an actual vote of the House will point out that a political defection from the opposition to the government, possibly the result of a promised cabinet position, pressure from the media, a new poll, sober second thought, the incapacity of a member of the House, and variety of unforeseen possibilities can cause political reality to change in the blink of an eye. In other words, there is no reliable way to predict the outcome of pending votes in the House, particularly in a charged political atmosphere.

democracy than denying dissolution because denying prorogation throws the question of confidence back to the House to resolve.[8] Dissolution, on the other hand, puts an end to the House and, as in the King-Byng affair, could signal an electoral show-down between the prime minister and the governor general.

The governor general offered no reasons for accepting Prime Minister Harper's advice and proroguing Parliament in December, 2008.[9] The outcome of that decision seems to have been reasonably popular with public opinion in the country (Russell 2009, 146). A new election, within several months of the most recent one, proved unnecessary. The coalition agreement quickly fell apart. Even in advance of the governor general's decision, it was known that the coalition leader was resigning as head of the official opposition in the wake of poor electoral results blamed on him, the positions of the Bloc and of the other opposition parties on the crucial issue of national unity were diametrically opposed, and the coalition was bitterly rejected in the West (Skogstad 2009). The arrival of the economic recession and the willingness of the government to change its economic policies to cope with this new reality won it support from the

---

[8]Canada. *Constitution Act, 1982*, being Schedule B of the *Canada Act, 1982* (U.K.), 1982, c.11: s. 5 provides: "There shall be a sitting of Parliament … at least once every twelve months." This point is made by Desserud 2009, 45–47.

[9]In an interview as she left office, Governor General Michaëlle Jean commented on her motives in taking over two hours before granting the Prime Minister's request for prorogation. She indicated that she needed time to reflect and hoped, with the heavy media coverage, that people would be helped to understand "our institutional realities … and our political system." [Canadian Press 2010]

One Canadian governor general sought to have his opinion published simultaneously with an exercise of his reserve power. However, he abandoned the idea under pressure from the prime minister. The October 29, 1925, federal election gave Arthur Meighen's Conservatives 115 seats, incumbent Prime Minister Mackenzie King's Liberals 100 seats, and third parties 30 seats. King advised Governor General Byng to call the House immediately in order to hold a confidence vote. Byng agreed to accept this advice but indicated that he wished King's press statement to note that the governor general would have instead preferred to call on Meighen to form a ministry. King told Byng that he objected to any public expression of the governor general's opinion: "… I must protect the Sovereign & His Representative by not letting His Ex's [Excellency's] name in any way be drawn into the public discussion" (C4333). Byng acquiesced. According to King's diary, the prime minister's press release, issued at 11 p.m. on November 4, 1925, with Byng's consent, stated that the governor general was "pleased to accept" King's advice (C4333-34). No reference was made to Byng's opinion that Meighen should have been called. King recorded that, "All I insisted on was that it shld not be His Ex. [Excellency] who was expressing his view" (C4333). I am grateful to Dr. Peter Neary for drawing my attention to this example. [King Diaries]

The only time that a governor general has offered formal written reasons explaining his exercise of his reserve powers was on November 11, 1975, when Sir John Kerr issued a statement explaining his reasons for dismissing Australian Prime Minister Gough Whitlam. The reasons offered simply added fuel to the intense controversy surrounding the decision. http://whitlamdismissal.com/documents/kerr-statement.shtml

Liberals and the continuing confidence of the House, immediately upon the resumption of sittings.

It is not likely that the governor general's decision would ever have enjoyed the kind of acceptance which it did had she given reasons for it. By remaining silent, all sides could read whatever justification they wished into the decision. Reasons would inevitably have become polarizing and been used as political fodder. The decision to follow the prime minister's advice could be seen as "business as usual" by those who thought that she was bound by convention, following the November 27 confidence vote, to do so. Those who held that the governor general ought, when exercising her discretion, to take into account a broader range of considerations, could find solace in thinking that she may have done exactly that and concluded, after considering those factors, that circumstances were not so extraordinary as to warrant rejecting the prime minister's advice.

For those who argue that the governor general ought to consider a broad range of factors in judging whether extraordinary circumstances exist, the outcome of the exercise of her discretion becomes less predictable than it would be if she were simply to ascertain if a confidence vote had been taken in the House. This has led some in this group to suggest codification of a series of new conventions that would specify outcomes in a multiplicity of circumstances.[10] Others in this group have suggested that the governor general ought to be required to give reasons to explain the exercise of her discretion. These reasons would then be available both to hold the governor general accountable and to form binding precedents for the future. The interesting question that arises, therefore, is whether codifying conventions, and/or requiring reasons, is a good idea.

Codifying Conventions; Requiring Reasons

While conceding that the "crisis" of December, 2008 passed, Peter Russell argues that it revealed dangerous confusion and division over the content of conventions governing prorogation and dissolution. His solution is to have constitutional scholars codify the applicable rules:

> The lack of political consensus on fundamental principles of our constitution poses a serious threat to the stability of our parliamentary democracy ... This puts the governor general ... in the position of refereeing a game without an agreed-upon set of principles. This situation suggests to me that the time has come to bring those spooky unwritten constitutional conventions down

---

[10] There may be a conflict of interest here. If you are a constitutional expert and you successfully make the case for new and written constitutional conventions, you might be called upon to author these new norms. The opportunity to immortalize oneself by formulating a part of the Constitution must be very seductive.

from the attic of our collective memory and try to see if we can pin them down in a manner that is politically consensual and popularly accessible (Russell 2009, 147; also, Stilborn 2009).

Sossin and Dodek share Russell's concern. Their remedy, however, is to have the governor general give reasons for the exercise of her reserve powers in cases of prorogation and dissolution. They suggest that saying nothing is outdated: "… this practice is inconsistent with the 'culture of justification' that has emerged as a key constitutional value in Canada" (Sossin 2009, 94). Elsewhere, Sossin suggests that the lack of transparency "is inconsistent with where our constitutional democracy has gone in the 21st century over the notion of accountability for crucial public decisions" (*Lawyer's Weekly* 2009).

Sossin and Dudek go on to enumerate three specific reasons why the governor general ought to provide reasons for a decision: "First, justification allays the concern that a decision has been motivated by improper, ulterior motives, such as currying the favour of the government of the day. Second, justification ensures that the decision is reasonable and based on legitimate and valid factors. Third, justification promotes transparency and accountability and, in so doing, enhances public confidence in the country's democratic institutions" (Sossin 2009, 94).[11]

Those championing this position face several initial hurdles. Any attempt to legislate reasons as a condition of the exercise of the governor general's discretion, or to legislate restrictions on the advice that a prime minister could offer, would, in all likelihood, run afoul of the constitutional amending formula.[12] S. 41 (a) of the *Constitution Act, 1982*, provides that any amendment to the office of the governor general requires the unanimous consent of the Senate, the House of Commons and the legislative assemblies of each province. There are two approaches to dealing with this objection, both unconvincing. The first maintains that such legislation would be constitutionally valid so long as it contains a clause stipulating that the power of the governor general to prorogue or dissolve remains unaffected. A restriction on the prime minister's prerogative to advise, however, necessarily constrains the ability of the governor general to exercise her discretion to prorogue or dissolve. This approach attempts to do indirectly what the constitution forbids doing directly. Such an approach,

---

[11] Other scholars have advocated that the governor general issue reasons (Hicks 2009a and b), as have some citizens in blogs (Kelly 2010).

[12] Along these lines, by a vote of 139-135, the House of Commons passed the following motion, which is advisory only, on March 17, 2010: "That, in the opinion of the House, the Prime Minister shall not advise the Governor General to prorogue any session of any Parliament for longer than seven calendar days without a specific resolution of this House of Commons to support such a prorogation."

when used to legislate fixed election laws, has recently been cast into doubt by the Federal Court (*Conacher* 2009, paras. 48–59; Hawkins 2010).

The second approach suggests that legislation setting out conditions for the governor general's exercise of her reserve powers, such as a requirement to give reasons, does not require s. 41 (a) unanimity so long as the legislation does not impair the fundamental characteristics of the office of the governor general (OPSEU). This theory distinguishes between impairing the governor general's discretion and regulating its exercise. This is a fine line. The constitution gives the governor general absolute discretion in the matters of prorogation and dissolution. To limit the scope of that discretion or the means by which it is exercised in any meaningful way compromises it. Either the governor general has an unqualified discretion or she does not. One cannot have it both ways (contra. Tremblay 2010, 16–17).

Can these constitutional impediments be avoided through the development of conventions that regulate the discretion to prorogue or dissolve? Conventions, while not legally enforceable, are considered politically binding. The Supreme Court of Canada has accepted the three-fold Jennings test for the establishment of a constitutional convention: what are the precedents? what are the beliefs of the actors in the precedents? and what is the reason for the practice? (*Patriation Reference*, 1981, 888-909). As will be discussed below, the reasons for codifying conventions or requiring reasons are questionable when the pros and cons are considered. Some scholars maintain that conventions can also be established when unanimously adopted by all of the actors involved (Heard 1991). It is difficult to imagine that both the prime minister and the governor general, the relevant actors in the case of prorogation and dissolution, would consent either to a restriction on the kind of "advice" that the prime minister could offer, or on the exercise of the governor general's discretion, whether by requiring reasons or otherwise. Moreover, it is unclear how such an agreement would bind their successors.

Conventions must be sufficiently precise to be identifiable and operational (Hawkins 2010, 129). As discussed, constitutional commentators are not even able to agree on the kinds of extraordinary events, let alone the specifics of those events, that would justify the governor general in refusing to follow a prime minister who had established the support of the House. Consensus might be obtained by devising conventions of great generality, but that would defeat the certainty sought by codification exercise.

Finally, it is not clear that 21st century democracy is defined by a "culture of justification" or whether the "practice of non-disclosure" is always applicable in a democracy. There are significant examples where outcomes are announced without the expectation that they will be accompanied by reasons. Cabinet debates leading to government decisions are secret. The prime minister makes cabinet and other appointments and dismisses cabinet ministers without giving reasons. Freedom-of-information laws contain exceptions where secrecy is preserved. Much of foreign affairs is conducted in secrecy despite the domestic impact that might result. Even the Supreme Court decides leave-to-appeal applications without giving reasons.

The Supreme Court has provided some guidance on when reasons are desirable, albeit in another context. The Court's 1999 *Baker* decision clarified and expanded the obligation of administrative decision-makers to justify their exercise of discretionary statutory power (*Baker* 1999). According to the decision, fairness requires a senior administrative officer to provide reasons for his recommendation that an applicant for permanent resident status not be granted an exemption from certain regulations on humanitarian and compassionate grounds. However, *Baker* does not hold that reasons are necessary in all situations. While reasons help ensure "that issues … are well articulated and, therefore, more carefully thought out," and while reasons "reinforce public confidence," fairness is, nonetheless, "eminently variable and its content is to be decided in the specific context of each case" (*Baker* 1999, paras. 21 and 39). Fairness requires reasons only "in certain circumstances." The circumstances in *Baker*, which involved the application of a particular regulation to a specific individual, in the context of a concrete dispute, can easily be distinguished from the exercise of broad discretion by the governor general in dealing with a polycentric matter of high political and constitutional import.

What factors should be considered in deciding whether reasons should be required or detailed codification should be attempted? In identifying these factors, the claim for transparency in democratic decision-making certainly stakes out the high road. Any argument to the contrary seems counterintuitive, indeed reactionary. However, there are good reasons related to the role of the governor general, and to the nature of the issues before her, that counsel, on balance, against developing codes and requiring reasons.[13]

THE POLITICIZATION OF THE RESERVE POWERS

In most cases, the governor general's action in summoning, proroguing and dissolving parliament amounts to little more than switching the

---

[13] Of course, the governor general might choose to give reasons, as did the governor general of Australia in the 1975 Whitlam affair. That may, however, violate the convention guarding the secrecy of discussions between the prime minister and the governor general and it may, for the same reasons that reasons should not be obligatory, be a bad idea.

chamber lights on and off. It is the executive that governs in accordance with the will of the people. In very rare cases, where it is unclear whether the government enjoys the confidence of the chamber, the governor general's role is to decide how to break the impasse so that responsible government can function. While the considerations that ought to go into that decision may be debatable, what is not debatable is that she, and she alone, has a constitutional duty to decide. She is the umpire who must keep the game going.

Her decision gains legitimacy from the fact that she is neutral. She is uniquely placed to make the call because the constitution makes her the most disinterested player, perhaps the only disinterested player, in the political game. If she were to give reasons, those reasons would be subject to interpretation, and would be put to partisan use by the politicians. The reasons would prompt speculation as to whether they were her "real" reasons for the decision, whether they actually reflected her true motivation, or whether they hid some vice-regal bias. Some would think the reasons self-serving. One side or the other would argue that the reasons were based on political as opposed to constitutional considerations. Depending on whether the reasons adopted the prime minister's rationale, or rejected it, the governor general would find herself in an adversarial position vis-à-vis either the prime minister or the leader of the opposition. If the governor general sought to avoid all of this by making the reasons sufficiently general as to be innocuous, one group of partisans or the other would criticize the reasons for lacking candor, for being formulaic or for being merely "archival."

Reasons would, therefore, inevitably draw the governor general into the political fray. The fact that she must make a choice already risks this. If, however, in addition to determining the outcome, she were to seek to justify her decision by issuing reasons, the danger of the politicization of her office would be greatly magnified. That politicization would undermine the very source of the legitimacy of her constitutional exercise of discretionary power and ultimately could completely destroy the utility of her constitutional role.

Requiring reasons in this context would hinder rather than promote democracy. In the highly charged political atmosphere of a prorogation or dissolution controversy, reasons risk undermining the governor general's neutrality. Yet it is precisely this neutrality that enables the governor general to act as the guarantor of responsible, democratic government. Any appearance of partisanship resulting from the reasons, even if involuntary and even if unfair, would be seen as undemocratic. It would also impair the governor general's ability to incarnate the nation, and to act as a symbol of its unity (Craven 2004, 7–8). Her role is unique. The constitution contemplates neither the politicization, nor the judicialization, of that role.

THE JUDICIALIZATION OF THE RESERVE POWERS

The governor general will not be able to function as arbiter in defence of responsible government unless the exercise of her discretion is final. By creating a record upon which a legal challenge could be built, reasons risk the judicialization of the governor general's reserve powers. Were the exercise of that discretion to be made subject to judicial oversight, the ultimate decision in matters of prorogation and dissolution would be shifted from Rideau Hall to the courts.

Protagonists in the charged political atmosphere surrounding the extraordinary use of reserve powers would use reasons to suggest that the governor general's discretion had been illegally exercised. They would allege that she had not taken into account relevant considerations, or that she had taken into account irrelevant ones. They would argue that her reliance on, or rejection of, various conventions, or her interpretation of those conventions, amounted to an error of law. They would maintain that their right to fairness had been denied by her failure to consult with them, or her failure to consider material that they had submitted.

Even without reasons, it is possible that a disappointed political faction might seek judicial review of the governor general's decision. Such a move would likely fail both because a court would be reluctant, on separation-of-powers grounds, to interfere with the operation of an executive function, and because a court would be cautious before considering this kind of political question a justiciable matter (Conacher 2009). Should reasons exist, courts would still, in all likelihood, be cautious. However, the chances of judicial review being attempted on the basis of those reasons, and the possibility of eventual success before an interventionist court, would increase significantly.

If reasons were required in the context of prorogation and dissolution, by the same logic reasons would quickly be sought for all exercises of vice-regal discretion. Sooner or later, someone dissatisfied with the reasons given for, say, the appointment or dismissal of a cabinet member, or perhaps the naming of a judge, reasons which would in fact be those of the prime minister, would mount a judicial challenge. While presumably such a challenge would be resisted by the courts, no one could be certain for how long that resistance would continue. The office of the governor general would be impoverished to the benefit of the judiciary, a development not foreseen by the Constitution, and a problem that the courts would likely prefer not to face.

THE IMPRACTICALITY OF CODES AND REASONS

The circumstances that generate constitutional controversy around prorogation and dissolution are fact-driven. The context is highly political.

The conventions and traditions that govern are well established (Monahan 2010). Outcomes are a matter of vice-regal judgment arrived at after weighing and balancing polycentric considerations. In these situations, reasons for decision would add little. The decision will speak for itself. The unique circumstances of each case make for precedents of limited utility. There is no reason to want to facilitate appeal or judicial review given that nothing would be gained by substituting the opinion of one decision-maker, a judge, for that of another, the governor general, especially when the latter is better positioned to make the final decision.

Even more than the reasons for a decision, what matters is that a decision is made. If the governor general "gets the decision wrong," it will not be so much because she has made an error in choosing one constitutional principle over another. Rather, it will be because the House, in the case of prorogation, or the electorate, in the case of dissolution, disagrees with the governor general's choice. In either case, the House, when recalled, or the electorate, if the House is dissolved, will get the opportunity to resolve the matter democratically (Franks 2009, 45). What really matters is that by making a decision, any decision, the governor general permits responsible government to continue functioning.

Attempts at exhaustively codifying conventions will also be frustrated by the unique situations in which difficult prorogation and dissolution cases arise. Boyce, citing Forsey, explains how codification is inappropriate in these fact-specific circumstances:

> …, there seems to be general recognition among political practitioners and academic commentators on the functioning of monarchy within Westminster-derived systems that the range of political circumstances in which the reserve powers might be needed is so vast that codification could never encompass them all or provide precise formulae for their use. Many would probably still accept Eugene Forsey's warning: "To embody them in an ordinary law is to ossify them. To embody them in a written constitution is to petrify them" (Boyce 2008, 61 and Chapter 3, fn. 37).

CONCLUSION

Some argue that by giving reasons, or adopting codes, the governor general could help educate the public in the complexities of the Westminster system of democratic government. This education, it is said, would increase public confidence in the governor general's exercise of her discretion.

These are laudable objectives, but they are misplaced. The Constitution, and the conventions which make it operational, do not make giving civics lessons part of the governor general's job description. There is good reason for this. If the governor general is to act as an impartial umpire in the defence of responsible government, she must remain neutral and be seen to remain neutral. Neutrality requires that she not prejudge hypothetical fact situations which may arise in the future and for which the factual picture is incomplete. As in common law adjudication, sticking to actual facts, avoiding speculation on hypotheticals, and deciding only what needs to be decided, focuses decision-making. In addition, the narrow exercise of vice-regal discretion is vital because of its absolute nature and the enormous consequences which it carries.

If not the governor general, who then is to explain to the public the operation of the Constitution? If the constitutional commentary on the events of late 2008 is any indication, politicians, scholars, columnists and the media are more than up to the task. These groups will identify and debate areas of controversy and explain that even in matters of state some uncertainty is inevitable.[14]

By arguing against the politicization and judicialization of the reserve powers and by casting doubt on the utility of reasons and codes in this context, issue is taken with Sossin and Dodek in their chapter entitled, "When Silence Isn't Golden" (Sossin and Dodek 2009; par contra Craven 2004, "The Goldenness of Silence"). Preferable is the approach suggested by the former *Daily Telegraph* editor, Sir Max Hastings, in describing the reigning monarch's success:

> At the heart of the Queen's brilliant success for almost 60 years is that we have been denied the slightest clue as to what she thinks about anything but dogs and horses. Her passivity has been inspired, because her subjects can then attribute any sentiments they choose to her. She has never said a word to raise a hackle. … The best hope for the future is to maintain the Queen's great tradition of being all things to all her subjects by remaining a smiling, but silent, monarch (Hastings 2010).

References

Aucoin, P. and L. Turnbull. 2004. "Removing the Virtual Right of First Ministers to Demand Dissolution." *Canadian Parliamentary Review* 27(2).

Baker v. Canada (Minister of Citizenship & Immigration, [1999] 2 S.C.R. 817 (S.C.C.).

Boyce, P. 2008. *The Queen's Other Realms – The Crown and its Legacy in Australia, Canada and New Zealand*. Sydney: The Federation Press.

Brun, H. 2008. "Michaelle Jean n'a pas le choix." *La Presse*. 4 décembre, A17.

---

[14] Boyce states: "Any governor general … who dares to raise publicly the possibility of an emergency situation which might involve recourse to the reserve power is likely to arouse fierce debate and political resentment if three Canadian examples contain any moral. In each case the vice-regal representative had admitted to the media that situations might arise which required dissolution of the legislature without advice." Interviews given by Governor General Schreyer after he left office were given as an example (Boyce 2004, 59).

Canada. Parliament. House of Commons. Motion. 2010, 17 March. (adopted by a vote of 139 – 135): "That, in the opinion of the House, the Prime Minister shall not advise the Governor General to prorogue any session of any Parliament for longer than seven calendar days without a specific resolution of this House of Commons to support such a prorogation." Available online at http://www.parl.gc.ca/HouseChamberBusiness/ChamberVoteDetail.aspx?Language=E&Mode=1&Parl=40&Ses=3&Vote=6

Canada. 2008, 5 December. "Proclamation Proroguing Parliament to January 26, 2009." *Canada Gazette* EXTRA 142(6). Accessed online at http://www.gazette.gc.ca/rp-pr/p2/2008/2008-12-05-x6/html/si-tr144-eng.html.

Canada. 2008. "Government of Canada: Announcement." 28 November. Accessed online at http://www.marketwire.com/press-release/Government-of-Canada-Announcement-925167.htm

Canadian Broadcasting Corporation. 2010, 2 October. "PM Gave Jean Pledges in Prorogation Crisis.". Accessed online at http://www.cbc.ca/canada/story/2010/10/01/harper-jean-prorogation.html.

Canadian Press. 2010, 28 September. "Michaelle Jean Breaks Silence on Prorogation." Accessed online at http://www.ctv.ca/CTVNews/TopStories/20100928/gg-jean-100928/

Clarkson, A. 2009. "Foreword." In *Parliamentary Democracy in Crisis*, eds. P.H. Russell and L. Sossin. Toronto: University of Toronto Press.

— 2006. *Heart Matters*. Toronto: Viking Canada.

Conacher v. Canada (Prime Minister), 2009 FC 920.

Craven, G. 2004. "The Developing Role of the Governor-General: The Goldenness of Silence," *Federal Law Review* 32(2): 281–90.

Desserud, D.A. 2009. "The Governor General, the Prime Minister and the Request of Prorogue," *Canadian Political Science Review* 3(3): 40–54.

Dickerson, K. 2010. "Protests Prompt Parliamentarians to Propound Prorogation Prescriptions, as Pundits Pronounce on Proposal' Prospects." *Centre for Constitutional Studies*. Accessed online at http://www.law.ualberta.ca/centres/ccs/news/?id=346

Forsey, E. 1968. *The Royal Power of Dissolution of Parliament in the British Commonwealth*. Toronto: Oxford University Press.

Franks, C.E.S. 2009. "To Prorogue or Not to Prorogue: Did the Governor General Make the Right Decision?" In *Parliamentary Democracy in Crisis*, eds. P.H. Russell and L. Sossin. Toronto: University of Toronto Press.

Hastings, M. 2010. "Why Prince Charles is too dangerous to be King." *The Daily Mail*. 20 December. Accessed online at http://www.dailymail.co.uk/debate/article-1339707/Prince-Charles-dangerous-king-This-eccentric-royal-imperil-monarchy.html

Hawkins, R.E. 2010. "The Fixed Election Law: Constitutional Convention or Conventional Politics." *Constitutional Forum constitutionnel* 19(1): 129–35.

Heard, A. 1991. *Canadian Constitutional Conventions: the Marriage of Law and Politics*. Toronto: Oxford University Press.

— 2009a. "The Governor General's Suspension of Parliament: Duty Done or a Perilous Precedent?" In *Parliamentary Democracy in Crisis*, eds. P.H. Russell and L. Sossin. Toronto: University of Toronto Press.

— 2009b. "The Governor General's Decision to Prorogue Parliament: A Chronology & Assessment." *Constitutional Forum constitutionnel* 18(1): 1–12.

Hicks, B. 2009a. "Lies My Fathers of Confederation Told Me: Are the Governor General's Reserve Powers a Safeguard for Democracy?" *Inroads: The Canadian Journal of Opinion* 25: 60.

— 2009b. "Guiding the Governor General's Prerogatives: Constitutional Convention Versus an Apolitical Decision Rule." *Centre for Constitutional Studies* 18(2).

Hogg, P.W. 2010. *Constitutional Law of Canada 2010 Student Edition.* Toronto: Thomson Carswell.

Jennings, I. 1960. *The Law and the Constitution.* 5th ed. London: University of London Press.

Kelly, R. and T. Nardi. 2010. "Open Letter to the Governor General of Canada." *Ottawa Citizen.* 21 January. Accessed online at http://communities.canada. com/ottawacitizen/blogs/thegargoyle/archive/2010/01/21/dear-governor-general-we-get-open-letters.aspx.

Lawyers Weekly. 2009. "Unravelling a Constitutional Crisis." 16 January. Accessed online at http://www.lawyersweekly.ca/index.php?section=article&article id=834

Library and Archives Canada. 29 October–4 November 1925. *The Diaries of William Lyon Mackenzie King.* C4323-C4335. Accessed online at http://www.collections canada.gc.ca/databases/king/001059-119.02-e.php?&page_id_nbr=9504& interval=20&&PHPSESSID=6vhr78jgg93bd8v8nns0

Monahan, P. 2010. *The House* [radio interview]. The Canadian Broadcasting Corporation. 2 October. Accessed online at http://www.cbc.ca/theHouse/2010/10/october-2-2010.html

Neary, P. 2009. "Confidence: How Much is Enough?" *Constitutional Forum Constitutionnel* 18(2): 45–48.

Ontario (Attorney General) v. OPSEU, [1987] 2 S.C.R. 2, p. 46-47.

Re Resolution to Amend the Constitution, [1981] 1 S.C.R. 753 (*Patriation Reference, 1981*).

Russell, P.H. 2009. "Learning to Live with Minority Parliaments." In *Parliamentary Democracy in Crisis*, eds. P.H. Russell and L. Sossin. Toronto: University of Toronto Press.

Smith, D.E. 1995. *The Invisible Crown: The First Principle of Canadian Government.* Toronto: University of Toronto Press.

— 2006. "Clarifying the Doctrine of Ministerial Responsibility as it Applies to the Government and Parliament of Canada." In Canada, *Commission of Inquiry into the Sponsorship Program and Advertising Activities (Gomery Commission) Report, Phase 2: Restoring Accountability – Research Studies: Volume 1 Parliament, Ministers and Deputy Ministers.*

Sossin, L. and A. Dodek. 2009. "When Silence Isn't Golden: Constitutional Conventions, Constititutional Culture, and the Governor General." In *Parliamentary Democracy in Crisis*, eds. P.H. Russell and L. Sossin. Toronto: University of Toronto Press.

Skogstad, G. 2009. "Western Canada and the 'Illegitimacy' of the Liberal-NDP Coalition Government." In *Parliamentary Democracy in Crisis*, eds. P.H. Russell and L. Sossin. Toronto: University of Toronto Press.

Stanbury, W.T. 2008. "Write it Down: Codify the Unwritten Conventions for Canada's Sake." *The Hill Times.* 15 December.

Stilborn, J. 2009. "The Role of the Governor General: Time to Revisit the Visits," *Policy Options* 30(7): 98–103.

Tremblay, G. 2010. "Limiting the Government's Power to Prorogue Parliament." *Canadian Parliamentary Review* 33(2): 16–17.

Tyler, T. 2008. "Politicians, Scholars Say Governor General Must Dispel Secrecy." *Toronto Star*. 6 December. Accessed online at http://www.thestar.com/News/Canada/article/549450

Valpy, M. 2009. "The 'Crisis:' A Narrative." In *Parliamentary Democracy in Crisis*, eds. P.H. Russell and L. Sossin. Toronto: University of Toronto Press.

Henry VII (r. 1485–1509)
King of England and Lord of Ireland

Portrait by unknown artist, 1505
© National Portrait Gallery, London

The following portraits of the Sovereigns grace the Foyer and
Salon de la Francophonie of the Canadian Senate.

François I (r. 1515–47)
King of France

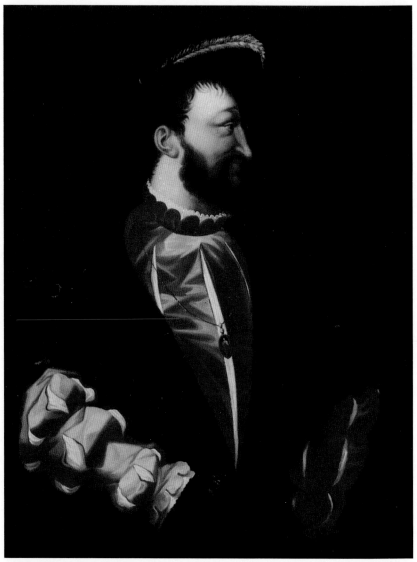

Portrait after Titian, circa 1820

National Capital Commission, Official Residences Crown Collection, Gift of the Honourable Serge Joyal, P.C., O.C., through the Canadiana Fund

Henri III (r. 1574–89)
King of France

Portrait by School of François Clouet, circa 1580
National Capital Commission, Official Residences Crown Collection, Gift of the Honourable
Serge Joyal, P.C., O.C., through the Canadiana Fund

Henri IV (r. 1589–1610)
King of France and Navarre

Bronze effigy after Barthélémy Tremblay, circa 1830

National Capital Commission, Official Residences Crown Collection, Gift of the Honourable
Serge Joyal, P.C., O.C., through the Canadiana Fund

Louis XIII (r. 1610–43)
King of France and Navarre

Portrait by Studio of Philippe de Champaigne, circa 1630
National Capital Commission, Official Residences Crown Collection, Gift of the Honourable
Serge Joyal, P.C., O.C., through the Canadiana Fund

Louis XIV (r. 1643–1715)
King of France and Navarre

Portrait by Studio of Hyacinthe Rigaud, circa 1700

National Capital Commission, Official Residences Crown Collection, Gift of the Honourable Serge Joyal, P.C., O.C., through the Canadiana Fund

Louis XV (r. 1715–74)
King of France

Portrait by Studio of Carle Van Loo, circa 1740

National Capital Commission, Official Residences Crown Collection, Gift of the Honourable Serge Joyal, P.C., O.C., through the Canadiana Fund

George III (r. 1760–1820)
King of Great Britain and Ireland

Portrait by Studio of Sir Joshua Reynolds, circa 1779
Senate of Canada / Sénat du Canada

George IV (r. 1820–30)
King of the United Kingdom of Great Britain and Ireland

Portrait by Sir Thomas Lawrence, circa 1822
National Capital Commission, Official Residences Crown Collection, Gift of the Honourable
Serge Joyal, P.C., O.C., through the Canadiana Fund

William IV (r. 1830–37)
King of the United Kingdom of Great Britain and Ireland

Engraving by Frederick Christian Lewis, 1831, from a drawing by Sir Thomas Lawrence in 1827

National Capital Commission, Official Residences Crown Collection, Gift of the Honourable Serge Joyal, P.C., O.C., through the Canadiana Fund

Victoria (r. 1837–1901)
Queen of the United Kingdom of Great Britain and Ireland

Portrait by John Partridge, 1842
Senate of Canada / Sénat du Canada

Edward VII (r. 1901–10)
King of the United Kingdom of Great Britain and Ireland, and
of the British Dominions beyond the Seas

Portrait by Luke Fildes, originally painted in 1903
Senate of Canada / Sénat du Canada

George V (r. 1910–36)
King of the United Kingdom of Great Britain and Ireland, and
of the British Dominions beyond the Seas

Portrait by Luke Fildes, originally painted in 1913
Senate of Canada / Sénat du Canada

Edward VIII (r. January to December 1936)
King of the United Kingdom of Great Britain and Ireland, and
of the British Dominions beyond the Seas

Photolithograph by Carl Vandyk, 1936, London (from a photograph taken in 1922)

National Capital Commission, Official Residences Crown Collection, Gift of the Honourable Serge Joyal, P.C., O.C., through the Canadiana Fund

George VI (r. 1936–52)
King of the United Kingdom of Great Britain and Ireland, and of the British Dominions beyond the Seas

Portrait after Sir Gerald F. Kelly by Robert Swain, 1955
Senate of Canada / Sénat du Canada

Elizabeth II (r. since 1952)
Queen of the United Kingdom, Canada and Her other Realms and Territories, Head of the Commonwealth

Portrait by Lilias Torrance Newton, 1957
Senate of Canada / Sénat du Canada

THE CROWN
AND CIVIL
SOCIETY

8

STATE CEREMONIAL: THE CONSTITUTIONAL MONARCH'S LITURGICAL AUTHORITY

PAUL BENOIT

Ce chapitre s'intéresse au rôle traditionnellement subjectif joué par la monarchie dans la vie sociale par rapport à son rôle traditionnellement objectif à l'échelle du gouvernement et du pays. L'auteur tente ainsi de répondre à ces deux questions :

1) Comment expliquer que l'État, qui a graduellement cherché en Occident à se démarquer des religions organisées, en soit venu à jouer un rôle religieux ou quasi religieux en suscitant le rassemblement affectif de la population et son élévation même passagère à un niveau de conscience supérieur ?

2) Quelles conventions devraient régir cette forme laïque et moderne de liturgie ?

L'auteur offre en conclusion quelques suggestions pratiques visant l'amélioration de deux des principales cérémonies d'État au Canada, soit l'intronisation du gouverneur général et l'ouverture du Parlement, et des trois jours fériés liés au développement et à la défense du pays.

> The monarchical constitution is the constitution of developed reason: all other constitutions belong to lower grades of the development and realization of reason (*Hegel* 1971, 270).

A DISPLAY OF AUTHORITY, NOT OF POWER

When thinking about Canada's constitution, or indeed the constitution of any country, one must bear in mind more than just the written laws or major institutions of the country. What should also be included are the unwritten rules or conventions that govern the behaviour of members of society and make up what we call its governance. These conventions are of two sorts: some pertain to the functioning of government and are meant to facilitate the resolution of issues; others pertain to the cultural life of society and reveal something of a society's distinctive character.

The latter are as important as the former. Indeed, history has shown that government resolutions can only go so far in ensuring the cohesion of society. More is required on the part of a country's citizens than formal compliance with its enactments; there must be a deeper, subjective engagement for a society to be strong and united. Without the cultural conventions that appeal to the senses and to the heart, there would be no larger purpose for which members of society would be prepared to sacrifice, nothing to compel the spirit and inspire noble deeds.

The monarch, under our constitution, has conventional roles to play in both areas. In this chapter, we will be concentrating on the cultural rather than the governmental – on the monarch's subjective engagement with civil society rather than her objective engagement with the prime minister. But before examining these conventional roles performed by the Queen, we need to understand clearly their authoritative basis.

As Hannah Arendt has explained, "authority is commonly mistaken for some form of power or violence" (Arendt 463). Authority is less palpable than power. It stems from an unquestioning recognition that some person or office is superior in some way and is therefore worthy of our respect and deference. By contrast, power comes from a consent that is freely given in an explicit or tacit manner; it increases as the will of more and more people is united through agreement, cooperation, and organization.

The relationship between authority and power is complex. The more power one has, the more one can act; the more authority one has, the less one needs to act. Authority may be kept in check by power but it can never be totally controlled by it. History has shown how foolish it is to decree that, from such and such a date, such and such an individual's authority shall cease to obtain. In the attempt to abolish it, one is very likely to increase it, which brings us to Arendt's second differentiation. Authority should not be confused with different forms of coercion – with the "sticks and carrots" used for ensuring compliance – as when "authoritarian" is used as a synonym for autocratic or dictatorial.

The right to go first, to set an example, to offer advice, or to issue a command is something that is granted spontaneously to some individuals quite apart from the surrounding configurations of power or the instruments of coercion at hand. The advantage of having a hereditary monarch to carry out certain conventional roles is that her performance is free from the play of power and the divisiveness that ensues from power's principle: the principle of election.

THE MONARCH'S LITURGICAL AUTHORITY

Her Majesty's nine-day tour of Canada at the end of June and the beginning of July 2010 highlighted the exercise of her cultural as distinct from her governmental authority. Indeed, millions of Canadians from different parts of the country were given the opportunity to witness directly the Queen's personal involvement in civil society. Through the organization of dozens of events, they got a glimpse of her carrying out her more subjective roles. One of those roles, I shall argue, was liturgical: indeed, during her tour, the Queen had occasion to carry out a form of worship on behalf of the public.

Just as on the governmental side, we can distinguish between the more particular role that the Queen plays as one of the three bodies of Parliament (the Queen-in-Parliament) and the more universal role she plays as embodiment of the State and its sovereignty (the Queen-in-Council), so, on the cultural side, can we distinguish between her more particular role as the font of all honours, bestowing marks of recognition on citizens who have made an outstanding contribution to the well-being of their country (as when the Queen unveiled a sculpture of Oscar Peterson, the jazz pianist, in Ottawa) and her more universal and liturgical role as mediator between society and the realm of spiritual values.

When we refer to Her Majesty's liturgical authority, it should be understood that the form of worship she carries out is secular, not sacred. In less exalted fashion, secular worship can include a range of events: paying homage to those who have sacrificed their lives in the defence of their country; marking anniversaries of important events in the history of one's country (as the Queen did on July 1st); and giving thanks to Providence for the blessings bestowed on one's country.

In considering the transformation from sacred to secular forms of worship and its impact on the constitutional development of Western countries, including Canada, this chapter will seek to answer two questions:

1) How did it come to pass that the state, which in the West sought over time to differentiate itself from organized religion, has nevertheless come to play a religious or quasi-religious role, in the sense of binding people together emotionally and transporting them, however briefly, onto a higher plane of existence?
2) What are the conventions that should govern this modern secular form of worship?

Finally, this chapter will make practical suggestions on the enhancement of the two most important ceremonies of State in Canada – the installation of the governor general and the opening of Parliament – and the three statutory holidays that pertain to constitutional development and defence. These ceremonies and holidays involve the monarch as the embodiment of the state. A clear understanding of the monarch's liturgical authority can help us to develop more thoughtful protocols that serve to strengthen the emotional bonds uniting Canadians and thereby contribute to an overall richer sense of Canadian citizenship.

Homo Religiosus

For most of man's history, religion has been the most important factor determining his outlook on life. Until very recently, being emotionally bound to some higher force was paramount. It was deemed *sacred* to the point that all other human experiences paled in comparison and were relegated to the *profane*. Only the sacred was real; it alone could impart significance to man's existence. As Mircea Eliade, the historian of religions, put it:

> Whatever the historical context in which he is placed, *homo religiosus* always believes that there is an absolute reality, the *sacred*, which transcends this world but manifests itself in this world, thereby sanctifying it and making it real. He further believes that life has a sacred origin and that human existence realizes all of its potentialities in proportion as it is religious – that is, participates in reality (Eliade, 202).

What made the religious experience so overwhelming was that it could seamlessly tap into man's profoundest emotions, resonate equally with all members of society, and leave everyone with a sense of being part of a larger cosmic whole. The deep and all-encompassing nature of the experience ensured that, for much of mankind's history, religion provided the sole source of legitimate governance. The order of Melchizedek was the norm. (As recounted in *Genesis* 14, at the time of Abraham, before the levitical priesthood was established, Melchizedek was both king and priest.) Tithes preceded taxes.

Challenges to the Primacy of the Religious

Out of the merging of ancient Greek, Roman and Hebraic traditions, the Christian West was faced with a number of challenges if it wanted to preserve the primacy of place for the religious experience. Six specific factors can be identified that over the course of eighteen centuries all drove organized religion in the West to the margins of the public domain and left an emotional gap in the body politic.

1) *Politics as a Competing Sphere of Authority.* From the outset, Christ's teachings made clear that there was a break between the things that

were owed to God and the things that were owed to Caesar. While in traditional societies there was always the distinction between the sacred and the profane, the profane in itself had no merit. As Eliade has explained, only if it became infused with the sacred did it take on any significance. Now, with Christianity, the profane took on importance in its own right. It became a legitimate sphere of human endeavour. The human condition, it was recognized, could be improved if the things belonging to Caesar were well managed.

2) *Philosophy as Another Competing Sphere of Authority.* Yet another important differentiation occurred in the West, which also had the effect of more clearly determining the specific nature of the religious experience. Carried forward from the ancient Greek and Roman civilizations was the tradition of cultivating a class of learned men who were neither priests attached to God nor ministers attached to Caesar. These were philosophers and men of science devoted to the pursuit of wisdom independently of any vested interests. Thus, even before the advent of the modern age, we find social order in the West resting unevenly on three different pillars of authority: religious authority located in the Church; political authority located in the Imperial State; and the authority of learned scholarship located in academies and universities. Each one of these realms had its own legitimate contribution to make to the well-being of mankind.

3) *Voluntarism.* With the Renaissance, the greatest challenge of all began to confront Western man's experience of religion. It was no longer just a matter of respecting other fields of competence and authority; there now arose an insistence that social order rest on freedom: that is, that all rules governing human behaviour, be they written or unwritten, should rest on ethical norms voluntarily adhered to by a substantial part of the population. Religious authority, like political authority and scientific authority, could henceforth be contested: it was the price to pay for keeping all rules alive and ensuring that they were internally compelling, not just something to be externally complied with. Sooner or later, and for different reasons, norms were contested in all spheres of public life in the West.

4) *Divisions in the Church.* In this context of trying to reconcile the demands of personal freedom with the demands of social order, the Church, the custodian of religious experience, itself became divided. The rules that made up public worship were contested as never before. Where once they reflected a consensus, they were now the source of division. Disputes ensued over not just theoretical definitions but also the practical implications of Christ's teachings. Disputes turned into civil wars as believers on one side or the other were persecuted and killed for their beliefs. It was one thing for Christians to fight Muslims in the Holy Land or on their borders; it was quite another for Christians to wage civil war amongst themselves within Western societies.

5) *An Urban and Commercial Way of Life.* Adding to the challenges facing the maintenance of public worship in Western societies was the fact that, with the growth of commerce and cities, man became increasingly cut off from nature. Religious traditions had always counted on nature as a primary revelation of the divine. The natural ties of family, of an agricultural way of life, of living with animals, and the close observance of natural cycles, all of which could be read for spiritual lessons and guidance, became increasingly frayed. The essential correspondence between man's life, the life of nature, and the grander order of the cosmos appeared to be broken.

6) *A Mechanistic Way of Thinking.* With the Enlightenment, a stricter demarcation was drawn between the realm of science, or the objective study of nature, and the realm of the spirit, or man's subjective state of consciousness. This break was the theme of a speech delivered in June 2010 by HRH The Prince of Wales. Prince Charles explained that the break has led to a "deep, inner crisis of the soul. It is a crisis in our relationship with – and our perception of – Nature, and it is born of Western culture being dominated for at least two hundred years by a mechanistic and reductionist approach to our scientific understanding of the world around us" (HRH The Prince of Wales 2010). The Prince continued, stating that this "imbalance, where mechanistic thinking is so predominant, goes back at least to Galileo's assertion that there is nothing in Nature but quantity and motion. This is the view that continues to frame the general perception of the way the world works and how we fit within the scheme of things. As a result, Nature has been completely objectified – 'She' has become an 'it' – and we are persuaded to concentrate on the material aspect of reality that fits within Galileo's scheme" (ibid.). More radical followers of the Enlightenment went further and harshly criticized the Church for its alleged superstitions and for keeping members of society in a state of ignorance.

In the face of these challenges, and without losing the growing social differentiation that they brought about, was it still possible for Western society to devise a form of public worship that could continue to bind people together emotionally on a higher plane of existence without reneging on the use of one's intellectual faculties on the one hand or the carrying out of one's political obligations on the other?

Paradoxically, just as the level of debate became increasingly critical in both the scientific and political realms, so the need for a public liturgy – one that would transcend the divisions of the will and the divisions of the mind and open man to what he had in common with other human beings – became greater than ever.

ROUSSEAU AND THE WAY FORWARD

Rousseau was perhaps the first to see clearly the dilemma facing Western man. While one could still find people on the margins of Western society for whom the sacred was still a reality, for most human beings living in the mechanically advanced societies of the West, the very notion of public worship had become problematical. Privately or within the confines of a small local community, worship could be carried on as it had for centuries, but it could no longer really be thought of as public in the sense of freely engaging a large percentage of the population. The symbols and rituals that made up the public liturgy of any one church denomination no longer rested on a consensus. For a large part of the population, they had ceased to have any spiritual significance.

From the perspective of the State, which had to ensure the security of civil society, there seemed to be no other option but to deny to all churches an exclusive monopoly on the religious experience and consequently to have them all recede in varying degree from the public realm. This was the only legal and political solution that could prevent the powerful emotions at the base of the religious experience from destroying civil order in society.

In some countries, a compromise was worked out between State and Church. There was no need for the state to become involved in public liturgy so long as that role could still be filled by one or two or possibly three churches that agreed not to make any practical claims that could infringe on the freedom of the other churches, and together to cover off the emotional religious needs of nearly the entire population.

However, by the 18th century, even this compromise was proving untenable in many Western countries. There were further divisions within Christianity, with numerous churches all claiming to be the true faithful interpreters of Christ's teachings. The right of the Jews to practise their religion free of discrimination also became an issue.

The governmental solution of legal tolerance may have prevented civil strife, but it left an emotional vacuum among neighbours and fellow citizens. By default, the State now found itself in a position of having to take over the communitarian role that for centuries had been carried out by the Church.

THE SUBLIME AND THE POETIC MODE OF REPRESENTATION

The challenge that Rousseau put to his mid-eighteenth century contemporaries, and which we are still grappling with today, is how, in a society increasingly differentiated materially and intellectually and that has cut itself off from nature, is it possible for members of the society to overcome their growing sense of alienation, to reconnect emotionally, and to be spiritually re-energized? Or to put the challenge in more liturgical terms, how was one to give public expression to man's inner life in a manner that would capture the awesome quality of the traditional religious ceremony without invoking the element of fear or terror that was often mingled with it? What would be the staged equivalent of feeling overwhelmed, of suddenly finding oneself in the midst of an earthquake, a tsunami, or an explosion of some sort, but without feeling that one's life is in danger?

The answer to these questions lay in that tradition of poetry that sought to cultivate a very distinct emotional tone – the sublime.

The process of refining the religious experience and cultivating the sublime was begun with Greek drama, which itself was derived from sacred liturgy and more specifically from choral songs in honour of the god Dionysus. In his *Poetics*, Aristotle explained how the poetic mode of representation, through the depiction of great events and of human beings like ourselves suffering undeservedly, can refine our raw emotions, bring them into fuller consciousness, and produce those feelings of empathy so necessary for an ethical society. An obscure Greek writer of the 1st century AD, who is referred to as Longinus, devoted a whole treatise to this psychological process. As he put it, the sublime was not so much a formal style of poetry as it was a tone that had a special effect on the audience:

> For the true sublime naturally elevates us: uplifted with a sense of proud exaltation, we are filled with joy and pride, as if we had ourselves produced the very thing we heard (Longinus, 179).

Longinus captured the essence of the sublime when, towards the end of his work, he described the experience as the feeling of being not just spectators but eager competitors at some Olympic games of the gods:

> This above all: that Nature has judged man a creature of no mean or ignoble quality, but, as if she were inviting us to some great gathering, she has called us into life, into the whole universe, there to be spectators of her games and eager competitors; and she therefore from the first breathed into our hearts an unconquerable passion for whatever is great and more divine than ourselves (ibid., 277).

Taking their cue from Longinus, whose work had been rediscovered by Italian humanists of the Renaissance, 18th century men of letters such as Addison, Grey, and Burke went on to differentiate the sublime still further. It had to be distinguished from the artistic in general and more specifically from what we consider to be the beautiful. As a poetic mode of representation, it had to offer an alternative not just to the clarity, distinction, and limits that had been fostered by the Enlightenment, but, just as importantly, it had also to offer an alternative to the prettiness and pleasing superficiality of the Rococo and *style galant*. Both the Enlighten-ment and the Rococo, for all their impressive achievements, had indirectly drawn attention to the emotional gap left by the gradual disappearance of wonder and enchantment from the world.

As a proxy for the religious experience, the sublime was injected into all aspects of culture during the second half of the 18th century. Educated men and women sought to poeticize not just the fine arts but other forms of cultural expression, such as gardening, interior design and crafts. Some sought to experience the sublime directly by turning once again to nature, but now in its grandest and most extreme forms. Aspects of our planet which heretofore had been thought of as forbidding or dangerous were now deliberately sought out in order to re-experience or experience for the first time that sense of terror and awe, which appeared to have been banished from other realms of human activity. "Extreme tourism" got underway: oceans, mountains, great waterfalls could all move modern man emotionally and evoke quasi-religious feelings, while keeping the terrifying dimension in check. Switzerland became an attractive destina-tion for those on tour in Europe.

These direct, emotional experiences of nature served as a touchstone for poets, as they strove to achieve the same uplifting effects in their works of representation. But it was in the performing arts, more than the literary or visual, that the stirring of deep emotions best lent itself to expression. Theatre, dance, music and opera, which, of all the arts, were the closest to the primal religious experience, were ripe for becoming the vehicles of choice for conveying the sublime. Mozart's operas became the supreme embodiment of this new poetic spirit.

The social exigencies of the late 18th century put additional pressure on the traditional forms governing the performing arts. If the event was to be truly public, it had to be accessible and even appealing to as many people as possible, nor should its content be too complex. Concerts and plays had to take to the streets and parks. Festivals became the most appropriate venue for framing a ceremonial public event: the modern, secular equivalent of the sacred feast days.

GERMAN NEO-CLASSICISM VS GERMAN ROMANTICISM

It was in German-speaking lands that poets and philosophers took up Rousseau's challenge most seriously. Within a period of half a century and centered in the relatively small duchy of Saxe-Weimar, two differ-ent traditions emerged that provided superficially similar but radically different responses to the need for a new kind of secular, quasi-religious community.

On the one hand, we find poets and philosophers, such as Lessing (who was influenced by Burke), Schiller, Goethe, Schelling and Hegel, who sought to take the classical humanist tradition to its next stage of development. On the other, moving in the same circles was another group led by such thinkers as Herder, the Schlegel brothers, and Fichte, who sought a simpler and more forceful expression and who gave birth to the *Sturm und Drang* and romantic movement. A close analysis of the difference between these two currents of thought, which are often confused, is fundamental if we are to understand and critically evaluate the basis of modern public ceremonial.

In trying to capture the integrative power of the religious experience and to convey it to modern men and women by way of sublime poetry, Schiller saw the challenge in terms of producing poetry that would embody or realize an ideal. He called this kind of poetry *idyllic* in the sense that it would combine the best of naive poetry, centered in nature, with the best of sentimental poetry, centred in man's freely operating intellect. It was up to the poet, he said, to "create an idyll that also realizes [or embodies] that pastoral innocence in those subjected to culture and to all the conditions of the most active and passionate living, the most comprehensive thinking, the most sophisticated art, and the highest social refinement, in a word, an idyll that leads to *Elyseum* the human being who now can no longer return to *Arcadia*" (Schiller 232). In other words, a new reconciliation had to be achieved between man's inner freedom and the exigencies of a highly differentiated society. Inspired by Schiller, Hegel placed this reconciliation at the heart of his philosophy.

For Hegel, the public realm was a mixture of infinite spirit and well-defined forms; spirit could be embodied in great political deeds, in constitutions, in the arts, customs and enjoyments of society. But it finds its finest embodiment in religious poetry; for there, the universal content of religion is blended with the more universal form of poetry. A spiritual unity is achieved whereby man's self-consciousness finds itself at home in the universe. The one comprehending is fundamentally reconciled to what is comprehended (Hegel 1970, 276–77).

Romantics glorified man's emotions and wanted to give their impulses free reign. The heart could not err and all one's effort should go into tapping into that subjective force and giving it voice as purely and profoundly as possible. In contrast, neo-classicists wanted to give man's emotions expression but to keep that expression within the bounds of reason. There were always objective factors that weighed in the balance and had to be taken into consideration by thoughtful human beings. The kind of reason that neoclassicists had in mind was comprehensive reason (*vernunft*), reason that can grasp overarching patterns and has insight into the purpose of things; it was not the instrumental reason of the Enlightenment, which was a mere understanding (*verstand*) that refuses to move beyond isolated categories and knows only *raisonnement* (Hegel 1967, 182).

Neoclassicists argued that in going back to one's roots and trying to uncover a pure expression of the self, romantics were driven to two extremes: the naive extreme of self-abandonment and the deliberate extreme of self-affirmation.

It may be argued that the first extreme, the naive expression of self (Rousseau's *l'amour-de-soi*) is built into human nature and can be discovered, as Herder did, in old folk tales and folk songs; or in the customs of tribal folk still unaffected by Western civilization; or even in today's young folks' spontaneous instinct for generating their own cult of celebrities, of identifying fanatically (i.e., as fans) with popular actors and singers and athletes who have captured their imagination. (This last kind of manifestation of raw emotion is especially evident wherever authorities, ignoring the importance of public ceremonies and the role that they can play in educating popular sentiments, have left an emotional vacuum in society.)

For neoclassicists, this return to a simpler stage of development is regressive; it undermines Western man's whole endeavour of continuous learning, of all-round cultural improvement and education (*Bildung*). One cannot turn back the clock and ignore the differentiations that have been achieved, often painfully, in man's individual and collective development.

More ominous is the other romantic extreme, in which we find public ceremonies deliberately designed to bring about the affirmation of a collective self rather than the transcendence of individual selves. This is the opposite of rendering homage to the nobility manifest in the deeds of others, and which are worthy of our emulation. Here the sense of self, rather than being softened and opened up onto a larger horizon, is aggrandized and hardened in the assertion of a collective identity.

Thus, in the wake of the French Revolution and Napoleon's conquest of Prussia in 1806, do we find Fichte devoting the rest of his life (he died in 1814) to forging a sense of community among German-speaking people scattered in dozens of states of differing size. This sense of community was based on the active positing of an individual's own self-consciousness as absolute; practically, this infinite willing was then given limited definition and necessary support through the ethno-linguistic world of a specific people or folk.

Instead of celebrating, in a spirit of patriotism, the noble deeds accomplished by others and how we have benefited from them and can emulate them, romantics, in a spirit of nationalism, celebrate what we are in and by ourselves and despite others. If the former community is animated by an empathy for (and an indebtedness to) others, the latter is animated by a wilful assertion of one's self to the exclusion of others.

This new form of community based on a spirit of nationalism quickly spread throughout German-speaking lands and was soon replicated among the people of Eastern Europe, as they too began to define themselves as different peoples. It was not long before this kind of self-affirmation spread to other parts of the world. Thus, German nationalism became the prototype not only for all forms of nationalism, but for all subsequent forms of group theorizing and identity-based politics, all of which are characterized by a wilful self-righteousness that continues to plague us two centuries later.

THE SYMBOLS OF COMMUNITY

The contrast between neoclassical and romantic definitions of community becomes apparent when we consider the role of symbols in public ceremonial. Symbols are real, tangible objects meant to stand in for some spiritual quality or virtue. In trying to do justice to that quality, no effort is spared to make the actual symbols as impressive as possible. For this is the most accessible way humans have of trying to bridge the inevitable gap between the world of the senses and the world of spirit. In the same vein, symbols are handled with care out of respect for the spiritual energy they are meant to embody, and are presented with dignity in order to allow that energy to radiate as fully as possible.

The monarch's coronation ceremony provides the finest example of the traditional use of symbols. The sword girt about the monarch symbolically invests her with the might necessary to defend the realm. The ring placed on her finger symbolizes her espousal to the realm. A sceptre with a cross and a sceptre with a dove are then presented to her, so that her steps may be taken in a spirit of justice and a spirit of mercy. Finally, at the climax of the ceremony, a crown, the symbol of glory, is placed on her head. While all these symbols may be admired aesthetically, their real purpose is to express a psychological truth, the significance of which can only be grasped if the correspondence between the material object and the spiritual quality is understood.

Under the influence of the romantic movement, the spiritual dimension, which forms the psychological backdrop governing the use of symbols, has receded, leaving only the naturalistic dimension of objects in its wake. Flags have taken the place of symbols. But flags are not symbols. They may contain representations of symbols, as when they depict elements drawn from a coat of arms, but in themselves they are not symbols; they are simply signs. They serve to signal one's national identity, usually in opposition to others of a different nationality. Individuals may invest their flag with qualities that go beyond their affiliation to a certain political and legal entity, but those meanings are not clear and settled. Hence, the ambiguity and confusion of today's flag-waving ceremonies: for some, it may be a patriotic act of rendering homage; for others, it may be a nationalistic act of self-assertion. And for as long as there is no consensus at an emotional level on the spiritual purpose of men and women living together, there is no human community.

A Framework for State Ceremonial

By turning to poets and philosophers operating within the neoclassical humanist tradition, who grappled two centuries ago with the same social challenges that we face today, we hope to have shown how a cultivation of the sublime is the key to fostering a sense of common purpose and founding an ethically based community. The formal structure for achieving that poetic effect can also serve as a framework for organizing state ceremonial. It is a structure that is dynamic, moving through three distinct stages or moments. For a production to be sublime and achieve that awesome, uplifting effect, it has to unfold along the following lines:
    First, the setting.

- The event should clearly mark a break from people's day-to-day preoccupations and the divisions of will and ambition that characterize civil society.
- It should appeal to as broad an audience as possible, making it truly public.
- It should be impressive so as to trigger a sense of awe (free of fear), an emotion that comes naturally to children, but more difficultly to adults with very settled mental habits.
- It should celebrate the noble deeds of ordinary human beings – the secular derivative of the sacred celebration of the lives of saints or of the mysteries related to supernatural beings.

Second, the transformation.

- With the boundaries usually defining their self blurred (a remnant of Dionysus), participants in the ceremony are moved by the nobility of the deed and come to partake of its essential goodness, a goodness that is felt to lie beyond ordinary existence and that is bestowed on human beings as a spiritual gift or blessing.
- The limits of one's personal and social existence are transcended, as one feels, if only for a moment, transported onto a higher plane.
- An ethical community, nourished from a common goodness, is established among all those participating, which is quite different, on the one hand, from the communion or mystical union sought after in sacred religious ceremonies or, on the other, from biological communities based on physical affinities.

Third, the prolongation.

- Having glimpsed their own lives within a grander State narrative, participants leave the ceremony with a greater sense of purpose and

thus better equipped psychologically to confront whatever material and physical challenges they face in their daily lives.
- Having recollected the noble deeds of those who came before, participants may be encouraged to emulate them to the extent possible.
- Having opened themselves consciously to others and their influence, participants leave the ceremony with a sense of empathy, with a sense of the profound mutuality of the human condition.

The installation of Canada's new governor general, David Johnston, on October 1, 2010, provided a good example of a ceremony of State that achieved sublimity, that special effect sought after by poets since the 6th century BC. The ceremony was a celebration of the impressive historical continuity and uniqueness of the office, which can be traced back through four centuries of continuous constitutional development to Samuel de Champlain, who was appointed governor in 1627 by Louis XIII. Johnston is our 65th. But, even more importantly, the ceremony was a liturgical service that invoked the many different spiritual qualities that the new incumbent would require to carry out the duties of the office.

The setting for the ceremony was most impressive. Gathered in the Senate chamber, before the empty vice-regal throne, were leading figures from all the estates of the realm: ministers of the Queen's Privy Council for Canada were seated around a table in the middle of the chamber; Supreme Court justices clad in their scarlet robes were present; the Chief of the Defence Staff of the Canadian Forces, Walter Natynczyk, was granted the special and most appropriate role of accompanying Mr. Johnston into the Chamber; senators occupied their seats; the speaker and representatives from the lower house were in attendance, as were the lieutenant governors of the provinces, diplomats and special guests, including former governors general and prime ministers. In the words of the Prime Minister, "today we are celebrating the entire Canadian Crown."

The program itself was profoundly coherent, with a balanced mixture of elements pertaining to the responsibilities of the office and elements designed to express the new incumbent's tastes and priorities. The ceremony began with a moment of prayer and reflection, calling on the Creator Spirit to bestow on David Johnston the spiritual gifts required for carrying out his duties. The most solemn moment of the ceremony occurred when Mr. Johnston took the oath of allegiance followed by the oath of office, after which he and his wife were invited to take their places on the vice-regal thrones. The national chief of the Assembly of First Nations, Shawn Atleo, then offered up for their new Excellencies a prayer of embarkation, calling on the Creator Spirit to protect them and make their voyage a success. His Excellency was presented with the chains of office making him Chancellor of the Order of Canada, of the Order of Military Merit, of the Order of Merit of the Police Forces, and of the Heraldic Authority.

He was then presented with the Great Seal of Canada, the seal used to give formal expression to Canada's sovereignty as a State. The seal was returned to a minister of the Crown (in this case, it was the minister of industry), who since the advent of responsible government has custody of the seal and whose counter-signature must be affixed.

In his inaugural address and through his choice of artistic perform-ances, David Johnston revealed something of his character and his prior-ities. He let it be known to the public, first of all, that he has been clearly influenced and shaped by the women in his life; secondly, that ensuring that all young Canadians have access to good teachers is something that matters very deeply to him; and, finally, that he wished to emulate one of his predecessors, Georges Vanier, who in his own inaugural address said: "In our march forward in material happiness, let us not neglect the spiritual threads in the meaning of our lives. If Canada is to attain the greatness worthy of it, each of us must say, 'I ask only to serve.'"

On leaving the Senate chamber, the Governor General, now as commander-in-chief of the Canadian Forces, carried out his first review of a guard of honour. Their Excellencies then got into the landau and headed back to their new home at Rideau Hall, but not without making a symbolic gesture of their own. They stopped by the war memorial to lay a bouquet of 26 red and white roses, two for each of our provinces and territories – an emotionally touching gesture that demonstrated the power of symbols to achieve a sublime effect.

The only shortcoming of the ceremony was that it was not witnessed by very many Canadians. In principle, all Canadians should stop doing what they are ordinarily doing for two hours and take part in this secular religious ceremony – the most important in Canada, in which once every five years we are emotionally bound together and our common aspira-tions renewed.

The opening of Parliament is another ceremony of State during which the Queen or her vice-regal representative has occasion, if only briefly, to exercise her liturgical authority. As in the case of the governor general's installation ceremony, all the constitutional elements of our society are gathered together in the upper chamber: what we habitually think of as a legal document becomes a *tableau vivant*. The procession of the (vice) regal personage to the throne is a sublime moment that captures the full achievement of our constitutional development and gives precise mean-ing to the phrase "freedom wears a crown." Of course, the main purpose of the ceremony is for the Queen or her representative to inform both chambers of what her government's legislative agenda will be for the session about to begin. But before getting down to business, in what is another liturgical moment, she reflects briefly on events of the recent past that have marked the country as a whole and have been occasions for the display of spiritual qualities. Concluding her speech, the Queen or her representative reverts back briefly to her priestly role with the following prayer: "That the blessing of God may rest on your counsels" or "That divine Providence guide you in your deliberations."

Of Canada's statutory holidays, three are of a public nature and occasions of State, in the sense that they pertain to the country's constitutional development and defence: Canada Day (celebrated July 1), Victoria Day (May 24), and Remembrance Day (November 11). All involve the Queen or her vice-regal representative as the embodiment of the State.

CANADA DAY

Originally and more precisely called Dominion Day, this holiday marks the uniting of two maritime colonies, Nova Scotia and New Brunswick, to the central Canadian colony of Canada and their transformation into a new confederation called the Dominion of Canada. From a constitutional perspective, Confederation also marked another step in the gradual devolution of authority from the United Kingdom to its former colonies in British North America. Thus Canada acquired its own Parliament and its own freedom to legislate in domestic matters. But the real emphasis of Canada Day is on the integration of heretofore separate colonies and regional cultures. In a country as vast as Canada it makes sense for us to celebrate the coming together of regions far distant from one another.

If the theme of the governor general's installation ceremony – The Smart and Caring Nation: A Call to Service – was in the neo-classical tradition of reaching out to others, the theme for the 2010 Canada Day ceremony – Our Year to Shine: Canada Welcomes the World – was in the romantic tradition of self-centredness. Fortunately, the Queen was able to rescue the situation by testifying to how Canada had remained "true to its history, its distinctive character and its values. This nation has dedicated itself to being a caring home for its own, a sanctuary for others and an example to the world." She then went on to salvage a bit of sublimity from the occasion by turning the success of the Olympics and a gold medal in hockey away from a tone of self-congratulation to something more altruistic by pointing out how "a sense of common purpose had been renewed within this country" and how a welcome of "extraordinary warmth and enthusiasm" had been extended to the rest of the world.

The focus of celebrations on Canada Day should be on the achievements of those statesmen who have responded to the call to service by rising above their local interests and contributing to the unity of the country. One appropriate way of doing this would be to have a particular province provide the theme of the celebrations for a given year; the sequencing of provinces could be determined in part by important anniversaries. The day could begin with a pageant re-enacting key events in the province's history, followed by a presentation of the achievements of some of the province's outstanding sons and daughters, and winding up with poetry and music performed by her leading artists. The lieutenant-governor of Saskatchewan's centennial gala, which took place in Regina in 2005, provides an excellent example of this kind of ceremony.

VICTORIA DAY

Originally established to mark the birthday of Queen Victoria in 1819, the May 24 holiday has now become the official holiday of the reigning monarch. Unfortunately, it is a holiday that has lost most of its sparkle, becoming not much more than a day off work with occasional fireworks in the evening for the benefit of the young. Even worse, the event is not celebrated in the province of Québec, which has chosen to celebrate Dollard des Ormeaux instead, and has moreover transformed the feast day of St. John the Baptist, which occurs on June 24, into a nationalist celebration.

Being the oldest of the three major civic holidays, Victoria Day should be the occasion for marking the most important stages in Canada's constitutional development. Just as on July 4, Americans enjoy commemorating that day in 1776 when Thomas Jefferson made public the Declaration of Independence, as well as 1787, the year during which a satisfactory constitution between the different states and the new federal entity was framed at a national convention in Philadelphia, so should Canadians be celebrating two important years from the same era. Indeed, the *Québec Act* of 1774 and the *Constitutional Act* of 1791, events which bracket, as it were, the American dates, are arguably more impressive. Those two Acts not only became the foundations for all subsequent constitutional developments but reflected a policy intent that has largely been respected ever since: the former recognizing local institutions (such as the French civil law, the seigniorial system, and the rights of the Roman Catholic Church to collect tithes) and designing a special oath that allowed Roman Catholics to take office without compromising their religious beliefs; the latter providing the full range of institutions that make up our system of government: a (lieutenant) governor, an executive council, an appointed legislative council, and an elected legislative assembly.

In philosophical terms, these constitutional events represented an advance on or a correction of the early 18th century Enlightenment thinking that prevailed among the American Founding Fathers, in that they embodied the neoclassical sensitivity to the needs of community that emerged in the second half of the 18th century. Our regime is, in spirit, more akin to Goethe than Newton.

A third year that merits celebration as part of Victoria Day would be 1849, the year in which the colonies in British North America became self-governing: i.e., henceforth the appointed governor was obliged to follow the advice of the minister enjoying the confidence of the lower chamber.

The program for Victoria Day, staged on the grounds of Rideau Hall, could consist of a historical re-enactment of these important watershed events. It could serve to educate Canadians, young and old, newly-arrived and well-established, of the agreements that were achieved and that have become the underpinnings for our living together. They have made for a peaceful and orderly society, and one with good governance practices.

Remembrance Day

Originally established to mark the end of hostilities at the end of World War I, Remembrance Day has now become a day to pay homage to all those men and women who have lost their lives fighting to defend freedom in military conflicts. The liturgy governing Remembrance Day has evolved in keeping with the need to reflect the diversity of religious practices to be found in Canada. Beginning with the oldest established churches in Canada, the Roman Catholic and Anglican, it has also included ministers from the Presbyterian and Methodist Churches and then the United Church. More recently, we have seen the inclusion of Aboriginal spiritual leaders along with Jewish rabbis and Muslim imams. The next step in this evolving liturgy would be for the governor general, who usually presides at the ceremony, to go beyond the multicultural approach and try to establish a coherent liturgy that would integrate common religious elements from all of these traditions.

Canada's involvement in the war in Afghanistan has added a very poignant and contemporary dimension to this celebration. It has meant that wartime sacrifices have been made real to a younger generation of Canadians.

If designed to appeal to citizens' intellect as well as their emotions, such public ceremonies could achieve what 18th century poets called the sublime: enthralling Canadians, inspiring them, and leaving them with feelings of gratitude for those who have built and defended our country and of empathy for one another.

References

Aristotle. 1995. *Poetics*, tr. Stephen Halliwell. Cambridge, Mass.: Harvard University Press.

Arendt, H. 2000. *The Portable Hannah Arendt*, ed. Peter Baehr. London: Penguin Books.

Benoit, P. 1982. "Remembering the Monarch." *Canadian Journal of Political Science* XV:3: 575–587.

Burke, E. 1980. *On the Sublime and Beautiful*. Danbury, Conn.: Grolier Enterprises.

HRH The Prince of Wales. 2010. "Islam and the Environment." Presented 9 June at Sheldonian Theatre, Oxford. http:www.princeofwales.gov.uk

Eliade, M. 1959. *The Sacred and the Profane*, tr. Willard R. Trask. New York: Harcourt Brace Jovanovich.

Hegel, G.F. 1967. *Philosophy of Right*, tr. T.M. Knox. Oxford: Oxford University Press.

— 1970. *Introductory Lectures to the Realm of Absolute Spirit*, ed. J. Glenn Gray. New York: Harper & Row.

— 1971. *Hegel's Philosophy of Mind: Being Part Three of the Encyclopaedia of the Philosophical Sciences*, tr. William Wallace. Oxford: Clarendon Press.

Longinus. 1995. *On the Sublime*, tr. W. H. Fyfe. Cambridge, Mass.: Harvard University Press.

Schiller, F. 1993. *Essays*, ed. Walter Hinderer and Daniel O. Dahlstrom. New York: Continuum.

9

THE CROWN AND HONOURS: GETTING IT RIGHT

CHRISTOPHER MCCREERY

Le Canada possède un système complet de décorations et de titres honorifiques étroitement lié au modèle fondateur de la royauté et dont l'origine remonte à la création, en 1934, de la Médaille d'ancienneté de la Gendarmerie royale du Canada. La participation royale à l'élaboration de ce système et à sa représentation symbolique est une constante de notre histoire récente. Au fil du temps, le système de décorations et de titres honorifiques canadien s'est enrichi de nombreuses distinctions qui en ont fait l'un des plus complets du monde. Ce chapitre fait la chronique du rôle central de l'engagement royal et vice-royal en la matière, tout en examinant l'évolution récente du phénomène et les domaines auxquels il est urgent d'apporter des améliorations.

In the words of that early scholar of Commonwealth autonomy, Professor Arthur Berriedale Keith, "The Crown is the fount of all honour" (Keith 1929, 237). The role of the Crown as the fount of all official honours in Canada is a precept that is as old and constant as is the place of the Crown in our constitutional structure. Since the days of Louis XIV, residents of Canada have been honoured by the Crown for their services with a variety of orders, decorations and medals.

The position of the Crown in the modern Canadian honours system is something that is firmly entrenched, despite consistent attempts to marginalize it in recent years. Indeed, honours are not something separate from the Crown; they are an integral element of the Crown, a part that affords individuals official recognition for what are deemed as good works or, in the modern context, exemplary citizenship. In 2009, we witnessed the Queen's direct involvement in the honours system when she appointed former Prime Minister Jean Chrétien a member of the Order of Merit. While many commentators and officials in Canada seemed confused as to just what this honour was – the highest civil honour for service – people did realize how significant it was, in large part because it came not from a committee or politician, but directly from the Sovereign.

This chapter will delve into the central role the Crown and Sovereign play in the creation of honours. It will also explore the areas of the Canadian honours system that require reform. The focus is primarily upon honours bestowed at the federal level, although provincial honours and their positive role will be intertwined into this larger discussion.

CREATING HONOURS OF THE CROWN

Although it is not widely acknowledged, the cornerstone of the Canadian honours system was placed in 1934 with the establishment of the Royal Canadian Mounted Police Long Service Medal. Now, this does not fit into the official history of our honours system that holds 1967 as the magical year in which the system came into being, with the creation of the Order of Canada (Thomas 1991, 12). But the official history, which has been around for more than 40 years, is misleading. Some of the information has only recently been revealed as the result of research into the creation of the RCMP Long Service Medal and the Canadian Forces' Decoration (McCreery 2010). The creation of these two honours played a significant role in ensuring the central place of the Crown in the creation, administration and symbolism of honours, not to mention the personal role of the Sovereign in the honours system.

The establishment of the RCMP Long Service Medal by King George V in March of 1934 marked the first time that an honour specific to Canada for services in Canada had been created by the Sovereign in Right of Canada. Previous honours such as the North West Canada Medal and the Canada General Service Medal, created in 1886 and 1899 respectively, may have been awarded to Canadians for services in Canada, but they were also awarded to British service personnel and the medals were created by the Sovereign in Right of the United Kingdom. The project to create the RCMP Long Service Medal began in 1920 when the Royal North West Mounted Police Veterans Association petitioned the Commissioner of the RCMP to support the creation of a long service medal – the grassroots nature of this early beginning of the Canadian honours system is an interesting side-bar.

By 1928 cabinet had sanctioned the creation of an RCMP Long Service Medal and an RCMP Officers' Decoration. Then the entire project languished as the Department of External Affairs vacillated as to how to seek permission from the King to create the two honours. The Under-Secretary of State, O.D. Skelton and the Assistant Under-Secretary of State, W.H. Walker, who could never have been accused of being keen on the Crown, made regular reference to that old chestnut, the Nickle Resolution of 1918, and embarked upon a three-year process of delay.[1]

In January of 1932 the newly appointed Commissioner of the RCMP, Sir James Howden MacBrien, went directly to Prime Minister R.B. Bennett to reactivate the RCMP Long Service Medal project. By January of 1933 an order-in-council was signed by the governor general and the RCMP Long Service Medal began its new life in earnest.

The next step was to seek the King's approval and this was done through the Dominions Office. The description of the Medal was sent to the Secretary of State for Dominion Affairs in February 1933. It was up to the Dominions Office to submit the proposal to the King on the advice of his Canadian ministers. This was an imperfect system, as it still involved a department of the British government, but other than the governor general, the Canadian government of the day had no direct conduit to the Sovereign.

Since Canada had become independent from Britain in December 1931 with the passage of the Statute of Westminster, officials on both sides of the Atlantic were unsure as to how to proceed. No one had experience in the creation of a Dominion-specific honour.[2] Prior to 1931, the Colonial Office and Treasury Department in Britain would have been heavily involved; however, the British government was aware of Canada's autonomy and endeavoured not to become involved without direction from the Canadian government. Given that the Dominions Office had some experience in

---

[1] The Nickle Resolution was a non-binding resolution of the House of Commons passed in 1918. The original resolution sought to end the bestowal of all peerages, baronetcies and knighthoods (titular honours) upon British subjects ordinarily resident in Canada. The Nickle Resolution has invariably become conflated with Order-in-Council 668-1918 and the Report of the Special Committee on Honours and Titles, 1919. The 1918 order-in-council brought an end to Canadians being summoned to the peerage or awarded baronetcies (hereditary knighthoods) with the consent of the Canadian government and placed control over all honours recommendations in the hands of the Prime Minister of Canada – it allowed for the continuing bestowal of knighthoods. The Report of the Special Committee reaffirmed the Nickle Resolution, 1918, and further sought to extinguish the hereditary character of peerages and baronetcies awarded to those ordinarily resident in Canada. The Report additionally considered the abolition of the titles "Right Honourable" and "Honourable," although this was not fully endorsed by the committee. The recommendation that the hereditary quality of certain honours already awarded to residents of Canada be extinguished was never actioned. R.B. Bennett utilized Order-in-Council 668-1918 as the basis for the bestowal of knighthoods during the 1930s, and the placing of authority over recommendations for honours in the hands of the Prime Minister of Canada (until 1972 when it was transferred to the Office of the Governor General) was of central importance to the development of the modern Canadian honours system.

[2] New Zealand had created a number of honours, including the New Zealand Cross and several long service medals, none of which received official sanction until long after established.

drafting royal warrants, it was left to them to create the royal warrant constituting the RCMP Long Service Medal. While the order-in-council passed by the Canadian cabinet signified its authorization of the creation of the Medal, final royal approval was deemed necessary to make the honour official.

By the fall of 1933 Commissioner MacBrien became concerned that, as in 1928, the project to create the Medal was stagnating. He wrote to the Under-Secretary of State, Ephraim H. Coleman, to find out the reason for the delay. As it turned out, the Dominions Office had been stalling the entire project on account of George V. The King wanted police forces throughout the Empire and Commonwealth to have a single standardized long service medal. Such a solution had been adopted in 1930 when the Efficiency Decoration and the Efficiency Medal were established for members of the various militia and reserve forces throughout the Commonwealth, and George V thought that this would be an equally good idea for the various police forces.[3] In addition, the King was proposing that changes be made to the criteria for the King's Police Medal. The conflation of these three issues related to medals for police was the real cause of the delay. George V had always taken a direct interest in the administration of his honours system and was somewhat of an expert on orders, decorations and medals (Nicholson 1953, 514).

The Keeper of the Privy Purse, Sir Frederick Ponsonby, again wrote Governor General Lord Bessborough to explain that "insuperable difficulties were found. The King therefore abandoned the idea of having a medal for the whole Empire, and decided that each of those Dominions that wished to have a medal of this description should be able to do so. I only want to explain why there was so much delay in dealing with a letter from the Canadian Government which came early last year" (Ponsonby 1934). Finally, on March 6,1934 at Windsor Castle, King George V signed the royal warrant constituting the Royal Canadian Mounted Police Long Service Medal. It was not until December 15, 1934 that the royal warrant was countersigned by Prime Minister R.B. Bennett – a legal necessity to signify that the King was acting on the advice of his Canadian ministry.[4]

With this drawn-out series of events, the first national Canadian honour came into being. Shortly after passage of the *Statute of Westminster*, the role of the King in Right of Canada was still being defined and this explains the continuing involvement of the Dominions Office. It was also through the Dominions Office that official communications to the King were transferred. The process served as a model that would be used by

---

[3] While the Efficiency Medal and Efficiency Decoration for use throughout the Commonwealth were of the same basic design, each carried a suspender bar bearing the name of the colony or Dominion in which it was awarded.

[4] Of course this should have been signed prior to the King signifying his approval.

other Dominions in the creation of Dominion-specific honours in the period immediately following passage of the *Statute of Westminster*.

By the outbreak of the Second World War, the relationship with the Crown in terms of honours was much more direct and unencumbered, and an administrative structure was established to aid in the development of honours policy. The Awards Coordination Committee (ACC) was established in 1940 to deal with all questions related to honours. Chaired by the Under-Secretary of State and reporting to the Prime Minister, the committee included members from the Department of National Defence, the Department of External Affairs, the Privy Council Office and the Office of the Governor General. The ACC dealt with all honours-related issues. It was instrumental in the development of the ill-fated Canada Medal and the highly successful Canadian Volunteer Service Medal (McCreery 2005a, 48).

The honours creation process was further refined in the late 1940s. In the post-war period the leadership of the various services – the Royal Canadian Navy (RCN), Canadian Army and the Royal Canadian Air Force (RCAF) – became interested in the establishment of a long service award for their service personnel. Canadians were eligible for ten different long service awards that were dependent upon rank, branch and length of service. The system was cumbersome and the Minister of National Defence, Brooke Claxton, was keen to see uniformity and efficiency brought to this area. A decorated veteran of the Great War, Claxton was a confident Canadian nationalist who sought to create Canadian symbols. Along with the Canadian Forces' Decoration, he was instrumental in the widespread usage of the Canadian Red Ensign (Bercuson 1993, 130).

As with the process of creating the RCMP Long Service Medal, the process of creating the Canadian Forces' Decoration (CD) was equally laborious. However, it served to further entrench the personal role of the Sovereign in the honours creation process. This process commenced in 1946 and would not be concluded until 1949.

Claxton was anxious to see the CD created in an expeditious manner. Although cabinet had approved the establishment of the CD in October 1947, by Christmas Claxton was dissatisfied with the pace at which the process was moving and he proposed a shortcut. In October, King George VI had approved new Letters Patent constituting the Office of the Governor General. These Letters Patent authorized the governor general to exercise – on the Sovereign's behalf – many of the powers of the King. Being a lawyer, Claxton was aware that this gave the governor general a much wider scope to act on the Sovereign's behalf. What Claxton was not aware of was that the King had specifically asked to retain direct control over a number of elements of the royal prerogative, and included in this list was the power to create honours. Claxton believed that the Letters Patent offered him a rapid mechanism to have the CD created. On December 23, Claxton wrote to the Clerk of the Privy Council, Arnold Heeney, to ask that the prime minister write to the governor general and request that the CD be created. Heeney responded, noting that a letter exchanged between Prime Minister Mackenzie King and the Private Secretary to King George VI clearly outlined that the authority and power to create new honours was to remain in the hands of the King and be delegated to the governor general only when "exceptional circumstances made it necessary to do so" (Heeney 1947).

Throughout the CD creation process, George VI was personally involved in the details related to design and the regulations that governed the decoration. Early designs for the insignia were void of the King's effigy. Claxton was not fixated on the precise details or logistics, but when the proposal reached the cabinet table, Prime Minister Louis St. Laurent and Secretary of State Colin Gibson were horrified that the medal had no symbolic connection to the Crown. Gibson surveyed every member of the cabinet and ex-servicemen who were members of the Liberal caucus and "in every case it was strongly urged that the head of His Majesty should be shown on the medal .... There was also considerable feeling that the recipients of the award would appreciate having the head of HM on the obverse as an indication that it is a decoration awarded on behalf of HM" (Gibson 1949). The design was quickly altered, the prime minister sent a formal submission to the King, and on August 20, 1949 the George VI approved the creation of the CD. With the King's approval the Privy Council drafted an order-in-council creating the CD (*Order-in-Council, PC 1949-6335*).

Our modern honours creation process was born out of the experience garnered in the establishment of the RCMP Long Service Medal and the Canadian Forces' Decoration. It was a process that placed a significant level of importance on the Crown and the Sovereign's involvement and assent. Today, proposals for the creation of new honours come from the Chancellery of Honours or the Department of National Defence, although they occasionally emanate from organizations or individuals. The Chancellery researches the proposed honour to ensure that it is needed and that it conforms to Canadian honours policy. A proposal can then be brought forward to the Honours Policy Committee (HPC), which is a committee composed of senior public servants. If the HPC agrees that the honour is needed, the Chancellery is directed to propose regulations and to draft an order-in-council. Designs for the insignia are then devised by the Canadian Heraldic Authority. The HPC then reviews the proposal again and, if it is approved, it passes to the prime minister for concurrence. Once the prime minister has agreed to the new honour, an order-in-council is passed. On the advice of the prime minister, through the governor general, the letters patent and design for the new honour are sent to the Queen for consideration. It is only when the Queen signs the Letters Patent and design that the honour is officially created. Amendments to the criteria for Canadian orders, decorations and medals do not have to be approved by the Queen once an honour is created; changes can be made by the governor general as the representative of the Sovereign.[5]

THE SOVEREIGN'S ROLE TODAY

Despite the Queen's central role in the Canadian honours system, there have been regular attempts to marginalize it. This marginalization began in the mid-1980s with the removal of references and photos of the Sovereign from official publications. In addition to this, despite numerous visits to Canada since the establishment of the Order of Canada, the Queen has only held one full-scale Canadian investiture and this took place in 1973 at Rideau Hall. Since then, it has only been the insignia of the Order of Canada and Order of Military Merit that Her Majesty has presented to newly appointed governors general. Even this tradition was hastily discarded in 2005 when Adrienne Clarkson insisted on presenting the insignia to Michaëlle Jean; thankfully the tradition was restored in 2010 following the appointment of David Lloyd Johnston as Governor General.

In 2009 a reference to the Queen was added to the various web pages related to honours on the Governor General's website, so there has been some positive movement in this area, but the changes are small. Unfortunately, Michaëlle Jean never once mentioned the role of the Queen in the honours system in any of her dozens of investiture speeches. It seems counter-intuitive that, while the Crown is the fount of all official honours, those who administer the system at the federal level have often attempted to remove the person of the Sovereign from the system. The most recent attempt to marginalize the Crown in the honours field occurred in relation to the Sacrifice Medal, which was almost created without the Sovereign's effigy on the medal. In the end it was officials in the prime minister's office who insisted that the Queen's likeness be included on the medal.

One of the most unusual events related to the Order of Canada and the Crown occurred in 2000 when Queen Elizabeth The Queen Mother was made an honorary Companion of the Order of Canada (CC). This is a distinction that at least one other member of the Royal Family has refused because the individual firmly believes appointment as an honorary CC is tantamount to saying that he/she is a foreigner and not a Canadian. The issue of the citizenship of members of the Royal Family, beyond the Sovereign, is a difficult one. However, in terms of the Order of Canada, there has always been a mechanism to have members of the Royal Family appointed without using the honorary designation. Our obsession with "citizenship" when it comes to honours seems antithetical to our multicultural makeup as a country. The Letters Patent constituting

---

[5] Except design and designation.

the Order make it clear that the Sovereign has ultimate authority over the Order and, on advice, the Sovereign could appoint any person, including a member of the Royal Family, as a regular (non-honorary) member of the Order. Similarly, an ordinance of the Order of Canada could be adopted allowing for members of the Royal Family to be appointed as regular members of the Order. Yet another alternative would be to create an extraordinary division for governors general and spouses (who are currently in limbo) and members of the Royal Family. Australia, New Zealand and Papua New Guinea are much more flexible in this area. Despite numerous nominations for members of the Royal Family to be appointed to the Order of Canada, aside from the Queen Mother there have been no such appointments. The advisory council of the Order of Canada has long suffered from a phobia on the subject of recognizing the service of the Sovereign's spouse and progeny.

Recent Developments

The Order of Canada came under great scrutiny following the appointment of Dr. Henry Morgentaler as a Member of the Order in July 2008. Despite the uproar surrounding his appointment and with the exception of six resignations, the Order weathered the most controversial honours appointment in Canadian history fairly well. A few things were revealed as a result of the appointment. The main one was the thin understanding of the honours system held by the media and general public. Many members of the general public believe that politicians decide who receives the Order of Canada and other honours. The Morgentaler appointment also exposed the perception amongst some that the Order of Canada is only given to artists and promoters of left-wing causes. One has only to consult the register of the Order to disprove this theory, but the perception persists.

As someone who has spent fifteen years studying the honours system, I was particularly disappointed to learn that the model of consensus that had been used by the advisory council of the Order of Canada to select names for submission to the governor general has been abandoned. For at least thirty years of the Order of Canada's history, the consensus model was employed with great success and it is a pity that this highly collegial mechanism is no longer employed.

Another concern with the Order of Canada has been the bending of rules to expedite appointments. Most glaringly, this happened in October 2009 when Ian Andrew Vorres was appointed a Member of the Order of Canada on October 22 and then invested with the Order by then-Governor General Michaëlle Jean while she was on a state visit to Greece only a few days later. It was only five months after the insignia was presented that the name was published in the *Canada Gazette*.[6] The entire process was expedited to allow the governor general a photo opportunity, a step that only serves to trivialize the honours system. Historically, appointments have only been expedited if the individual is terminally ill (McCreery 2005b, 201). The recipient in this case does not appear to have any health issues that necessitated this, so the example is highly unusual and one hopes it will not be repeated.

There have also been muted complaints by former members of the advisory council that Madame Jean became overly involved in promoting particular nominations for membership in the Order of Canada. This is something that previous governors general assiduously avoided. As chancellor of the Order of Canada, the governor general is supposed to serve as a neutral arbiter, not a promoter of nominations – this precept was first enunciated by Roland Michener in 1967 and later by Ray Hnatyshyn in 1991. The Chancellery of Honours must guide governors general away from such involvement, lest the neutral position of the governor general become compromised through inadvertently using the position to advance friends and champions of whatever personal interests they might have.

GAPS IN THE SYSTEM: GETTING IT RIGHT

Given that the honours are so closely intertwined with the Crown – they are dependent upon the Crown for their existence at an official level – it is valuable to reflect upon the state of the Canadian honours system. The system has done something particularly remarkable over the past four decades: it has largely filled the honours vacuum that existed in this country for nearly fifty years. While Canadians do not necessarily understand the nuances and intricacies of our various national and provincial honours, there is a general level of respect for those who have been honoured by the Crown.

Canada has one of the most balanced and well-structured honours systems in the world. This does not mean that the system is perfect. Despite success in many areas, the Canadian honours system still has a number of gaps, and there have been recent failures in terms of the overall functioning of the system. I am not going to drill down to the minutia, so I have chosen to focus on a few key areas. Logistical issues relate to the continuing absence of mixed investitures at the national level, the need for greater publicity of the honours system, appointments to the Royal Victorian Order, substandard insignia quality, long delays in providing

---

[6] Published in the *Canada Gazette* on March 20, 2010. With the exception of the Royal Victorian Order, until recently an honour was not presented until it was gazetted.

appointment scrolls to honours recipients, the lumping of all three levels of the Order of Canada into one part of the order of precedence, and the poor quality of official publications and brochures.

The remaining gaps in our honours system are relatively few. We are one of the only polar nations that does not bestow a polar medal to recognize service in the north despite the north being such a integral part of our national identity (Ipsos Reid Poll 1 April 2009) and the significant amount of service rendered in the region by the Canadian Forces and RCMP. Canadian public servants receive no official honours in recognition of outstanding service or even long service. Prior to 1952 there was the Imperial Service Medal, and prior to 1946 there was the Imperial Service Order, yet there has been no attempt to fill these gaps. The Order of Canada has always been beyond the reach of even the most capable public servant, other than the clerk of the privy council, who has almost invariably been appointed to the Order sometime after retirement. There has long been an interest on the part of senior public servants to see an honour created to recognize federal, provincial and municipal service; however, there remains no champion for this cause. The Order of Merit of the Police Forces achieves the same sort of recognition across many different police organizations, so there is no reason that the same could not work for public servants.

Since the creation of the Order of Merit of the Police Forces in 2000, there have been calls from the various fire services to have an Order created along the lines of the OMPF. Quite rightly, firefighters look to the honours awarded their police colleagues and wonder why there is not equivalent recognition of their service to the community. The honours system is not going to be able to resist this call much longer, and it is certain to be followed by similar entreaties by the correctional and peace officers, emergency medical services and coast guard. At present our honours system totally ignores the meritorious services rendered by the various protective services, other than the police. There is of course the option of creating a myriad of Orders of Merit: Order of Merit of the Fire Services, Order of Merit of the Correctional Service, Order of Merit of the Coast Guard, Order of Merit of the Peace Officers, Order of Merit of the Emergency Medical Services. Such proposals are impractical and our honours system would become cluttered with what amounts to vocation-specific honours – this was the situation in France prior to the 1960s, where every department from Tourism to the Post Office had their own order.

In an ideal world, the Order of Merit of the Police Forces and Order of Military Merit would be converted into a Canadian Order of Merit, with a civil and military division. The Order of Military Merit would simply serve as the military division, while the civil division would become open to all of those serving in protective services that receive long service awards from the family of Exemplary Service Medals. This issue is one of fairness and equity in providing national recognition for the various protective services that play an important role in maintaining the safety of our communities.

Canada has a distinguished history of creating honours that are never awarded – the most notable example of this was the Canada Medal. Established by King George VI in 1943, the Canada Medal was meant to serve as Canada's foremost civil and military award for distinguished service. There was one small problem: the prime minister of the day, William Lyon Mackenzie King, could not decide who was to receive the medal. So for the ensuing twenty-three years the Canada Medal was on the books as our pre-eminent honour, yet no awards were made. The demise of the Canada Medal came in 1966 when it was abolished, just ahead of the creation of the Order of Canada.

Two awards in our modern honours system which are approaching the same fate as the Canada Medal are the civil division of the Meritorious Service Cross (MSC) and the Meritorious Service Medal (MSM), collectively known as the Meritorious Service Decorations (MSDs). There have been no awards of the civil MSC since 2004 and no civil MSMs since 2005, despite continued nominations coming from the general public and organizations. The military division of the MSDs, which is largely driven by the Department of National Defence, has been a highly successful program over the past decade,[7] which makes the demise of the civil division all the more bizarre. Since 2006 officials at the Chancellery of Honours have been assuring members of the general public that a review of the civil MSDs is underway and that a restructured advisory committee is being considered. We have yet to see the fruit of more than four years of effort that we are assured has been put into reforming this important part of our honours system.

When the civil division of the MSDs was established in 1991, the decorations were intended to become the workhorse of the Canadian honours system, with the MSDs serving as a mechanism to reward contributions that fell short of membership in the Order of Canada and also to recognize single meritorious acts. It is the civil MSDs that are supposed to serve as a stepping-stone towards membership in the Order of Canada.

Our closest honours cousins, Australia, Britain, France and New Zealand, all make liberal use of intermediate awards.[8] Unfortunately for Canadians, it is the Order of Canada, a provincial order, or nothing. Given the necessity for only a small number of annual appointments to

---

[7] Since 2000, 288 military division MSDs have been awarded.

[8] In New Zealand this is achieved with the Queen's Service Order, Queen's Service Medal and membership in the most junior level of the New Zealand Order of Merit; Australia uses the Medal of the Order of Australia; Britain uses the most junior level of the Order of the British Empire; France uses the chevalier level of l'Ordre des arts et lettres, the Ordre national du mérite and the Légion d'honneur.

these orders, there is a desperate need for the civil division of the MSDs to be reactivated.

Along with the civil MSDs, another element of the honours system that is approaching the same fate as the doomed Canada Medal is the honorary division of the Order of Canada. Honorary appointments to the Order of Canada are a true rarity. For the Order's first thirty years of existence, only one honorary appointment was made. In 1998 it seemed that some progress had been made in establishing a protocol and process for appointing non-Canadian citizens to the Order. Since then, however, only sixteen additional honorary appointments have been made. A valuable tool for recognizing non-citizens who play a role in promoting Canada abroad and within Canada is left to gather cobwebs. When this is compared with the significant number of appointments that Britain and France make to non-citizens, the inference could be drawn that Canada is an isolationist country that does not welcome people from abroad and does not allow its citizens to travel abroad.

Certainly we should not go the route of some countries that actively use their honours system as a tool of foreign policy. One only has to examine the parade of distasteful world leaders who were adorned with diplomatic honours, from Robert Mugabe to Nicolae Ceausescu. However, there is much we could learn from the use of appointments to non-citizens as a highly valued reward for promoting culture, language and economic interests. Part of the issue is the trickle of nominations and the cumbersome nature of the advisory council's existing structure. There is no reason why the various Canadian heads of mission could not draw up a list of potential candidates on an annual basis. Canadian organizations involved overseas should be encouraged to do the same. Another way to remedy the situation would be to establish a sub-committee of the advisory council of the Order of Canada to consider honorary appointments. Such a sub-committee could be composed of those active in the international field. Similarly the civil division of the MSDs could be used quite successfully to recognize the service of non-citizens. The military division of the MSDs has been used successfully in this way.

Our national honours system continues to do a poor job of recognizing exemplary volunteers. While there was a long tradition of 20-25 appointments to the Order of Canada per annum in recognition of voluntary services (period 1997–2007), this plummeted to a mere 16 appointments in 2008 and a paltry 8 appointments for 2009.[9]

Of course there is the Caring Canadian Award, but this is not a national honour – it is a lapel pin with a certificate.

---

[9] This tally is calculated on the basis of citation content, not merely the individual category used by the Chancellery of Honours. Thus a person recognized for public service who was also a noted volunteer would be included in this calculation.

In the realm of recognizing volunteers, only Ontario, Quebec and Saskatchewan have been active.[10] This is an area in which the various provincial honours systems or indeed the national system could expand, especially given the high value that Canadians place on voluntary service. The civil division of the MSDs was intended, in part, to recognize voluntary service that did not meet the bar for admission to the Order of Canada; yet, as we have seen, the program is dormant.

Many retired members of the Canadian Forces and various protective services often complain that they and their comrades are never considered for the Order of Canada in recognition of their service. Since the early 1980s the military and protective services have been almost entirely shut out of the Order of Canada. Over the past thirty years there have been only twenty-six appointments in this area, the most recent one in 2006 when Major-General Lewis MacKenzie was appointed a CM. Certainly members of the Canadian Forces and Police Forces are eligible for the Order of Military Merit and the Order of Merit of the Police Forces, but this is often given part way through an individual's career. Why are more members of the Canadian Forces and protective services not appointed to the Order of Canada at the conclusion of their career? It is not as though we are lacking worthy candidates.

Over the past decade there has been a proliferation of what can euphemistically be termed unofficial or "fake medals." These are honours created by individual organizations or government offices that end up being worn with official national and official provincial honours. Numerous police forces, provincial fire marshals' offices and provincial departments have fallen into this habit, as have some Canadian veterans associations. Most of these unofficial awards duplicate existing honours, whether it is for meritorious service or long service. Inexplicably, even members of the Royal Canadian Sea, Army and Air Cadets are now permitted to wear unofficial medals on the left side of their uniforms. All of this is in violation of federal *Order-in-Council P.C. 1998-591.* The federal government has done almost nothing to enforce the rules, so the rules are ignored. Organizations should at the very least follow the example of the Royal Canadian Legion which only permits internal awards to be worn on the right side, while official national and provincial honours are worn on the left, or Crown side.

Quite simply, if you wear an unapproved insignia (order, decoration or medal) you should be sanctioned, either through a fine or through the revocation of your national honours. Only the Canadian Forces (excluding Cadets) and RCMP have enforced the rules in this regard. The proliferation of unofficial medals worn with official provincial and national honours

---

[10] In Quebec appointments at the Chevalier level of the Ordre national du Québec are often for volunteer services, Ontario awards the Ontario Medal for Good Citizenship and Saskatchewan awards the Saskatchewan Volunteer Medal.

diminishes the importance of official honours and make the entire system look like a farce in which anyone can wear anything.

On the topic of enforcement, section 419 of the Criminal Code is in desperate need of updating. This is the section that prohibits individuals from wearing war medals to which they are not entitled. The section does not extend to the Order of Canada, service medals for time in Afghanistan or other Canadian honours. Some provinces have penalties for wearing their provincial orders, but this is not universal. Thus, anyone can legally buy an Order of Canada replica and a Star of Military Valour and General Campaign Star and wear them without any penalty – only the possibility of public ridicule. Australia has a comprehensive and short section in their Defence Act that we could well duplicate to prevent this sort of honours-related offence (*Australia Defence Act, 1984, s.80B(3)*).

In the realm of foreign honours, Canada has one of the most restrictive and cumbersome policies in the world. The existing policy, which grew out of the 1956 foreign honours policy, makes the presentation of even low-level decorations into an exercise of diplomatic gymnastics. The general phobia of Commonwealth and foreign honours ties directly back to the Nickle Resolution of 1918 and a fear that foreign governments would bestow honours on Canadians in an effort to enlist their support in causes that were not necessarily sympathetic to the government of the day. When a foreign government wishes to honour a Canadian, they have to apply through the Department of Foreign Affairs; the request is then sent to the Canadian Honours Policy Sub-Committee, which makes a decision based on a set of criteria that are widely open to interpretation.

Again, we could learn much from the policies used in France and New Zealand. In these jurisdictions citizens are permitted to accept an order, decoration or medal from a foreign government. It is then up to the recipient to apply through their own honours system for permission to wear the insignia. The Canadian system for approving foreign honours is best explained by this analogy: A friend has helped me move into a new house and I want to give him a gift. However, before I can give him the gift I have to check with his landlord to make sure it is ok for me to give him the gift. The landlord then sends my request to a Byzantine committee and after many forms are completed and considered, they make a decision. Only after the landlord and committee have given their approval am I allowed to present the gift.

This process is antiquated and widely ridiculed amongst our allies for its draconian structure. Many Canadians who would otherwise be recognized by foreign governments go unrewarded because of the highly restrictive process. More frequently, however, foreign governments ignore entirely the Canadian regulations and simply bestow whatever honours they wish.

Finally, there are ongoing issues with what can politely be referred to as the "details" of an honours system. The quality of the insignia of the

Order of Canada, Order of Military Merit, some provincial orders, the Meritorious Service Decorations, the Star and Medal of Military Valour and the Star of Courage and the Medal of Bravery is below the standard of what we should be allowing the Crown to bestow upon exemplary citizens. Poor enamel quality and poor detail on struck items make it seem as though we do not take the honours business seriously. Over the past six years the Department of National Defence has made very significant advances in the quality of service medals and the Canadian Forces Decoration and they have escaped the mugs' game of "low cost bidders." When you consider that these honours are for a lifetime of achievement, is it too much to ask that attention be paid to the detail that goes into the lasting record of recognition?

CONCLUSION

Two factors give the Canadian honours system its legitimacy: the Crown and the calibre of the recipients of our national and provincial honours. Without the Crown, honours would lack the mystique and symbolic capital with which they imbue the recipient. Our honours system is a resilient and durable institution, a living and evolving institution. However, the myriad of past successes are increasingly being overshadowed by serious challenges, gaps and issues that have gone ignored for the past decade. Radical change is not necessary, but a balanced approach to reform and review of the Canadian honours system would serve to strengthen and better secure the future of the Crown's honours and the pride Canada has in those who have been recognized for their exemplary citizenship in many different fields.

The position of the Crown as the fount of all official honours is not something that is often challenged; strangely, however, over the past thirty years there has been a penchant, at the federal level, for marginalizing the role of the Sovereign as the giver of honours. A key element of reforming our honours system must be to acknowledge and explain the role of our head of state in the honours system.

REFERENCES

Bercuson, D. 1993. *True Patriot: The Life of Brooke Claxton, 1898–1960.* Toronto: University of Toronto Press.

Gibson, C. Library and Archives Canada [LAC] RG 24 Vol 24634, Gibson to Brooke Claxton, 18 March 1949.

Keith, A.B. 1929. *The Sovereignty of the British Dominions.* London: Macmillan Press.

Heeney, A.D.P. LAC, RG 24 Vol 24634, Sir Alan Lascelles to William Lyon Mackenzie King, 7 August 1947 quoted in a letter from A.D.P. Heeney to Brooke Claxton, 30 December 1947.

McCreery, C.P. 2005a. *The Canadian Honours System*. Toronto: Dundurn Press.
— 2005b. *The Order of Canada: Its Origins, History and Development*. Toronto: University of Toronto Press.
— 2010. *The Canadian Forces' Decoration*. Ottawa: Department of National Defence.
Nicholson, H. 1953. *King George the Fifth; His Life and Reign*. London: Constable Press.
Ponsonby, F. LAC, RG 18 Vol 1481 File 19-N, Ponsonby to the Earl of Bessborough, 6 March 1934.
Thomas, W. 1991. *The Register of Canadian Honours*. Toronto: T.H. Best Printing Company.

10

The Honour of the First Nations – The Honour of the Crown: The Unique Relationship of First Nations with the Crown

David Arnot

Fondées sur l'honneur et le respect, les relations par traités qui unissent la Couronne aux Premières Nations sont à ce point privilégiées qu'elles ont toujours eu préséance sur toute interaction avec l'État. Or les gouvernements successifs ont généralement ignoré le caractère unique de ces liens et terni par conséquent l'honneur de la Couronne à laquelle ils prêtent pourtant allégeance. Ce n'est que dernièrement que nos tribunaux ont reconnu l'élément d'honneur inhérent à ces traités et l'obligation fiduciaire de nos gouvernements, agissant au nom de la Couronne, d'en assurer l'application. Et c'est tout aussi récemment que ces traités ont été reconnus en tant que composantes fondamentales de notre pays. Les Premières Nations les considèrent comme un pacte qu'elles ont conclu avec la Couronne et le Créateur. Pour l'ensemble des Canadiens, l'honneur de la Couronne doit ainsi s'incarner dans les notions de justice et d'équité.

What Are the Treaties?

A simple definition of "treaty" is that it is a contract, the instrument that has become a large part of our professional and domestic lives. A contract is an agreement between two groups of people to do things for each other. This agreement may be in writing or verbal, and it may be neither. Many contracts are implied (a restaurant expects you to pay for the meal you order). Whatever form a contract takes, it embodies an element of morality and must be based on trust. The courts may invalidate a contract that involves sharp practice, misrepresentation or fraud, or if it results in unjust enrichment or unsatisfactory performance. Both contracts and treaties can have commercial or noncommercial objectives.

"Treaty" is more frequently used to identify a formal beneficial agreement or contract between countries. The North American Free Trade Agreement and the proposed global treaty to cut greenhouse gases are functional examples. "Peace treaties," on the other hand, do not enjoy such bilateral support if they are written by the victors and imposed on the vanquished. Therefore, in cases such as the 1919 Treaty of Versailles, the word "treaty" may be a misnomer. Usually treaties continue only if the signatories find them advantageous and will include an escape clause.

These examples do not adequately depict the agreements between the Crown and Canada's First Nations. Unlike commonplace contracts, the First Nations treaties have no time limit: they last forever. Unlike normal treaties, they cannot be broken by either party: they contain no means of escape. Finally, they are unlike peace treaties because there was no war: neither party held a dominant position. In fact, the only manner by which they resemble typical treaties is that they were intended to benefit both parties. Canada's courts have described these treaties as *sui generis* or unique (*R. v Guerin* 1984, 335). They outline what the Europeans who came to the part of North America that is now Canada pledged to First Nations in exchange for access to their land.

If the usual definitions of "treaty" are imperfect and render the word inadequate for the historic understanding reached with First Nations, what word should be used? I prefer "covenant," a word with biblical origins, which religious cultures apply to their affiliation with God. A covenant is also a formal promise under oath, or an agreement that will survive forever. A religious ceremony forging a promise between two parties and God establishes a covenant. Common law distinguishes a covenant from a normal contract with a seal to signify the unusual solemnity of the promise. At the conclusion of each treaty negotiation the parties shared a pipe, a ceremony as solemn for First Nations as the seal was for Europeans. During treaty discussions, missionaries sat with Crown representatives, an affirmation of the Crown's solemn position.

Danny Musqua, a Saulteaux Elder from my province, put it aptly when he described Treaty 4, made by his forebears: "We made a covenant with Her Majesty's government, and a covenant is not just a relationship between people; it's a relationship between three parties, you (the Crown) and me (First Nations) and the Creator" (Cardinal and Hildebrandt 2000, 32). First Nations view treaties and the treaty relationship as sacred.

Why Were Treaties Made?

The origins of treaties in North America between First Nations and Europeans can be found in the 1500s when fur traders made business agreements with First Nations for furs and provisions (Canada 1996a). In the following century, treaties were negotiated between the colonies that would eventually become the United States and the Iroquois Confederacy. An important precedent was the Great Peace of 1701 when 1,300 representatives of 40 First Nations gathered in Montreal to make a treaty that ended a century of war between the confederacy and New France (Havard 2001). Later in the 1700s there were peace and friendship treaties between First Nations and Maritime colonial governments that allowed European settlement.

The British Crown had long used treaty-making around the world to acquire new territories, establish military and economic alliances, and build peaceful relations with other nations. On the other side, First Nations also had a long-standing tradition of making treaties between tribes to settle land disputes and end wars, and to make trade and marriage arrangements.

The legal framework for making treaties with First Nations in the last 250 years is the *Royal Proclamation* of King George III. It was issued in 1763, four years after the defeat of France, and established strict procedures for British territorial expansion in North America. Regarded by Canada's First Nations as their *magna carta*, the proclamation recognized them as nations and stipulated that only the British government could acquire their lands, thus preventing acquisition by private individuals or companies. And the only means by which First Nations' lands could be acquired was through treaty with the Crown.

The first application of the *Royal Proclamation* and its treaty-making provisions was in the area north of the Great Lakes, designated as Upper Canada in 1791. The methodology would be later employed to make the 11 numbered treaties in the territories Canada purchased from the Hudson's Bay Company in 1870. Although this region was beyond the jurisdiction of the proclamation, the Canadian government recognized that First Nations there had the same rights to their ancestral land as did those in Upper Canada.

The need for treaties was simple: First Nations possessed territory the Crown wanted settled by Europeans. This was especially the case with the numbered treaties. At the same time, First Nations appreciated the benefit of European technology and were willing to share their land with farmers under certain conditions. The economic benefits offered in negotiations convinced First Nations to sign the treaties and allow settlement. However, not everything discussed was documented. The omissions were not deemed significant because First Nations negotiators could not read and write. Besides, treaty dialogue did not focus on barter, but on accommodation and trust. The two sides were talking about harmoniously sharing an immense and abundant territory. First Nations were promised the choice of continuing their hunter-gatherer economy or adopting the settlers' agriculture economy and receiving the necessary training and implements.

The numbered treaties were meant to initiate an ongoing liaison between First Nations and the Crown for as long as the sun shines, the waters flow and the grass grows. They were not meant to be land sales, but a structure for establishing political, economic and social associations between First Nations and newcomers. The promises made by Crown negotiators reflected First Nations' world views and philosophies.

Where Have Treaties Been Concluded?

Pre- and post-Confederation governments have made 68 treaties with First Nations, covering most of Ontario and the Prairies, and parts of Vancouver Island, the Northwest Territories and Atlantic Canada. These do not include peace and friendship treaties.

The numbered treaties, their year, their area in present-day Canada and the First Nations who are parties to them are as follows:

- Treaties 1 and 2, 1871, southern Manitoba and Saskatchewan, Ojibway and Cree
- Treaty 3, 1873, Lake of the Woods region of Ontario, Saulteaux (Ojibway)
- Treaty 4, 1874, southern Saskatchewan (Qu'Appelle region), Cree and Saulteaux (Ojibway)
- Treaty 5, 1875, central and northern Manitoba, Saulteaux (Ojibway) and Swampy Cree
- Treaty 6, 1876, central Saskatchewan and Alberta, mostly Plains and Woodlands Cree
- Treaty 7, 1877, southern Alberta, Blackfoot and others
- Treaty 8, 1899, northern Alberta and northeast corner of B.C., Cree, Dene, Dogrib and others
- Treaty 9, 1905, northern Ontario (James Bay region), Ojibway, Cree and others
- Treaty 10, 1906, northern Saskatchewan (Peace River region), primarily Dene and Métis
- Treaty 11, 1921, western part of Northwest Territories, primarily Dene and Métis of the Mackenzie region

Why Did Canada Enter into Treaties?

In the area of Canada managed by the Hudson's Bay Company (the North West or Rupert's Land), relations between First Nations and Europeans developed in pace with the fur trade's expansion. Company agents learned First Nations' protocols and used this knowledge to cultivate alliances with their hosts. However, when the new government of Canada bought Rupert's Land from the Hudson's Bay Company in 1870 for 300,000 British pounds, First Nations leaders, not surprisingly, were enraged. This territory had been sold without their consent and they received no money for it. So conflict resulted. Surveyors sent by the government were barred, as were other non-First Nations, making settlement impossible. In the meantime, American territorial ambition threatened, causing anxiety for the Canadian government. Preventing appropriation by the United States necessitated upholding Canadian sovereignty by settlement and by laying a transcontinental railway, pursuant to Prime Minister John A. Macdonald's National Policy. These measures were unachievable without access.

When the United States pursued its western expansion it waged wars against the indigenous inhabitants, a venture that practically bankrupted its government. Canada's government wisely decided on a peaceful policy. Fortunately, First Nations were amenable to the approach.

WHY DID FIRST NATIONS ENTER INTO TREATIES?

First Nations' chagrin over the Rupert's Land transaction was tempered by changing economic reality: commercial slaughter of buffalo and other wildlife diminished hunting opportunities; meanwhile, fur prices had dropped. Lacking immunity to European diseases, First Nations faced health problems.

Salvation lay in the new economy, First Nations believed, and this meant learning the ways of the newcomers and acquiring new skills, such as farming. They did not, however, want their way of life to be assimilated to the European culture. They believed that through treaties they could advance economically and protect their traditions. Most important, they also wanted peace.

WHAT TREATIES AND THE CROWN MEAN TO FIRST NATIONS

Throughout treaty negotiations, First Nations leaders stressed their need for education. They saw agriculture as the way to sustain their people. From their oral tradition we have learned they were willing to share their land, not surrender it, in exchange for the Queen's generosity and security. This was not exactly what Ottawa had in mind: it needed dominance, not sharing, to exercise sovereignty and enable settlement. That prerogative eluded the understanding of First Nations negotiators and had they realized it there might have been a different outcome.

The treaties have two components – written documents and First Nations' understanding based on their oral history. This second element covers verbal undertakings made by Crown negotiators. To comprehend the spirit and intent of treaties, it is necessary to recognize the validity of both components. Essentially, treaties were a blueprint for harmony. When the treaty parties came together, they were basically trying to answer the question, "How are we going to live together?"

The idea of a treaty being created for mutual gain appears to have governed the thinking of First Nations leaders. Chief Peguis, anticipating settlement and its consequences as early as 1857, wrote to the Aborigines Protection Society in England demanding that before whites "take possession of our lands we wish that a fair and mutually advantageous treaty be entered into with my tribe" (Great Britain 1857).

During negotiations for Treaty 3 in 1873, the principle of mutual advantage was advanced by Chief Mawedopenais:

> All this is our property where you have come …. This is what we think, that the Great Spirit has planted us on this ground where we are, as you were where you came from …. Our hands are poor but our heads are rich, and it is riches that we ask so that we may be able to support our families as long as the sun rises and the water runs …. *The sound of the rustling of the gold is under my feet where I stand*; we have a rich country; it is the Great Spirit who gave us this; where we stand upon is the Indians' property, and belongs to them (*The Manitoban*).

First Nations view treaties as sacred agreements and hold both treaties and the Crown in great reverence. While serving as treaty commissioner I heard representatives of the Federation of Saskatchewan Indian Nations (FSIN) and Elders speak about treaties and the Crown in consistent terms: treaties created a lasting relationship with the Crown and her subjects, with the Creator as witness. The FSIN further stated that treaties are referred to in reverence – reverence for the ancestors who signed them with the Crown with the Creator as witness. The treaty commissioners who represented the British Crown demonstrated a great reverence for their Queen who was head of state and church.

Treaty 6 Cree Elder Norman Sunchild said that when First Nations negotiators finally agreed to the treaty, the commissioner took the promises in his hand and raised them to the skies, placing the treaties in the hands of the Great Spirit (Cardinal and Hildebrandt 2000, 7). Alma Kytwayhat, another Treaty 6 Cree Elder, said, "It was the [Queen] who offered to be our mother and us to be her children and to love us in the way we want to live" (ibid., 34). These sentiments were voiced time and again throughout Saskatchewan.

Honour of the Crown

Canadians have inherited the British tradition of acting honourably for the sake of the Sovereign. This convention has roots in pre-Norman England, a time when every yeoman swore personal allegiance to the king and anyone who was charged with speaking or acting on behalf of him bore an absolute personal responsibility to lend credit to the king's good name. Should he fail in this responsibility or cause embarrassment, he was required to answer personally to the king with his life and fortune. The Crown was not an abstract or an imaginary essence in those days, but a real person whose powers and prestige were directly dependent on the conduct of his advisers, captains and messengers.

The concept of the Honour of the Crown of course became more complex and bureaucratic as it evolved. The sovereign is now insulated from personal involvement in the affairs of state. It is noteworthy that the American colonists, during the 18th century agitations that preceded their revolution against British authority, appealed to the Honour of the Crown to protect them from men they described as "the king's evil ministers." They distinguished between the Crown *per se*, which traditionally stood for what is just and honourable, and the government of the day, which was susceptible to corruption and misconduct.

Appealing to the Honour of the Crown was recourse not merely to the sovereign as a person, but to a bedrock of principles of fundamental justice that lay beyond persons and beyond politics. It is precisely this distinction that rests at the heart of our ideals of "human rights" today.

The Supreme Court of Canada resurrected the notion of the Honour of the Crown in its 1984 landmark decision, *Guerin v. R.* S.C.C., where it first stated that the government has a fiduciary duty towards First Nations. By unanimously rebuking government privilege, the court marked a milestone in restoring a system of law based on principles rather than persons. Defining "fiduciary duty of the Crown," the court restored the concept of holding ministers to a standard of fairness that demands forethought as to what conduct lends credibility and honour to the Crown, instead of what conduct can be technically justified under the current law. The Supreme Court clearly rebuked the notion that a minister's reasons to act can be defended on the grounds of political expediency.

In *Marshall No. 1*, 1999, the Supreme Court outlined with clarity the principles that underlie the high standard of the Honour of the Crown as follows:

> This appeal puts to the test the principle, emphasized by the Supreme Court on several occasions, that the Honour of the Crown is always at stake in its dealings with Aboriginal people. This is one of the principles of interpretation set forth in the *Badger Case*, Supreme Court of Canada. Interpretations of treaties and statutory provisions which have an impact upon treaty or

Aboriginal rights must be approached in a manner which maintains the integrity of the Crown. It is always assumed that the Crown intends to fulfill its promises. No appearance of "sharp dealings" will be sanctioned.

This principle that the Crown's honour is at stake when the Crown enters into treaties with First Nations dates back at least to the Supreme Court of Canada's decision in 1895 in *Ontario v. The Dominion of Canada and the Province of Quebec*. In that decision Gwynne, J. dissenting, stated: "The terms and conditions expressed in treaty instruments that have to be performed by or on behalf of the Crown have always been regarded as involving a trust graciously assumed by the Crown to the fulfillment of which with the Indians, the fate and Honour of the Crown is pledged" (*R. v. Marshall*, 1999).

The Honour of the Crown is not limited to the interpretation of legislation, or the application of treaties. As I see it, the Honour of the Crown also refers to the same essential commitment that all Canadians understand as embodied in two words, "justice" and "fairness." The Honour of the Crown is much broader than a mere interpretation of s. 91(24) of the *Constitution Act, 1867*, which states that Canada has a fiduciary obligation with respect to First Nations and lands reserved for First Nations. In every action and decision the women and men who represent the Crown in Canada should conduct themselves as if their personal honour and family names depended upon it. The idea of the Honour of the Crown is not merely an empty slogan, but absolutely central to the historical relationship between the sovereign and the subject.

The people serving within our system of parliamentary government must sometimes choose between "blind obedience" to a political master and "justice." Which is the greater duty – to obey the ministers of the Crown or to respect the principles of justice for which the Crown stands? Honour truly lies in loyalty to the fundamental values that are behind the Crown's authority. This dialectical tension is inherent in our gradual evolution as Canadians, from colony to a country, and from a traditional constitutional monarchy to a modern liberal society, grounded in democratic practices and respect for human rights and their protection by an independent judiciary.

Honour of the First Nations

In its response to the Report of the Royal Commission on Aboriginal Peoples in January 1998, Canada reflected on the past and future place of its treaties. In *Gathering Strength: Canada's Aboriginal Action Plan*, the government acknowledged that

- the treaties between the Crown and First Nations are the basic building blocks in the creation of our country, and

- a vision for the future should build on the recognition of the rights of Aboriginal people and on the treaty relationship.

The Supreme Court of Canada will not allow the treaty relationship to go unrecognized in the future. Treaties are part of the Constitution and must be honoured.

First Nations take exactly the same view of honour as the tribal people who inhabited Britain when the Normans arrived. Tribal leaders owed their status and authority to their honesty and good names. Treaties were made between people and between families and secured by personal honour. Every individual was personally bound to uphold the agreement, and to honour and renew the living relationship among peoples that the treaty represented.

The challenge we face is to create conditions in Canada wherein all people and all communities enjoy a high quality of life. First Nations must take their rightful place in the Canadian state. The First Nations must be recognized as one of three founding groups of our country, along with the French and the British.

The treaties are unique. They created a fundamental political relationship. From the First Nations perspective, they have a strong spiritual component because they are covenants between themselves, the Crown and the Creator. A revitalized treaty relationship has the potential to be a unifying force that will redefine and enrich what it means to live together, as Canadians, today and far into the future.

The concept of honour was the basis of the First Nations leaders' understanding of what they were doing when they entered into treaties with the British Crown. They were entering into a personal relationship – a kinship – with British subjects and most crucially, a personal relationship with the British sovereign. The treaty was, therefore, about adoption and family within which a perpetual connection was modelled on the mutual respect and responsibilities of family members to one another. It was presumed, based on traditions and values, that the sovereign would assume personal responsibility to see that the spirit of kinship and mutual benefit was respected in practice.

FUTURE ROLE OF THE CROWN IN TREATY IMPLEMENTATION

There are important judicial and constitutional grounds for full treaty implementation. The *Reference re: Secession of Quebec, 1998* provides advice on how to approach this. The Supreme Court's decision recognizes the limitations of the law and the courts for conducting purely political processes. The decision comes from the court's detailed examination of the fundamental principles underlying the Canadian constitution, particularly the circumstances in which the duty to negotiate arises. As such, it offers considerable guidance in determining whether a duty to negotiate treaty implementation exists, as well as the legal enforceability of such a duty.

The court identified four fundamental principles of the Constitution: federalism, democracy, constitutionalism and the rule of law, protection of minorities. In describing these principles in general, the court stated:

> Although these underlying principles are not explicitly made part of the Constitution by any written provision, other than in some respects by the oblique reference in the preamble to the *Constitution Act, 1867*, it would be impossible to conceive of our constitutional structure without them. The principles dictate major elements of the architecture of the Constitution itself, and are as such its lifeblood (*Reference re: Secession of Quebec* 1998, 36).

The court observed that these principles help us to interpret the text and to delineate spheres of jurisdiction, the extent of rights and obligations, and what our political institutions must do. It also found that respect for these principles is vital to ongoing constitutional development. "Canadians have long recognized the existence and importance of unwritten constitutional principles in our system of government" (*Reference re: Secession of Quebec* 1998, 36).

With respect to the federalism component particularly, the court remarked that it is the political mechanism by which diversity could be reconciled with unity:

> The principle of federalism recognizes the diversity of the component parts of Confederation, and the autonomy of provincial governments to develop their societies within their respective spheres of jurisdiction (*Reference re: Secession of Quebec* 1998, 39).

The court thus links federalism and "the pursuit of collective goals" by cultural and linguistic minorities which form the majority within a particular province. And it explains the fundamental role of democracy in promoting self-government and accommodating cultural and group identities: "A sovereign people exercises its right to self-government through the democratic process" (*Reference re: Secession of Quebec* 1998, 42).

The court neatly connects the principles of constitutionalism and the rule of law, stating that the constitutionalism principle requires that all government action comply with the Constitution while the rule of law principle requires that all government action must comply with the law, including the Constitution. The court gave three additional examples of this principle:

> First, a constitution may provide an added safeguard for fundamental human rights and individual freedoms which might otherwise be susceptible

to government interference. Although democratic government is generally solicitous of those rights, there are occasions when the majority will be tempted to ignore fundamental rights in order to accomplish collective goals more easily or effectively. Constitutional entrenchment ensures that those rights will be given due regard and protection.

Second, a constitution may seek to ensure that vulnerable minority groups are endowed with the institutions and rights necessary to maintain and promote their identities against the assimilative pressures of the majority.

And third, a constitution may provide for a division of political power that allocates political power amongst different levels of government. That purpose would be defeated if one of those democratically elected levels of government could usurp the powers of the other simply by exercising its legislative power to allocate additional political power to itself unilaterally (*Reference re: Secession of Quebec* 1998, 47).

With respect to the protection of minority rights, the court stated: "We emphasize that the protection of minority rights is itself an independent principle underlying our constitutional order" (*Reference re: Secession of Quebec* 1998, 49). In this connection, the constitutional guarantees of First Nations and treaty rights were specifically mentioned as an underlying constitutional principle:

Consistent with this long tradition of respect for minorities, which is at least as old as Canada itself, the framers of the *Constitution Act, 1982* included in s. 35 explicit protection for existing Aboriginal and treaty rights, and in s. 25, a non-derogation clause in favour of the rights of Aboriginal peoples. The "promise" of s. 35, as it was termed in *R. v. Sparrow*, [1990] 1 S.C.R. 1075, at p. 1083, recognized not only the ancient occupation of land by Aboriginal peoples, but their contribution to the building of Canada, and the special commitments made to them by successive governments. The protection of these rights, so recently and arduously achieved, whether looked at in their own right or as part of the larger concern with minorities, reflects an important underlying constitutional value (*Reference re: Secession of Quebec* 1998, 50).

These fundamental principles of constitutional law have a direct application to treaty implementation. The federalism principle also has clear relevance to the treaties. In its 1996 Final Report, the Royal Commission on Aboriginal Peoples wrote:

The treaties form a fundamental part of the constitution and for many Aboriginal peoples, play a role similar to that played by the *Constitution Act, 1867 (formerly the British North America Act)* in relation to the provinces. The terms of the Canadian federation are found not only in formal constitutional documents governing relations between the federal and provincial governments but also in treaties and other instruments establishing the basic links between Aboriginal peoples and the Crown. In brief, "treaty federalism" is an integral part of the Canadian constitution (Canada 1996b, 194).

The principles of federalism are critical to an understanding of the treaty relationship as well as the Canadian constitution. The principle of democracy exists to secure the legitimacy of representative institutions exercising the right to collective self-determination on behalf of self-determining individuals. The principles of constitutionalism and the rule of law have particular relevance in light of the *Marshall No. 1* decision, which clarifies that the Crown has not conducted itself in accordance with its legal and constitutional duties to respect the treaties. The application of the principle of protection of minorities, including the protections of section 35, is self-evident.

The jurisprudence on treaty interpretation in cases such as *Marshall No. 1* shows that despite the fact that existing treaty rights have been given constitutional protection by section 35(1) of the *Constitution Act, 1982*, the rights arising under the treaties are not what they may seem on the face of treaty documents. What was recorded in a treaty text may be incomplete and even misleading as a guide to the intentions of the parties. The constitutionalism principle requires that all government action comply with the law and the constitution. To fulfill this most elementary expectation of constitutional law, the government must at minimum be able to know what legal rights, duties and corresponding constitutional constraints arise from the treaties.

The *Reference re: Secession of Quebec* makes it equally clear that a duty to negotiate exists to ensure that our constitutional arrangements respect both the legality and legitimacy of a liberal democratic society.

In the case of First Nations treaty rights, reconciliation is also a prominent theme in the jurisprudence. In decisions such as *Van der Peet*, *Gladstone* and *Delgamuukw*, the Supreme Court has stressed the theme of reconciliation between different groups of people with different rights. In *Van der Peet*, reconciliation is described as the rationale of the constitutional guarantee of existing Aboriginal and treaty rights in section 35(1) of the *Constitution Act, 1982*:

> …what s. 35(1) does is provide the constitutional framework through which the fact that Aboriginals lived on the land in distinctive societies, with their own practices, traditions and cultures, is acknowledged and reconciled with the sovereignty of the Crown. The substantive rights which fall within the provision must be defined in light of this purpose; the Aboriginal rights recognized and affirmed by s. 35(1) must be directed towards the reconciliation of the pre-existence of Aboriginal societies with the sovereignty of the Crown (*R. v. Van der Peet* 1996, 45).

The Supreme Court of Canada in the *Haida Nation* (*Haida Nation v. British Columbia* 2004) case has made it clear that treaties serve to reconcile First Nations' "pre-existing" sovereignty with the "assumed" sovereignty of the Crown. Thus, on an issue like sovereignty, something vital has been settled but new questions have arisen. It is going to be important for the treaty parties to reach an understanding on how the treaties reconciled sovereignties, and further, what this reconciliation implies for future governance arrangements. These are political questions and require a principled, careful political resolution, as the Supreme Court of Canada made clear in the *Reference re: Secession of Quebec*.

The Supreme Court simultaneously linked the pre-existing sovereignty of the First Nations to the reconciliation achieved in the treaties. This judicial observation points the way to an examination of the treaty relationship as one of political reconciliation. It also suggests that treaty implementation can be the vehicle which puts discussion of sovereignty within a framework that emphasizes sharing, accommodation and mutuality as opposed to unilateralism and separation. There is even an existing theoretical basis for this framework of treaty implementation – treaty federalism.

The commitments made in the treaties bind the Crown, regardless of internal divisions between federal and provincial governments. In the federal structure of Canada, the federal government has inherited the duty to honour the treaties and the companion duties to implement them. In the words of Lord Denning of the English Court of Appeal, "No Parliament should do anything to lessen the worth of these guarantees. They should be honoured by the Crown in respect of Canada..." (*R. v. Secretary of State for Foreign and Commonwealth Affairs*, 1982).

In a federal state, although other levels of government have important roles to play, it is the Canadian government that has the constitutional responsibility to take leadership on treaty implementation. The role of provincial governments is controversial among First Nations. They say, correctly, that they made treaties with the Crown. If the Crown has chosen to complicate matters by dividing up authority to make laws among different layers of government, that is an internal matter to the Crown. The Treaty First Nations often refer to their "bilateral" relationship with the Crown, and to the treaty implementation process as a "bilateral process" involving only the Treaty First Nations and the Crown in right of Canada.

In theory the Crown is indivisible; in reality the Crown's authority is fragmented. In theory the Crown is sovereign, with absolute power; in reality, we live in a democratic state, in which theoretically absolute sovereign authority came under the rule of law centuries ago and is now exercised by a Parliament elected by popular support, by an executive branch of government drawn from that Parliament, by an independent judiciary, and constrained by a complex web of written constitutional texts and unwritten principles and conventions. The Supreme Court has been clear that Crown constraints are a part of the framework of subsection 35(1). As the court observed in *R. v. Sparrow*:

> Section 35 calls for a just settlement for Aboriginal peoples. It renounces the old rules of the game under which the Crown established courts of law and denied those courts the authority to question sovereign claims made by the Crown (*R. v. Sparrow* 1990, 33).

Crown sovereignty, including provincial sovereignty, is constrained under subsection 35(1) by its obligations to First Nations peoples. The courts have jurisdiction to question the Crown's actions. Freedom is increased when the Crown is obliged to observe constitutional limitations on its power; section 35(1) falls within this tradition (Borrows 2007).

CONCLUSION

To date, the Canadian government has not formulated a policy to guide its officials in the implementation of treaties or, to put it in terms that Canada might more comfortably embrace, to reconcile the divergent views on the treaties of the Crown and First Nations. It can be argued that the *Royal Proclamation of 1763* already contains such a policy because it committed the Crown to a method of acquiring First Nations lands with their informed, collective consent. This was clearly a major source of Crown policy when it made the numbered treaties. The proclamation, however, did not suggest how the treaties, once made, should be honoured, fulfilled or implemented. Perhaps it is time for a new proclamation.

The federal government now acknowledges that the policies of the past were harmful and that the continuation of these policies demands reconciliation. In recent decades, the federal government has made advances in addressing such concepts as the inherent right to self-government and to reconciliation with respect to residential schools. Over the last 40 years, the federal government has increasingly empathized with First Nations' distinctive cultural and societal characteristics, their right to political autonomy within the Canadian federation and the need for economic development so they can fully participate in the Canadian economy. Contemporary federal policy is based on the implicit recognition that past strategies of promoting cultural assimilation of First Nations or confining them to reserves are no longer legitimate.

Despite these acknowledgements, the national political processes have failed to correct the problems and have left us all with an unfinished agenda. The Royal Commission on Aboriginal Peoples (RCAP) made recommendations that would have dramatically altered the landscape for First Nations, but so far they have been disregarded for the most part.

One RCAP recommendation that was implemented called for establishing treaty commissions in the appropriate provinces and territories. These commissions were to be permanent, independent and neutral forums where treaty negotiations could take place. However, the commissions' mandate must be expanded to achieve concrete results.

It can be argued that Canada's current policy towards the treaties is a legalistic approach and has the appearance of deliberate avoidance of the issues. In the absence of a policy to redress treaty injustice, and seemingly by default, the courts have been given the task of determining the meaning of treaties. But beyond making such determinations the courts have little power in what is essentially a political issue (*Delgamuukw v. British Columbia* 1997) and certainly cannot take a proactive approach. That is the task of government.

It is clear that existing laws and policies of the Canadian government do not attempt to reconcile the divergent views on the treaties or advance their implementation. The situation appears stymied and reveals an apparent contradiction in our parliamentary system. Ministers, on the one hand, are servants of the Crown with a duty to act honourably and defend pledges made on the Crown's behalf. On the other hand, they owe it to their party to gain the electorate's approval. They are always cognizant that a majority of voters may be reluctant to support initiatives that will benefit a minority, regardless of the Crown's guarantee. Ministers usually will put expedience before fiduciary duty, notwithstanding the courts' admonitions to do otherwise.

Perhaps treaty implementation is not something that can be entrusted to politicians. This is the unambiguous message of Robert J. Talbot's biography of Alexander Morris (Talbot 2009). As lieutenant governor of Manitoba and the North West Territories in the 1870s, Morris negotiated Treaties 3, 4, 5 and 6 and revisions to Treaties 1 and 2. However, Ottawa refused to uphold the promises Morris made on the Crown's behalf. It marked the beginning of a policy of treaty repudiation and First Nations' subjugation. Morris died a frustrated man.

I am not arguing against public accountability: it is the very foundation of democracy. However, if politicians are not equal to the responsibilty of treaty implementation, is it possible to remove it from the political arena and ask others to fulfil the Crown's obligations? I am not thinking of another royal commission; its findings would be at the mercy of government. But an independent parliamentary officer, in the style of an auditor general, with an adequate budget and staff might get the job done. This would be a Chief Treaty Commissioner or a Chief Commissioner for Aboriginal issues who reports to Parliament. Such an office would monitor the progress of treaty implemenation and the Crown's response to its fiduciary duty to all Aboriginal peoples.

Treaties, by their nature, are agreements. One party to an agreement cannot undertake an investigation of its obligations without considering fully and fairly the views of the other party. This is especially true given the special relationship that exists between the Crown and First Nations, and the obligations of the Crown to deal honourably with First Nations in relation to their rights. While the Honour of the Crown is always at stake in the fulfillment of treaty rights, such fulfillment can also involve a fiduciary duty, as stated by the Supreme Court of Canada.

It is apparent that policies are needed to authorize the officials of both parties – First Nations and Crown – to undertake a joint process of determining what the treaties mean and of implementing their findings. This policy must be enabling, not restrictive. It must authorize officials to undertake treaty implementation discussions in a respectful manner. It must mandate serious exploration and negotiations. Each side must develop objectives and guidelines for a process that will produce practical as well as principled outcomes.

Independent provincial treaty commissions, such as Saskatchewan's Office of the Treaty Commissioner, have a critical role to play in this exercise. By fostering dialogue and understanding, they can help to build the trust that is the foundation for a renewed treaty relationship. Direct relationship building in a neutral forum, without the intervention of third parties, such as mediators or arbitrators, is superior to any other method. The results have greater value and are far more enduring than anything imposed on the parties simply because both sides have pride of ownership. Discussions of this kind are absolutely necessary to advance towards treaty implementation that everyone can live with.

The bifurcation of the Crown into two levels of government in the modern context requires a tripartite approach to treaty implementation. So in the case of Saskatchewan's numbered treaties, what is needed to affirm a mutual commitment to the treaty relationship is a joint declaration signed by the governor general of Canada, the lieutenant governor of Saskatchewan and the chief of the Federation of Saskatchewan Indian Nations. From a contemporary Canadian constitutional perspective this should not be seen as a controversial recommendation.

A more elaborate proposal is having the federal government ask the Queen to issue a new Royal Proclamation to govern a new treaty approach. Such a declaration would supplement the *Royal Proclamation of 1763* and restore the fundamental principles between First Nations and the Crown of the bilateral nation-to-nation relationship, the treaty making tradition and, most important, the method for treaty implementation and renewal.

Because the Crown also includes the provinces, Saskatchewan has developed policies on treaty land entitlement and negotiating First Nations' self-government. And as with the federal government, these policies authorize negotiations with First Nations with the objective of reaching agreements. However, Saskatchewan's government has traditionally taken the position that it was not a party to the treaties, since the province did not exist at the time all but one of the treaties were negotiated. Consequently it has no policy framework to mandate participation by the Crown in right of Saskatchewan in discussions to examine and implement the treaties and the treaty relationship.

This position of non-participation cannot be sustained if it becomes a barrier to treaty implementation. The process of treaty implementation, therefore, includes increasing the awareness and altering the mindset of government officials, who have been advised they have no role to play in implementing the treaties. Treaty implementation must include not only making large decisions at high levels, but the activities of all officials in both federal and provincial governments. These officials must be encouraged to appreciate the potential impact of their actions upon the rights and interests of Treaty First Nations and to recognize that treaties are a government wide responsibility, not just the responsibility of Aboriginal Affairs and Northern Development Canada or provincial Aboriginal affairs departments. Treaties can no longer be compartmentalized in the structure of government or the thinking of public servants. A change in approach would necessitate officials of all departments becoming fully aware of their fundamental constitutional obligations. This involves nothing less than a change in the culture of government, a general acknowledgment that treaty matters pervade all government business; that everything governments do must be viewed through the treaty relationship lens.

To achieve such a change more work has to be done internally to integrate the treaty relationship into the federal and provincial systems. I would like to see a government guideline that would require every meeting agenda to begin with the question: how will this affect First Nations and their treaties? A treaty perspective would thus become integral to all government programs and policies, and can be achieved without developing a broader treaty policy; all it takes is a change in attitude.

When the treaties are shown to have been dishonoured or ignored by the Crown, and treaty rights are shown to have been elevated to constitutional status in theory yet ignored and marginalized in practice, surely there is a duty to engage in negotiations to place these rights in their proper place. Failure to do so would represent profound disrespect for the Constitution, the rule of law and other fundamental principles that support our constitutional structure.

The treaties were negotiated agreements of a confederal nature and thus were inherently instruments of reconciliation when they were made. In *Reference re: Secession of Quebec*, the Supreme Court made it clear that a demand for secession is purely political and the resulting duty to negotiate secession is equally political. The task is to attempt to reconcile divergent interests, rights and duties, with no presumption this can be accomplished even if all parties approach the task in good faith.

By contrast, in the context of the treaties, demand for implementation of already legally protected rights is based upon principles of constitutionalism and the rule of law and must be enforceable by the courts. The concluding words of the majority judgment in *Delgamuukw* state:

> Ultimately, it is through negotiated settlements, with good faith and give and take on all sides, reinforced by the judgments of this Court, that we will achieve what I stated in *Van der Peet, supra*, at para. 31, to be a basic purpose of s. 35(1) – "the reconciliation of the pre-existence of Aboriginal societies with the sovereignty of the Crown." Let us face it, we are all here to stay (*Delgamuukw v. British Columbia*, 1997, 114).

Discussions to reconcile disparity between the words of treaty text and the true extent of the constitutional rights are inherently founded upon rights and obligations in the realm of law as well as politics. The rulings of the courts have built a compelling case for the Canadian government and First Nations to establish proper treaty implementation. The courts will compel the Crown and First Nations to negotiate in good faith. Both parties will be constrained by the principles of the treaties and the treaty relationship. The objective of a treaty implementation must be a real and lasting reconciliation.

REFERENCES

Borrows, J. 2007. "Let Obligations Be Done." In *Let Right Be Done: Aboriginal Title, the Calder Case, and the Future of Indigenous Rights*, eds. H. Foster, H. Raven and J. Webber. Vancouver: UBC Press.

Canada. 1996a. Royal Commission on Aboriginal Peoples. *Report on the Royal Commission of Aboriginal Peoples*. Vol. I, *Looking Forward, Looking Back*. Ottawa: Canada Communication Group.

— 1996b. Royal Commission on Aboriginal Peoples. *Report on the Royal Commission of Aboriginal Peoples*. Vol. II, *Restructuring the Relationship*. Ottawa: Canada Communication Group.

— 1997. *Gathering Strength: Canada's Aboriginal Action Plan*. Ottawa: Canada Communication Group.

Cardinal, H. and W. Hildebrandt. 2000. *Treaty Elders of Saskatchewan: Our Dream is That Our Peoples Will One Day Be Clearly Recognized as Nations*. Calgary: University of Calgary Press.

Delgamuukw v. British Columbia, (1997) 3 S.C.R. 1010.

Great Britain. 1857. Report of the Select Committee on the Hudson's Bay Company. House of Commons.

Haida Nation v. British Columbia (Minister of Forests), (2004) 3 S.C.R. 511.

Havard, G. 2001. *The Great Peace of Montreal of 1701*. Montreal and Kingston: McGill Queen's University Press.

The Manitoban, cited in Morris, A. 1991. *The Treaties of Canada with the Indians of Manitoba and the North-West Territories Including the Negotiations on Which They Were Based.* Saskatoon: Fifth House Publishers.

R. v Guerin, (1984) 13 D.L.R. (4th) 321, [1984] 2 S.C.R.

R. v. Marshall, (1999) 3 S.C.R. 456.

R. v. Secretary of State for Foreign and Commonwealth Affairs, ex parte Indian Association of Alberta, (1982) 2 W.L.R. 641.

R. v. Sparrow, (1990) 1 S.C.R. 1075.

R. v. Van der Peet, (1996) 2 S.C.R. 507.

Reference re: Secession of Quebec, (1998) 2 S.C.R. 217.

Talbot, R.J. 2009. *Negotiating the Numbered Treaties: An Intellectual and Political Biography of Alexander Morris.* Saskatoon: Purich Publishing.

THE CROWN IN
COMPARATIVE
PERSPECTIVE

11

THE AUSTRALIAN MONARCHY IN THE TWENTY-FIRST CENTURY

PETER BOYCE

En Australie, le débat public sur la monarchie porte rarement sur sa capacité de servir les arrangements constitutionnels du pays mais essentiellement sur l'importance ou non pour le chef de l'État d'être un Australien résident. Ce chapitre décrit l'élan républicain du début des années 1990, période où le premier ministre Keating dirigeait le pays, et les facteurs qui expliquent l'échec du référendum constitutionnel de 1999. Mais si le sentiment républicain s'est apaisé depuis le début du siècle actuel, les sondages d'opinion indiquent toujours qu'au moins la moitié des Australiens souhaitent rompre avec la Couronne à l'issue du règne d'Élisabeth II. Entre-temps, les adeptes d'une république australienne devront surmonter de sérieux obstacles politiques et constitutionnels. Car les républicains dits « minimalistes » rechignent à l'idée d'un président directement élu par le peuple, tandis que certains chefs des États du pays résisteraient vraisemblablement à tout amoindrissement du statut quasi indépendant de leurs gouverneurs.

Any discussion about monarchy in Australia is focused almost exclusively on whether it should be abandoned. Seldom is interest expressed in the possibilities of strengthening public respect for the Crown or its effectiveness within Australia's system of government. Nevertheless, following the loss of a constitutional referendum proposal to introduce a so-called "minimalist" republic in 1999, even the most vocal proponents of change allowed the matter to assume a lower priority on the national political agenda. The republican mood is currently quiescent, but opinion polls continue to record majority support for a republic, the latest, conducted in May 2009, showing 51 percent in favour and 30 percent against. Furthermore, 81 percent indicated that if there was to be a republic the head of state should be popularly elected (UMR Research 2009).

Although Australia had experienced outbursts of republican sentiment during the 19th century, especially in the years immediately prior to the granting of responsible government and the decade prior to federation, only non-revolutionary versions of republicanism were espoused and, somewhat surprisingly for colonies hosting a large Irish diaspora, it was generally settlers of English or Scottish background who drove republican sentiment, not Irish Australians (McKenna 1998, 1–11). During the early 20th century, criticism of the Crown centred on the importation of British governors and the perceived social elitism emanating from Government House. For much of the 20th century the platforms of state branches of the Australian Labor Party (ALP) included the objective of abolishing the office of governor, but neither at the federal nor state level did the party pursue this objective with any sense of serious commitment. At its 1991 national conference, however, the ALP adopted a pro-republic stance and in December of that year Paul Keating succeeded Bob Hawke as prime minister. Keating, of Irish descent, had become convinced that the cultivation of a stronger Australian sense of national identity necessitated the appointment of a local citizen as head of state, and that a severance of constitutional ties with Britain would greatly assist his foreign policy priority of closer economic and political engagement with Asia (Keating 2000). The Australian Republican Movement (ARM) was founded in Sydney that same year, initially headed by another Irish Australian, the author Patrick Keneally, and in 1992 Australians for Constitutional Monarchy (ACM) emerged as a vocal counterpoint organization, also in Sydney.

The Republic Referendum and Its Aftermath

For most of the 1990s, Australians were assailed almost daily by media discussion or political debate about the need for an Australian head of state. The campaign was formally launched by Prime Minister Keating's appointment of a Republic Advisory Committee in 1993, charged with the responsibility of examining possible models for a republic and conducting public forums across the nation. It was chaired by a prominent Sydney lawyer and merchant banker, Malcolm Turnbull, whose subsequent political career would lie within the Liberal Party, ultimately as its leader. Keating accepted the Committee's recommendation of a "minimalist" model for a republic – that is to say, the president would exercise a role as close as possible to that of the governor general, including exercise of the reserve power, but would be appointed by Parliament on the prime minister's nomination and in consultation with the leader of the opposition (Republic Advisory Committee 1993). Realizing that the procedure for amending the Australian constitution would require careful education of the electorate and persuasion of the opposition parties, Prime Minister Keating fixed no date for a constitutional referendum, relying largely on the propaganda of the Australian Republican Movement, now headed by Turnbull, and the generally sympathetic print media to promote the republican cause. That cause was also assisted by the sullied public image of some members of the royal family during the early and mid-1990s.

Although Keating had promised a constitutional convention to prepare the way for a referendum, his government lost office to the Liberal-National Party coalition in the February 1996 federal election. John Howard, the new prime minister, was a declared monarchist but had agreed during the election campaign to call a constitutional convention to consider the republic proposal. Half the delegates to this assembly, held in Canberra in February 1998, were popularly elected and half appointed by the Howard government. At the end of two weeks of vigorous and widely reported deliberation the conference resolved to recommend a minimalist republic, endorsing the model favoured by Keating's Republic Advisory Committee in 1993 (Report of Convention 1998).

Howard honoured his promise to present a proposal for constitutional change to the electorate but, with assistance from a firmly monarchist cabinet colleague, Nick Minchin, he shrewdly composed the referendum question to restrict voter choice to the minimalist republic model, avoiding the prior question of whether the Queen should be replaced by an Australian head of state. This had the intended effect of splitting the republican vote at the referendum held in November 1999. In the eighteen months between the Canberra Constitutional Convention and the referendum, a sizeable percentage of Australians had been persuaded that any president should be directly elected by popular vote rather than appointed by Parliament, and the vocal lobby for retention of the status quo, Australians for Constitutional Monarchy, successfully exploited this division within the republican ranks. Astutely, they emphasized that the selection of a republican head of state would be controlled by politicians, conveniently disguising the fact that current arrangements allow one senior politician to nominate the governor general. The ACM also minimized references to the Queen during the campaign and argued that the governor general was already Australia's head of state, an interpretation directly at odds with that of Canadian monarchists with regard to their own governor general.

The referendum's outcome was a rejection of the minimalist republican proposal in every state and territory of the Commonwealth except the Australian Capital Territory, 49 percent to 51 percent, notwithstanding that opinion polls in the two years preceding the referendum had indicated at least 60 percent in favour of change (Australian Electoral Commission 2000). Support for the republic was far stronger in inner metropolitan areas than in smaller cities or rural communities, and support was also correlated with income level and socio-economic status (Mackerras and Maley 2001, Higley and McAllister 2002). The convenor of Australians for Constitutional Monarchy during the campaign period, Kerry Jones, later contended that the several reasons for rejection of the republican proposal included a public dislike of elites and distrust of the media (both prominent in the "Yes" campaign), as well as a deep-seated respect for the Australian constitution and its monarchical framework (Jones 2002). Respect for the monarchy was also undoubtedly influenced by one's emotional attachment to Britain and its political tradition. Surveys conducted during the mid-1990s revealed that "emotion had a lot to do with attitudes to the republic, but it was emotion about Britain, not about Australia" (Kelley 2002, 119).

The public campaign for a minimalist republic during 1998–99 had included ringing and regular endorsements from all of the major metropolitan daily newspapers, including *The Australian*, Melbourne's *The Age* and the *Sydney Morning Herald*. A former governor general, two former chief justices and several former diplomats also offered strong support (Boyce 2008, 216–18). The endorsements of Sir Zelman Cowen, a distinguished constitutional lawyer and former governor general, and of two former chief justices of the High Court, Sir Anthony Mason and Sir Gerard Brennan, were particularly welcomed by the ARM, because they addressed the awkward questions of whether and how the royal prerogative could be transferred to and enshrined within a republican model of government. Against their assurances that such a transfer could be smooth and uncomplicated, another former chief justice, Sir Harry Gibbs, argued that any amendment to the status of the Crown would be messy and require amendment of the *Australia Acts* of 1986, which in turn would require the consent of all six states (Twomey 2006). The *Australia Acts*, enacted concurrently at Westminster and in the Australian federal Parliament, severed the residual constitutional links between Britain and the six states.

In the welter of campaign debate and propaganda, very little mention was made of the potential risk entailed in transferring the key conventions of Westminster-style responsible government to a republican context. The historian, Alan Atkinson, was one of very few who posed the question as to whether the moral and cultural authority of the Crown was sufficiently entrenched in Australia's political culture to survive the end of monarchy (Atkinson 1993), while a second historian, Neville Meaney, wondered whether the abolition of monarchy might have "unexpected and adverse consequences," especially for the practice of parliamentary democracy (Meaney 1996, 17). The constitutional lawyers pushing for change seemed relatively unconcerned by this prospect.

Whether the plethora of editorial opinion, specialist comment, letters to the editor and public platform debates during the late 1990s raised significantly the level of public understanding of the Crown's place in Australia's constitutional framework, and of the governor general's role in particular, is unclear, but it seems likely that most Australians developed a more focussed interest in the vice-regal office during this period than ever before. A report on the level of political literacy in Australia commissioned by Paul Keating and published in 1994 had revealed a disturbingly low level of familiarity with the structure of the political system as a whole, with barely 16 percent able to identify the role of the Queen's representative (Civic Experts Group 1994). By 1999 the report card would possibly have been more encouraging.

The more ardent protagonists for a minimalist republic suffered a sense of let-down after the referendum, and a weakened ARM, no longer chaired by Malcolm Turnbull, resolved to encourage discussion of models that would accommodate direct election of the president. But for Prime Minister Howard the issue was now off the national agenda, and his government retained office until December 2007. Furthermore, Labor state premiers who had endorsed the minimalist model were, with one exception, openly hostile to the idea of direct election and were therefore willing to let the republican cause be shelved until the general public could become better educated to its dangers. They were particularly alive to the probability that a directly elected president (and his or her state equivalent) would compete with the political executive for influence.

Republican sentiment was re-aroused in 2003–04 by the controversy which swirled around Howard's first nominee as governor general, Peter Hollingworth, who was Anglican archbishop of Brisbane (Boyce 2008, 197–201). The choice of Hollingworth was not received unfavourably by a majority of Australians, notwithstanding widespread comment that it might jeopardize the separation of church and state. The bishop had earned considerable public respect as executive director of the Brotherhood of St. Laurence, an influential social welfare agency. The new governor general was unlucky in having to fend off allegations that he had not taken sufficient investigative or disciplinary action against sexual abuse in Brisbane church schools while archbishop. He was unlucky in that the media at that time were reporting sexual abuse claims, especially those targeting the clergy or church schools, with fiendish enthusiasm. Hollingworth's somewhat clumsy attempts to explain or justify his actions through the media further compromised the dignity of the vice-regal office, and when the Labor opposition threatened to formally withdraw confidence, the staunchly monarchist prime minister was left with little choice but to ask for Hollingworth's resignation. The Labor leader, Simon Crean, quizzed Howard in the Parliament as to whether he had consulted widely before recommending Hollingworth to the Queen and proposed that a more consultative and bipartisan process be agreed for future appointments. His proposal was rejected.

During 2004 a Senate committee reviewed 730 public submissions addressing the preferred steps towards the achievement of a republic, confirming the need for a preliminary plebiscite and subsequent investigation of several models, but no dates for this process were suggested and the committee's report attracted relatively little public notice (Report of Senate Committee 2004).

Republicans revived their hopes for constitutional change in late 2007 with the election of a Labor government led by Kevin Rudd. Their hopes received a further boost in April 2008, when the new prime minister convened a two-day "Twenty-Twenty Summit" of "the best and the brightest" citizens to help him determine policy priorities for Australia's social and economic progress. Not surprisingly, the group designated to discuss the structure of government were nearly unanimous in calling for a republic. Rudd was sympathetic to their report but indicated that he would not move for constitutional change during the first term of his government. Nor did he subsequently offer any encouragement to the republican movement that he would give the matter high priority during his second term. Rudd was deposed as Labor leader by his own parliamentary caucus in June 2010, but there was no reason to suppose that his successor, Julia Gillard, would be in any hurry to re-open the republic issue. Nevertheless, a broad consensus has emerged among republicans across the political party divide as to the process to be followed when the issue regains a place on the parliamentary agenda. It would follow that outlined in the 2004 Senate committee report and earlier recommended at a people's conference held at Corowa in 2001.

Prime Minister Rudd's selection of Australia's first female governor general in June 2008 was well received across the political spectrum, the more so as Quentin Bryce had already served a term as governor of Queensland and was therefore assumed to be well prepared for the national role at Yarralumla. Moreover, many republican supporters now seemed willing to temper their demands for early constitutional change. The feminists among them may have been encouraged to do so by the knowledge that Ms. Bryce had spent much of her professional life as an advocate for women's rights. But the governor general designate attracted some negative media coverage when she requested a replacement of the official secretary at Government House even before taking up office (*The Australian*, 21 October 2009, 9). The retiring governor general, General Michael Jeffery, was reported to have sought to persuade Ms. Bryce to reconsider her demand, but he was unsuccessful.

Further negative comment followed a disclosure that the new official secretary, a career foreign service officer, was a friend and former colleague of the prime minister and that his partner was employed as personal assistant to the then prime minister's wife, Therese Rein. Although this new linkage of personnel between Government House and the prime minister's office could raise doubts about the governor general's independence, the choice of Stephen Brady as official secretary seems to have been soundly professional and merit based. Furthermore, the prime minister's wife was a highly successful businesswoman, whose international employment agencies operated at a considerable distance from her husband's office.

Quentin Bryce has undertaken considerable overseas travel, sometimes to meet with Australian service personnel in war zones, but also representational visits in her capacity as *de facto* or effective head of state. The most recent of these embroiled the governor general in controversy because the Rudd government unwisely allowed an announced itinerary of state visits to nine African capitals to be interpreted as a political mission on behalf of the federal government, explicitly to canvass support for Australia's bid for a Security Council seat (*The Australian*, 12 February 2009, 1, 2).

Dispute over ownership of the title "head of state" took a curious turn in February 2010 when Buckingham Palace announced that the Queen would address the United Nations General Assembly in July in her capacity as head of state of all her realms. Journalists observed that since the 1999 referendum it had become "a local convention" to recognize the governor general as head of state and that Prime Minister Rudd had so described Ms. Bryce in announcing her forthcoming round of state visits to Africa in 2009. He later withdrew the claim (*The Australian*, 12 February 2010, 1, 2). Most oddly, to a Canadian observer at least, the national convenor of Australians for Constitutional Monarchy, David Flint, disputed the prime minister's reassurance that the Queen was indeed the country's head of state: "Perhaps the Prime Minister believes we have two heads of state, or that they change from time to time" (*The Australian*, 13 February 2010). Flint's stance on this troublesome question follows the lead of Sir David Smith, a former, long-serving official secretary at Yarralumla, whose idiosyncratic argument that the governor general is already the *de jure* head of state has enjoyed wide circulation (Smith 2005). The current leader of the Liberal Party, Tony Abbott, who is a former convenor of ACM and author of a book-length defence of the Crown, *The Minimal Monarchy* (Abbott 1995), has studiously avoided recent public comment on the head of state identity question. It should be noted, however, that references to the governor general as "effective head of state" have enjoyed some currency among both monarchist and pro-republican commentators.

THE STATES: SIX SEPARATE CROWNS?

A serious constitutional and political complication facing advocates of an Australian republic is that a national referendum for change would carry no automatic effect on the Crown-in-right of the states or the office of state governor. The status of the Crown in each of the six states is determined by state constitutions, which are ordinary statutes, even though two states, Western Australia and Queensland, have partially entrenched those sections of their constitutions affecting the office of governor (Twomey 2006, 169–74). Without corresponding state legislation to parallel any Commonwealth initiated constitutional amendment in favour of a republic, the Crown would remain intact at state level. Presumably, if and when a fresh attempt is made to convert to a republic, prior agreement will have been sought from the state premiers to legislate amendments to their own constitutions. During the 1998–99 debates, several premiers indicated that they would not move to abolish the Crown without seeking public approval at a state referendum or plebiscite.

Because state governors reinforce state identity in a period of increasing centralization of government, even republican sympathizers among the premiers will be reluctant to see the office abolished. Furthermore, since passage of the *Australia Acts* in 1986, state premiers have enjoyed the right to communicate directly with the Queen, even if (by agreement with the Commonwealth and with the Palace) this right is normally exercised only in relation to the appointment of governors. Although such correspondence will seldom be controversial, this right of direct access highlights the full delegation of the royal prerogative to the states, and even republican premiers will want guarantees from the Commonwealth that any formula for transfer of the royal prerogative at the national level will be correspondingly practicable at the state level.

In discharging their community leadership role, state governors customarily enjoy a higher public profile within their own state than can ever be achieved by a governor general, and within a small state, Tasmania especially, the governor will be afforded opportunities to make contact with a sizeable percentage of the population.

Most governors complete their terms in office without having to exercise any discretionary authority or "reserve power," but several states have experienced indecisive election results or "hung parliaments," and serious abuse of core conventions of cabinet government are not unknown. The most recent (March 2010) Tasmanian state election saw the governor exercising discretion when, in the face of a deadlock between the two major parties, with a third party, the Greens, winning five seats, he rejected the initial formal advice of the premier to commission the leader of the opposition, requesting that the incumbent retain his commission and test the confidence of the Parliament, due to be reconvened within a few weeks. The governor, Peter Underwood, broke new ground in immediately publishing his reasons for such a decision (Underwood 2010).

How confident or courageous an Australian state governor might be in exercising his or her right to "warn" cannot be measured, because such attempts to influence a premier are normally exercised confidentially and remain unreported, but one can safely assume that the majority of governors feel considerably more comfortable exercising one of Bagehot's other two "rights" of the monarch – to "encourage."

Unlike their Canadian counterparts, Australian state governors chair all meetings of their Executive Councils, and most of them take this duty very seriously, requiring agenda papers to be delivered to Government House several days in advance. Most governors, especially those trained in the law or familiar with the machinery of government, will feel entitled to question submissions and even refer matters back to the relevant minister or department. Although there is no tradition of state premiers conferring on a regular basis with their governor, there have been encouraging signs in recent years of a willingness to experiment with scheduled open-ended, informal discussions.

The Australian states continued to receive British appointees as governor until the 1970s, with a Western Australian premier turning back the clock for another UK appointment as late as 1980. British appointees were serving two masters, because they dispatched regular confidential reports to the secretary of state for Foreign and Commonwealth Affairs, as well as having been appointed on the secretary of state's formal recommendation to the monarch. Most Australians were almost certainly unaware of these lingering, anachronistic signs of semi-colonial status. The quality of local appointees to state Government Houses has been generally high, notwithstanding that premiers from both sides of politics have been consistently reluctant to adopt a formalized consultative process before submitting their nominations to Buckingham Palace. Very occasionally a serious mistake is made, the most scandalous of which was committed by a Tasmanian premier in 2003 (Boyce 2008, 202–8).

The state vice-regal office enjoys a much higher level of funding support and administrative independence from the political executive than does the provincial vice-regal office in Canada. Furthermore, Government House itself is in every state a magnificent residential building in spacious grounds, each of them predating Federation. Governors entertain regularly and elegantly. In any average week they will host at least one formal dinner, a couple of evening receptions, and possibly a luncheon. In most states the capital city's main morning newspaper will carry a daily "vice-regal notices" column, listing the governor's activities for the previous day and identifying all guests and callers at Government House. This is seen as a contribution to public accountability and transparency.

In several states the official secretary to the governor enjoys the status of department head and in every state is "the accountable officer" in complying with the state's Finance and Audit Act. Official secretaries often serve lengthy terms and acquire influence and prestige within the state bureaucratic network. Charles Curwen was official secretary to the governor of Victoria for more than twenty years and had filled lesser offices at Government House before that. The current official secretaries to the governors of New South Wales and Western Australia have also enjoyed lengthy tenure. The acquisition of status by official secretaries is assisted by the fact that in every state except New South Wales the governor's work base is Government House, territorially removed from both the Parliament building and government offices. The premier waits on the governor at Government House, the clerks of Parliament present bills for the royal assent at Government House, and ministries are sworn in at Government House.[1] The state governors have gathered in informal conference on an irregular basis in recent decades, but the official secretaries try to meet at intervals of approximately eighteen months, and they always invite the governor general's secretary to join them.

Very few locally recruited state governors have been affiliated with a political party at the time of their appointment and most have been able to claim some familiarity with constitutional matters or with the machinery of government. The pattern of recruitment has been somewhat different from that discernible in Canada. Most governors in the past three decades have been judges, senior military officers or senior academics. Two of the six women who have occupied Government House at state level have been senior lawyers, one an academic, one a college head, one a diplomat, and the sixth a businesswoman-community leader. Only one male governor has been drawn from the world of commerce, and no indigenous Australian has been appointed since the short tenure of Sir Douglas Nicholls in South Australia during the 1970s. Several governors, perhaps most, are believed to acknowledge privately that abandonment of monarchy by Australia is inevitable, and one of their current number, South Australia's Rear-Admiral Kevin Scarce, declared himself in interview at the time of his appointment to be a republican.

COMPARING THE CROWNS

In broad constitutional and political terms, the Australian and Canadian Crowns are remarkably similar and, largely because of the two countries' parallel constitutional histories, their contemporary political cultures share many attributes. The formal powers of the governor general in Canberra are approximately the same as her opposite number in Ottawa and, following court challenges and appeals to the secretary of state for the colonies towards the end of the nineteenth century, the formal and applied powers of Canada's lieutenant-governors grew to parallel those of Australian state governors. Nevertheless, the fact that provincial representatives are still appointed by the prime minister (albeit increasingly in consultation with provincial premiers) and that the status of the Crown can be amended by Australian state legislation, suggests a lingering distinction between the two sub-national spheres. This distinction is further reflected in the nomenclature of vice-regal appointments, with state governors accorded the title of "Excellency."

---

[1] However, a republican premier of New South Wales, Bob Carr, announced in January 1996 that his state's governor would no longer reside at Government House and the governor's place of work was transferred to a suite in the Chief Secretary's Department. Carr made no secret of his wish to downgrade the office of governor (Boyce 2008, 165).

The Queen's representatives in each country retain access to the monarch's reserve powers, but the exercise of genuine discretion is seldom needed. It is noteworthy, however, that only in Australia has a prime minister been dismissed and only in Australia that the resignations of two vice-regal representatives been sought by the political executive. Furthermore, there appears to have been considerably more discussion of the reserve powers in Australian constitutional and political forums than in Canada (Boyce 2008, 53–60, 81–83, 130–35). As in Canada, the governor general has in recent years appropriated several functions formerly exercised by the Queen alone – the signing of letters of credence and recall for heads of diplomatic mission, for example.

In their capacity as president of Executive Council, Australian vice-regal representatives are afforded more opportunities to exercise at least marginal influence on the political executive than their Canadian counterparts are able to exercise through their lesser involvement in Privy Council or Executive Council meetings, though governors drawn from a legal or political background will be more likely than other appointees to question cabinet recommendations (Boyce 2008, 126–30, 158–60).

The impediments to any constitutional change to the vice regal office are more daunting in Canada than in Australia, though the requirement of approval by a majority of states and a national majority of voters at a national referendum is also very constraining. The quasi-independent state Crowns, however, can be modified by legislation, except in two states, Queensland and Western Australia, where approval by referendum is also required. The state Crowns (if we may be permitted to refer to them in the plural) are linked with the national Crown constitutionally in just one curious respect. Section 4 of the Commonwealth constitution allows for the most senior of the state governors to administer the Commonwealth in the extended absence or incapacity of the governor general, and this arrangement has worked well.

The Australian honours system, though modelled on Canada's, is administered somewhat differently. There are no state honours, but state governors conduct investitures for those recipients of Order of Australia awards resident in their home state. State premiers were allowed to submit nominations for imperial honours until the early 1990s, and this privilege was often abused, especially in nominations for knighthoods. Each state is represented on the Order of Australia Council, the secretary of which is the governor general's official secretary. Like its Rideau Hall counterpart, Yarralumla houses the Order's secretariat.

The Australian governor general's establishment is smaller than that based at Rideau Hall, and cost AUD $15.3 million in 2008–09 (Official Secretary 2009, 7). Moreover, it has been largely spared public criticism of its efficiency or any serious questioning of its modus operandi. The official secretary is a department head and represents the governor general in defending its expenditures before the Senate Estimates Committee.

PROSPECTS FOR STRENGTHENING THE VICE-REGAL OFFICE

If a generous measure of lateral thinking could help conceptualize the status and function of the sovereign as being distinct from that of the Australian head of state, the future of monarchy in Australia might be assured, but such a workable distinction is unlikely. That being so, one must try to identify more modest opportunities to strengthen popular acceptance and understanding of the Crown and its place in Australia's constitutional and political arrangements. The options are few.

The development of a procedure for ensuring an element of public input to the prime minister's selection of a governor general and of consultation with the leader of the opposition before a recommendation is made to the Queen would almost certainly win public approval. More imaginative public education programs might also assist the monarchist cause, and several Government House websites are now quite instructive, but pro-republican political leaders are unlikely to take initiatives in this direction. An increased frequency of visits by members of the Queen's family would not necessarily be a winning innovation, notwithstanding the apparent popularity of "working visits" in Canada, though occasional visits by the monarch herself, if prudently handled, are likely to be well received. A short unofficial visit to Sydney by Prince William in the summer of 2009 attracted very sympathetic media coverage.

One difficulty in projecting a public profile for the governor general is the tendency of recent prime ministers to assume a more presidential role, sometimes encroaching on traditional vice-regal territory. Prime Minister Howard, for example, wanted to open the Sydney Olympics, but the popular demand that this ceremony be performed by the Queen's representative, Sir William Deane, eventually forced a change of plan. Ardent royalist though he was, Howard was frequently irritated by the governor general's implied criticisms of his government in public speeches highlighting the plight of aborigines and other disadvantaged Australians. But Howard was also willing to sideline Deane's successor, General Michael Jeffery, in his fervour to farewell and welcome home contingents of Australian military units serving in various theatres of action overseas.

Without any doubt the biggest hurdle to retain public support for the monarchy centres on the question of how far the role of governor general can afford to be distanced from that of the sovereign without marginalizing the person of the Queen. Complaints that Rideau Hall has played down the Crown's constitutional and personal links to Buckingham Palace have had no parallel in the Australian media, but there is no doubt that Yarralumla and all six state Government Houses have quietly but steadily distanced themselves from the Palace. This year even Commonwealth Day (always accompanied by a message from the Queen) received no acknowledgment from the governor general.

The current public mood does not accord high priority to the early abandonment of monarchy, but a clear majority of Australians have consistently endorsed the view that change should occur at the expiry of the Queen's reign, a view shared by the current prime minister, most Labor state premiers, a former Liberal prime minister and by many senior Liberal parliamentarians. But just how the severance would be handled, politically and constitutionally, is another matter. The British rules of succession present difficulties, because in the event of the Queen's death or abdication their effect on Australia is an automatic elevation of Prince Charles to the Australian throne. But one can fairly safely predict that Charles' succession will not be acceptable to a large proportion of the Australian public.

Australians seem satisfied with the Crown as a pivotal institution in their Westminster-derived polity, even if relatively few would understand it as "the first principle" of their political system, but the overwhelming majority are likely to remain concerned by the national identity of their head of state. The claim by Sir David Smith, and a few other leading defenders of the status quo, that an Australian is already head of state – in the person of the governor general – does not carry much weight with the general community, and of course it would sit very uncomfortably with those Canadian monarchists who sound alarm bells whenever Rideau Hall dares to even imply that the governor general is Canada's head of state.

Canadians may be unaware that Buckingham Palace was drawn into the head of state identity argument during the republic referendum campaign in 1999. Prior to the campaign, the Queen's website declared that she was head of state in fifteen overseas realms, but just weeks before the referendum her website was mysteriously amended, with the words "head of state" replaced by "sovereign." The alteration was obviously requested or suggested by a well placed Australian monarchist. I assume that Canadian authorities were not consulted about the change.

Although the case against privileged heredity was regularly heard throughout the campaign for an Australian republic, there has been little evidence of any deep-seated hostility to the notion of royalty. Indeed, there has been continuing and widespread public interest in the fortunes of Denmark's very popular Crown Princess, Mary Donaldson, a Tasmanian girl, and her husband, Frederic. Their first official visit to Australia overshadowed a concurrent national tour by the Prince of Wales. Of course the couple's youth, striking good looks, sporting prowess, and relaxed dignity help explain the sympathetic public response, along with the increasing tendency to assess royal visitors by much the same criteria as popular entertainment celebrities. But over-riding these factors was surely Princess Mary's Australian identity.

While opinion polls continue to record majority support for a republic (though by narrower margins in recent years), it is difficult to determine how intensely they favour abandonment of the Crown. Opinion polls are not designed to measure the intensity of emotions or convictions, even if the questions put to the public are intelligently worded (which has not always been the case). Certainly it would be unfortunate if a majority of Australians, or indeed even a sizeable minority, were deeply unhappy about the identity or role of their head of state, but we have no hard evidence that this is yet the case. It would seem that relatively few Australians have become disenchanted with the constitutional role of the Crown as ultimate guardian of the democratic process, and notwithstanding Sir John Kerr's dismissal of Prime Minister Whitlam in November 1975, republicans on both sides of the party divide have accepted without complaint the proposal that in any minimalist model the head of state should retain access to the reserve power, including the capacity to dismiss the political executive.

Why has the drive for republic in Australia lost impetus? Firstly, the most active proponents of change were exhausted and disillusioned by the referendum loss, with the advocates for a minimalist republican model now painfully aware that the electorate would need to be carefully educated to reject the popularly favoured direct election of the head of state. Furthermore, because the deadline of the centenary of the federation for the installation of Australia's first president was missed, with no other historic milestone date imminent, any sense of urgency has been lost. Also significant has been the departure of the Australian Republican Movement's chief benefactor and most powerful organizer, Malcolm Turnbull – he who declared at the declaration of the referendum result that Prime Minister Howard had "broken the nation's heart." Turnbull would remain a republican but within a few years would be elected to Parliament as a Liberal, would serve in Howard's last administration, and would later assume the party leadership. With Paul Keating's departure[2] there followed a more relaxed approach to the twin questions of national identity and engagement with Asia, even if several senior diplomats with experience of Asian postings remained convinced that the monarchical connection with Britain was a net liability for Australian diplomacy.

Probably the most telling factor in explaining the abandonment of any concerted drive for a republic is the persistent evidence that an overwhelming majority of Australians would demand a directly elected head of state if the Crown were to be abolished, and this majority would appear to contain many monarchists. As already noted, those political leaders who endorsed the minimalist model for a republic tend to fear that direct election of the head of state would probably wreck the Westminster system of "responsible" government, because the office would be politicized and could become more powerful than the prime ministership

---

[2] See above. Paul Keating was Labor prime minister of Australia from 1991 to 1996 and in 1992 called for an "Australian head of state" by 2000 (Boyce 2008, 213–15).

unless it were stripped of the governor general's discretionary authority. There is general agreement among republicans that within such a model the key conventions governing the head of state's relationship to the political executive would need to be codified. It is clear, however, that the rank and file of Australians have not yet grasped the implications of direct election.

The call for abandonment of monarchy in Australia will not again become a high priority for government without bipartisan support, and because most current political leaders fear the consequences of a directly elective presidency, which is clearly the popular preference, they will not wish to tread this political and constitutional minefield without careful preparation. In the meantime it might be helpful if the concept of a bipartite head of state could gain acceptance in the public mind.

REFERENCES

Abbott, T. 1995. *The Minimal Monarchy*. Adelaide: Wakefield Press.
Atkinson, A. 1993. *The Muddle Headed Republic*. Melbourne: Oxford University Press.
Australian Electoral Commission. 2000. *Referendum 1999: Report and Statistics*. Canberra.
Boyce, P. 2008. *The Queen's Other Realms: The Crown and its Legacy in Australia, Canada and New Zealand*. Sydney: Federation Press.
Civic Experts Group. 1994. *"Whereas the People..."– Civics and Citizenship Education*. Canberra: Australian Government Publishing Service.
Higley, J. and I. McAllister. 2002. "Elite Division and Voter Confusion: Australia's Republic Referendum 1999." *European Journal of Political Research* 41(6).
Jones, K. 2002. "Why Australians voted No in the 1999 Republican Referendum." In *Constitutional Politics: The Republic Referendum and the Future*, eds. J. Warhurst and M. Mackerras. Brisbane: University of Queensland Press.
Keating, P. 2002. *Engagement: Australia faces the Asia-Pacific*. Sydney: Macmillan.
Kelley, J., et al. 2002. "Public Opinion on Britain, a Directly Elected President and an Australian Republic." In *Constitutional Politics: The Republic Referendum and the Future*, eds. J. Warhurst and M. Mackerras. Brisbane: University of Queensland Press.
McKenna, M. 1996. *The Captive Republic: A History of Republicanism in Australia 1788–1996*. Melbourne: Cambridge University Press.
Mackerras, M. and W. Maley. 2002. "1999 Republic Referendum Results: Some Reflections." In *Constitutional Politics: The Republic Referendum and the Future*, eds. J. Warhurst and M. Mackerras. Brisbane: University of Queensland Press.
Meaney, N. 1996. "The Commonwealth and the Republic: An Historical Perspective." In *Papers on Parliament*, No. 27. Canberra: Department of the Senate.
Office of the Official Secretary to the Governor-General. 2009. *Annual Report 2008-9*. Canberra.
Report of the Constitutional Convention, Old Parliament House, Canberra, 2-13 February 1998. 1998. Canberra: Department of Prime Minister and Cabinet.

Report of Senate Committee. 2004. Report of the Senate Legal and Constitutional Affairs Committee. *Road to a Republic*. Canberra.

Republic Advisory Committee. 1993. *An Australian Republic: The Options*. Canberra: Australian Government Publishing Service.

Smith, D. 2005. *Head of State: the Governor-General, the Monarch, the Republic and the Dismissal*. Sydney: Macleay Press.

Twomey, A. 2006. *The Chameleon Crown: The Queen and Her Australian Governors*. Sydney: Federation Press.

UMR Research. 2009. Accessed online at http//www.umrresearch.com.au/doc/republicmedia2009june.pdf

Underwood, P., 2010. "Reasons for commissioning Mr Bartlett to form a Government." Accessed online at http//www.govhouse.tas.gov.au/speeches

12

"THE CROWN DOWN UNDER": ISSUES AND TRENDS IN AUSTRALIA AND NEW ZEALAND

NOEL COX

Toute évaluation du rôle de la monarchie en Nouvelle-Zélande appelle inévitablement la comparaison avec la situation de l'Australie et, dans une moindre mesure, du Canada et du Royaume-Uni. Mais si ces pays ont plusieurs caractéristiques en commun, il est important de prendre la mesure exacte de ce qui les différencie. Car si tous sont des monarchies parlementaires fondées sur le modèle de Westminster et sont le produit d'une évolution graduelle, des différences majeures s'appliquent au cas de la Nouvelle-Zélande. Premièrement, elle ne possède pas de constitution écrite et dûment établie, à l'inverse d'autres royaumes, mais comme au Royaume-Uni. Deuxièmement, c'est le seul État unitaire des quatre. Mais surtout, les liens tissés entre la Couronne et la population indigène des Maoris ont procuré à la monarchie un réel ancrage en Nouvelle-Zélande. D'où les conséquences négligeables de l'absence d'inscription constitutionnelle de la monarchie. D'où également la relative inanité de l'agitation républicaine.

INTRODUCTION

Any appraisal of the position of the monarchy in New Zealand inevitably invites comparisons with Australia, and to a lesser extent Canada and the United Kingdom. We share many common attributes, though it is important to be mindful of the differences. I will begin by highlighting some of the differences and similarities between Australia, Canada and New Zealand.

AUSTRALIA, CANADA AND NEW ZEALAND

In common are our constitutional origins and underlying principles, both originally from the United Kingdom. We share a common Crown. This is not simply the same Queen, but a common perception of what it means to be a constitutional monarchy, and many of the principles inherent in a monarchical government on the British model. We share a belief in a system of parliamentary democracy, so that we both entrust the day-to-day government of our respective countries to politicians responsible to parliament and ultimately to the electorate. We also share the concept of the separation of powers, where no single branch or organ of government is entrusted with more power or responsibility than it can reasonably be expected to exercise. These are but a very few of the enormous range of similarities between our two countries.

But there are also marked differences between Canada and New Zealand. On the constitutional level, perhaps the most crucial is that we in New Zealand do not have an entrenched constitution. That is not so say that we do not have a constitution, but simply that there is no formal document which can be said to be the source of constitutional power in New Zealand. As a consequence of this situation there is no formal limitation upon the supremacy or sovereignty of Parliament. Although New Zealand shares this distinction with the United Kingdom, there are now limitations upon the sovereignty of the British Parliament as a consequence of its membership of the European Union.

New Zealand never acquired an entrenched constitution, for it was never required (as it was needed in Australia and Canada upon federation, to assign powers between the state and provincial legislatures, and the federal authorities). We were never the victim of revolution, or the beneficiary of a deliberate grant of independence. Like the United Kingdom, New Zealand evolved as a country over time. With particular respect to the monarchy, the immediate consequence of this situation is that the New Zealand Parliament could, in strict theory, pass an act establishing a republican form of government without recourse to a referendum. In practice it is almost certain that a referendum would be held, either because the government felt obliged to hold one, or because sufficient voters petitioned for one to be held. But, unlike in Australia, the outcome of such a referendum would not be binding on Parliament.

The Monarchy in New Zealand

New Zealand's form of government, in common with other countries established predominantly by settlers from the British Isles – excepting only the United States of America – is that of a constitutional (or limited) monarchy. In 1840 the monarchy meant the "British" monarchy. It was the Queen of the United Kingdom (not England as the Treaty styled her) who concluded the Treaty with Maori chiefs at Waitangi. With the growth of the newly settled colony, the British government progressively entrusted more powers and responsibilities to the colonial parliament and executive. This process was accelerated during the early part of the twentieth century when New Zealand, together with several other long-established British colonies, notably Canada and Australia, were granted the status of "dominions."

Each dominion shared allegiance to the Crown. Although the personification of the Crown was the sovereign, the Crown included the sovereign's advisers as well. Initially these were primarily based in the United Kingdom, but later came to include individuals resident locally. Over time, each dominion began to develop its own concept of the Crown. Beginning in the 1930s the sovereign acted in relation to New Zealand only on the advice of New Zealand ministers. As the Queen came to be regarded more and more as the Queen of New Zealand and only incidentally as the sovereign of these other countries, so a distinct New Zealand Crown evolved. Thus the once-single imperial Crown slowly evolved into a multiplicity of national Crowns. This meant that obligations once undertaken by the British Crown were now the responsibility of the New Zealand Crown. This can be illustrated with reference to the Crown's obligations under the Treaty of Waitangi. Although for all practical purposes such obligations were vested in the ministers of the New Zealand government, Maori continued to hold the sovereign responsible for upholding the terms of the Treaty. In 1984, for instance, Maori bypassed the New Zealand government by appealing to Queen Elizabeth to uphold the provisions of the Treaty. But it was the Queen of New Zealand rather the United Kingdom to whom they appealed.

This evolution of a distinct New Zealand Crown went hand in hand with the nationalizing of the office of governor general. During the early part of the twentieth century the governor general was seen as the local agent of the British government. Despite being granted a measure of personal discretion, successive appointees were expected to refer contentious matters to British ministers or senior Whitehall officials. Although this link began to attenuate from the 1920s, the essentially British nature of the institution persisted for as long as appointments were limited to those who were not only born, but also domiciled, in Britain. As well as representing the Crown, the office of the governor general in New Zealand had come to represent, to some extent, the values and attitudes of a particular slice of British society transplanted into New Zealand, namely the aristocracy.

The first New Zealand-born governor general, Sir Arthur Porritt,[1] was appointed in 1967, and while this did not produce any significant immediate change in the functions of the office, it did mark the beginning of a transition in its character and style. Porritt was an eminent surgeon and

---

[1] Freyberg was born in London, and, although largely brought up in New Zealand, had spent the greater part of his adult life abroad.

former Olympic sprint medallist who, at the time of his appointment, was an honorary member of the Queen's Household. Like other prominent expatriate New Zealanders, such as the scientist Ernest Rutherford, he became well known only after leaving New Zealand. However, having forged a dual New Zealand-British identity, Porritt was seen subsequently as an important transitional figure in the nationalizing of the office of governor general. When Porritt returned to Britain on the completion of his term, a former New Zealand high commissioner to London, Sir Dennis Blundell, became the first New Zealand-born governor general who was also a New Zealand resident. He held the post from 1972 until 1977. Because neither Porritt nor Blundell was a member of the British aristocracy,[2] there was no expectation among New Zealanders that they would conduct themselves as if they were. Moreover, while they represented the Queen, they did not in any sense represent Britain.

Thereafter every appointee has been a New Zealander, appointed (as indeed they have been formally since 1941 and informally since 1910) by the Queen on the advice of the New Zealand prime minister. While the powers of the office are limited, each modern incumbent has the potential to shape the character, and also the role, of the office of governor general in response to changing conditions and expectations. More recent appointments include the first Maori governor general (Sir Paul Reeves, 1985–90), followed by the first woman (Dame Catherine Tizard, 1990–96). Both were notable for stamping their distinctively New Zealand qualities and personalities on the office (Lange 1998). That two of the three most recent appointments (Sir Michael Hardie-Boys 1996–2001 and Dame Silvia Cartwright 2001–06) were former Court of Appeal and High Court judges respectively is a reflection of the potential for constitutional uncertainty surrounding the appointment and termination of coalition governments under the new electoral arrangements of the mixed-member plurality system (MMP). The current governor general, Sir Anand Satyanand, was both a District Court judge and ombudsman.

Although for most purposes the governor general is the head of state, the country is not a *de facto* republic, but rather a "localized" monarchy (Ladley 1997). Appointees derive their status from both their constitutional position at the apex of the executive branch of government and their role as representative of the sovereign. The office can be said to have three principal roles: community; ceremonial; and constitutional (Tizard 1997). It is perhaps in their community leadership role, which includes both public engagements and commenting on social trends and issues, that governors general are most conspicuous. According to Dame Catherine Tizard (1993, 4), it is the responsibility of the governor general to both

---

[2] Though, after his retirement, Porritt was to become a de jure British aristocrat. It was customary, though not invariably the practice, for the governor general to receive a peerage until Porritt's time.

acknowledge a sense of community spirit and affirm those civic virtues that give New Zealand a sense of identity and purpose. This aspect of the community role is not only demanding, but potentially perilous, with incumbents being required to tread a fine line between the bland and the politically controversial. The ceremonial role, in contrast, is constrained by New Zealand's lack of a strong tradition of overt symbolism, pomp, and ceremony. Events such as the State Opening of Parliament have rarely played a major part in public life in New Zealand. The dangers inherent in the community leadership role were illustrated in 2002 when Dame Silvia Cartwright was criticized in some quarters for suggesting that the parental right to discipline children should be reassessed. She attracted further controversy by observing that imprisonment was not an effective way to reform criminals. In both cases she was drawing upon her prior experience as a High Court judge rather than as governor general, but that did not isolate the office – and her – from criticism.

The third, constitutional, role flows from the position of the governor general as representative of the sovereign. This said, most of the powers of the office derive from statutes and regulations rather than the royal prerogative. The governor general assents to bills and orders in council, opens and dissolves Parliament, appoints ministers, and makes a range of other appointments. Once seen as an instrument of imperial will, the governor general is occasionally now seen as a constitutional safeguard against executive despotism.[3] However, arguments that the governor general can act as a guardian of the constitution appear to overstate the case. New Zealand's economic and social policies have been dramatically altered over the past two decades without intervention from the governor general. This reflects the fact that the governor general can only intervene to preserve the constitutional order itself. Like the sovereign, the governor general will almost always act only on the advice of ministers responsible to parliament. However, as we have seen, the importance of the constitutional role was doubtless an important factor in the selection of Hardie-Boys and Cartwright following the introduction of MMP in 1996.

While the office of governor general has evolved over time, so too has that of the sovereign and the monarchy as a whole. Just as the evolution of the executive government through the twentieth century often saw the diminution of the role of the governor and then governor general, a process seen as strengthening the political independence of the country, so the Queen's role has also diminished at the expense of the governor general and other members of the executive, especially (in recent years) the prime minister.

---

[3] Auckland District Law Society Public Issues Committee, The Holyoake Appointment, 1977, p. 7.

Republican Arguments in New Zealand

There is comparatively little tradition of republicanism in New Zealand. Republican sentiment in New Zealand has never been as strong as in Australia, but in 1994 Jim Bolger, then prime minister, raised the issue of New Zealand becoming a republic by the turn of the century. The reason given was that "the tide of history is moving in one direction," towards republicanism as a fulfilment of national identity. Although Mr. Bolger knew what he was proposing did not have popular support, he seriously underestimated the level of opposition to his proposal from within his own party and ultimately weakened his position within the government. Nor was the response from the left wing opposition as favourable as he might have wished.

The immediate origins of Bolger's call for a republic belong in the neo-liberalism adopted by successive governments since 1984. The wish to bury the colonial inheritance, to face towards multiculturalism, and to locate New Zealand firmly in Asia was a conscious, market-related choice forced by external developments. The argument is that New Zealand is a South Pacific nation that should train its focus on Asia. There were also political arguments around nationhood, what New Zealand stands for, and its feeling of self-respect. Most important among the symbolic issues, and that upon which Mr Bolger relied, was the idea of the inappropriateness of "the Queen of England" "to be Head of State and to have power to appoint a Governor General to exercise her royal powers on her behalf in New Zealand." National identity, the argument goes, requires a New Zealand head of state. Thus attacks upon the Crown have been motivated, not by criticism of the way in which the political system operates, but by the connection with the British monarchy.

The position of the Crown, however acceptable and useful the system of government may otherwise be, is potentially undermined by the very symbolism which is one of its strengths. This is the essence of the Australian republican movement. Yet this very aspect is of importance in New Zealand because of the Treaty of Waitangi and for other reasons. In short, recent changes in New Zealand society, economy and government do not necessarily indicate that a republic is likely to be adopted in the short to medium term, even if Australia opts for one. On the contrary, these changes, including the adoption of MMP, have left people exhausted and inclined to look with disfavour on proposals for further change.

The Fenian element, so significant as the historical intellectual basis of much of Australia's republican movement, was also largely absent from New Zealand politics. The Crown can be seen as equally representative of all people. It is not necessarily confined to those of British ancestry. It is also true that to equate Irish Catholicism with republicanism is both erroneous and harmful. Certainly it can be said that there is little evidence of such sentiment in New Zealand. For their part, to the Maori the Crown was often seen as an ally against the colonial (and later) government. For it is at least symbolically important that the Treaty of Waitangi was signed by the Maori chiefs with the representative of the Queen in 1840 and not with the European settlers.

Whilst most criticism of the monarchy focuses on what republicans call the "self-evident absurdity" of sharing a head of state with another country, people seem to be more concerned with the effectiveness of the political system. Symbolism is all very well, but the system works reasonably effectively. For most purposes the Australian head of state is the governor general anyway, and he has never been a partisan political figure.

The same cannot be necessarily expected of a president, especially one liable to removal by the prime minister. The inherent disadvantage of a republic, whether in Australia or New Zealand, would be that the highest office becomes a matter of partisan contest, or of factional division. This seems to be generally understood in New Zealand. A monarchical system of government removes the office of head of state from the realm of party politics. Any republican system risks the politicization of the highest office, whether the president is elected or appointed.

Public dissatisfaction with politicians is widespread, on both sides of the Tasman. There has yet to be shown any good reason for changing the role of head of state of Australia, or New Zealand, into just another prize for politicians.

Opinion polls showed that voters in Australia in the 1999 referendum were concerned by the details of the proposed republic. If they had to have a president, most would prefer one directly elected by the people, rather than appointed by politicians. It is unlikely, however, that New Zealanders would favour any constitutional reform which would increase the number of politicians, or the power they hold.

The success of the referendum in Australia did not silence the republicans in New Zealand any more than it did in Australia. But we have been preserved from more active republican agitation. New Zealand should learn from the Australian experience and not let a matter of national identity become the cause of division. The referendum campaign was, as could be clearly seen from across the Tasman, a hard-fought battle. It is not an experience I would wish anyone to have to face. Of course, New Zealand can choose go its own way, whatever Australia ultimately decides. We have our own unique political system, especially the Treaty of Waitangi, and fortunately lack the more noticeable nationalist republicanism that has bred across the Tasman.

One of the more amusing comments by a republican was that New Zealand should show its independence by following Australia (and holding a referendum). Such a simplistic argument is typical of the shallowness of the current debate in New Zealand – and this argument was used by former Prime Minister Helen Clark. At the time of the Queen's Birthday a few years ago the Republican Movement of New Zealand issued a bizarre "declaration" that the first Monday of June each year will now be known as Republic Day. I am pleased to note that the republicans have graciously condescended to suspend their festivities until New Zealand actually becomes a republic, if that ever occurs.

The advent of a republic in Australia or Canada would make a New Zealand republic neither more nor less likely in the short term, as we are a distinct country and society founded on a compact between the Crown and the Maori people. Any move to a republic in New Zealand would require careful consideration of the future role of Maori in society and government. If the protracted process of settling land disputes is any precedent, such a debate would require many years of effort before any conclusion could be reached.

Status of the Monarchy in New Zealand Today

In New Zealand today it can probably be said that there is only a small republican movement – if indeed it can be dignified with the term "movement." Although it received a reasonable degree of media attention at times, the movement can be said, with much accuracy, to depend upon the exertions of one man. Indeed, the Republican Party itself disbanded several years ago, though it has since been revived as a tiny fringe party. The major parties do not advocate a republic – though many members of the minority Green Party do so ideologically, as do many individual members of the Labour Party, perhaps the majority. Yet it has not been perceived as a popular option to promote, so it has been allowed to languish. We can be sure, however, that republican sympathizers watched events in Australia closely ten years ago.

The New Zealand National Party, the major government party, officially holds that loyalty to the Queen is the first principle of the party (although the issue of republicanism was first placed on the political stage by a National Prime Minister – to the dismay of his colleagues). Attempts recently to discuss the possibility of a referendum on the monarchy at some indeterminate time in the future were met with strong opposition from within the party.

More insidious is the idea that a republic is inevitable, that New Zealand will one day become a republic. Even some supporters of the monarchy seem blighted by this particular disease. The present prime minister, John Key, who is from the National Party, is a pragmatist. But he has been quoted on a number of occasions as saying that a republic is "inevitable." He has not proposed active steps to promote a republic because that would be contrary to National Party policy, and because he is conscious of the difficulties in the way of the republican option, including popular support for the monarchy, and the complication of the Treaty of Waitangi. Peter Dunne, Leader of the United Future Party and a junior government minister, challenged the prime minister to follow the Australian government's example and make a referendum a matter of priority (*New Zealand Herald*, 27 April 2009).

Although some commentators have spoken of the republican debate in New Zealand, there is not really a debate yet. The great majority of people either support the monarchy in a general sort of way, or they cannot be bothered to think about an alternative. The republicans see this, and rely on the inevitability argument (with a careful use of criticism of members of the royal family and a general effort to ignore the role of the Crown in New Zealand).

In early 2010 a private member's bill was introduced into the New Zealand Parliament by Green MP Keith Locke. Locke, like most republicans, was primarily interested in destroying what currently exists. He proposed no alternatives. Instead, he asked that the voters trust him to come up with a replacement that is just as good as the system we have now. He was asking people to give him the keys to their democracy. We should be wary of writing Locke and people of his ilk a blank cheque. The bill itself was also poorly drafted and the procedure it proposed ill-conceived. Fortunately common sense prevailed and the bill failed at its first reading.

The biggest threat to the monarchy in New Zealand is indeed its own success. A system which has worked successfully for two hundred years is one which is easily taken for granted. The level of ignorance of our constitutional system is appalling. Though the situation is somewhat different in Australia, I applaud any initiative which seeks to increase public awareness and understanding of our constitutional structures.

CONCLUSION

The majority of New Zealanders want the country to remain a monarchy. It is doubtful whether many of those who support a republic will approve of the Republican Movement's latest proposal. Indeed, their suggestion is so eccentric that it is quite comical. But the relatively lightweight nature of organized republicanism should not be allowed to mask a more dangerous and insidious threat. Their press release repeated the inaccurate claim that 40 percent of New Zealanders favour a republic. Such distortions are dangerous because of the support they give to the "inevitability" argument. It is no argument at all to say that it is inevitable that New Zealand will become a republic. The majority do not wish this to occur, although it may be that many believe New Zealand will eventually become a republic.

A clear majority, approximately two-thirds, support the status quo. The rest are divided between supporters of change, and the undecided. With such odds the monarchy should not be seen as beleaguered. But the onus is on us, as avowed advocates (or apologists) for the monarchy, to remind people of this. There is a regrettable complacency at large, and an even more dangerous perception (particularly amongst the news media) that the end of the monarchy is inevitable. That is far from being a foregone conclusion.

REFERENCES

Cox, N. 2008. *A Constitutional History of the New Zealand Monarchy*. Saarbrücken: VDM.
Lange, D. 1998. Interview with the Rt Hon David Lange, 20 May.
Ladley, A. 1997. "The Head of State: The Crown, the Queen and the Governor-General." In *New Zealand Politics in Transition*, ed. R. Miller. Auckland: Oxford University Press.
Tizard, C. 1993. *Crown and Anchor: The Present Role of the Governor-General in New Zealand*. Wellington: Government Printer.
— 1997. *The Role of the Governor-General of New Zealand*. Wellington: Government House.

CURRENT
ISSUES

13

Reflections on the "Canadianization" of the Crown: A Modest Proposal

Jacques Monet

Ce chapitre évoque les initiatives adoptées depuis 1952 en vue d'étendre l'exercice des prérogatives royales de sa Majesté au Canada. Au nombre de ces initiatives, citons la création d'un système canadien de décorations et de titres honorifiques, le transfert au gouverneur général du devoir de signer les lettres de créances des représentants canadiens à l'étranger, ou encore l'« inscription » de la Couronne dans la nouvelle Constitution.

Toutes témoignent de la nécessité de renforcer la charge de gouverneur général en ayant plus visiblement recours à notre Souveraine, non seulement en ce qui a trait aux nominations mais aussi en favorisant des consultations régulières entre les 11 premiers ministres du pays et les 11 représentants de la Couronne.

L'auteur propose un rituel qui présiderait à la nomination des gouverneurs généraux et préconise de multiplier les courtes « visites de travail » de sa Majesté au Canada pour mieux faire voir et comprendre comment s'exercent ses prérogatives royales.

On the evening of her coronation day in 1953, the Queen spoke to us by radio. She was the first of our thirty-two Sovereigns to be explicitly styled Queen of Canada. The morning's glorious ceremony, she said, was "not the symbol of a power and a splendour that are gone, but a declaration of our hopes for the future." Twenty years later, in Toronto, in June 1973, she added: "The Crown is an idea more than a person, and I would like it to represent all that is best and most admired in the Canadian ideal … I hope you will all continue to give me your help in this task." Now, after a generation, and coming within days of Her Majesty's twenty-second visit to Canada as well as of the appointment of a new governor general, those organizing the conference on the Crown held in Ottawa June 9–10, 2010 happily decided to consider and ponder the present reality and future options for the more or less unconscious, unplanned, and as yet unfinished process which has come to be known as the Canadianization of the Crown.

A few weeks after the Queen's accession, Vincent Massey was installed as governor general, the first Canadian in modern times to be so appointed (the real "first" was Pierre de Vaudreuil in 1755). Since then, in strict alternation between French- and English-speaking men and women, ten more have followed, each one from a different cultural background and walk of life; each one illustrating one or other of the many ways of being Canadian. Fifty odd years later, it is obvious that the cumulative effect of their witness, in addition to the Queen's, has given entirely new meanings to the Canadian Crown.

Many and varied initiatives have contributed to this, the most obvious, perhaps, being the creation of an entirely new system of honours, insistently encouraged by Vincent Massey, initiated by General Vanier and then, after approval by Her Majesty, put in place by Roland Michener in the centennial year, 1967. The deliberate placing of the Chancellery in Rideau Hall and under the exclusive authority of the governor general gave assurance that the new honours secretariat would remain absolutely impartial, one of the very few, if not the only one, in the world to be entirely free of partisan patronage and influence. Our "fountain of honour" thus acquired a new radiance and respect, and is a unique feature of a distinctly Canadian identity. This happened as well in 1988 when the Queen authorized Madame Sauvé to create an original and entirely Canadian Heraldic Authority.

Many such "Canadianizing" initiatives followed, most notable among them being the transfer to the governor general in 1977 of the duty to sign the letters of credence of Canadian representatives abroad. Another was the beginning, a year later, of the careful process of finding an amending formula to the Canadian constitution, together with a unique Charter of Rights and Freedoms for Canadians. Her Majesty took an encouraging and keen interest in the latter two, and in conversations with Governors General Léger and Schreyer as well as with Prime Minister Trudeau she helped with many suggestions to accelerate and patriate the new Canadian constitution ... in which Canadians had quite explicitly entrenched the "compound" Canadian Crown.

During the sessions of the June 2010 conference, several speakers used David Smith's term "compound" to describe the unique character of the Canadian Crown. As Michael Jackson underlined, the term expresses how the Crown encompasses and transcends both federal and provincial jurisdictions; how it reconciles unity and diversity.

Adapting the Crown in 1867 to our unique federal constitution was for the authors of Confederation a bold and daring innovation. The Crown was already bathed in evocative history, religious and cultural symbolism, as well as universal human values. The "Fathers" made it remind us as well that Canadian culture, history, identity and tradition are much too rich, that Canadian society is much too complex and diverse to be represented by a single person. Our Crown would be represented by a team of twelve: the Sovereign, the governor general and the ten lieutenant-governors. One and indivisible, our Crown is mysteriously "compound" as its powers and prerogatives are exercised by different people placed over different jurisdictions.

Each depends on the other. If they were not associated with the mysterious magic and mystique surrounding royalty and, currently, with the public's unbounded and universal admiration and respect for the Queen herself, the offices of the lieutenant governors, for instance, would enjoy no more prestige than that of a colonial relic. The governors general would be no more than honourable pensioners enjoying political rewards, and their high office held to be a matter of necessity, that is, fulfilling the need for an umpire during rare times of political strife. On the other hand, the Sovereign cannot properly discharge her duties as Queen of Canada without the help and support of the governor general and the lieutenant governors. Together, as a corporate personality, the twelve by their presence and work are continually giving to the "compound" Crown new and uniquely Canadian meanings and relevance.

Understandably, the "Canadianization" of the British Crown has led to serious concerns about the transfer to the governor general of so many of the Queen's prerogatives. Some observers, with small, more or less convincing, evidence, are convinced that covert republicans in the government, or even at Rideau Hall itself, are preparing to set up the governor general as head of state. The concern is groundless, in my view. On the other hand, it is harmful, since criticism of any member of the "compound" body hurts every other. It does not add to the Sovereign's indispensable role, for instance, to belittle or impugn her chosen personal representative, nor does it help the lieutenant governors to denounce the Sovereign as a foreigner.

I was impressed conversely by the serious and well-founded conclusion reached by knowledgeable observers as well as many colleagues at the 2010 conference that the governor general's office has been seriously weakened by the steady growth in power of the prime minister's. And this despite the transfer to the governor general of the exercise of so many of the Sovereign's prerogatives. It is a very legitimate point. And much more reflection should be devoted to it. Meanwhile, as elements of such reflection, may I ask a few questions, offer a few suggestions, and make a "modest proposal"? In this way I hope to enhance the Canadian public's awareness and understanding of the monarchy's role in our distinctive parliamentary democracy. It is important that the Sovereign be seen to be exercising her Canadian royal prerogatives in Canada, and likewise the governor general and the lieutenant governors.

Why can't the Sovereign, for instance, be invited regularly to open the first session of every Parliament?

As for the governor general, whose role has been to exercise the royal "right to be consulted, the right to encourage and the right to warn," let us focus on three "moments" in the relationship between the governor general and the prime minister. These are the manner of the governor general's appointment; the decision on the length of the governor general's tenure; and the formal "visits" for conversation between the governor general and the prime minister.

About the appointment, a bit of history. The appointment is made by the Queen on the advice of the prime minister. It used to be by the Queen, then by the King, advised by the prime minister of Great Britain, himself prompted by the colonial secretary. Later, beginning with the appointment of Lord Byng in 1921, the British prime minister tendered his advice to the Sovereign after consultation with the Canadian. A decade later, in 1931, when Lord Bessborough was appointed, the prime minister of Canada advised the King after consultation with the British prime minister. Finally, and ever since 1952, when Prime Minister St. Laurent advised the appointment of Vincent Massey, the prime ministers of Canada have tendered their advice confidentially to the Sovereign without any consistent process of consultation. In 1978, for instance, Prime Minister Trudeau recommended the appointment of Mr. Schreyer to the Queen after hearing of his name being mentioned in a discussion by a small group of people who had met by coincidence on a flight to Ottawa one afternoon, and who happened to be the secretary to the governor general, a senior cabinet minister from Western Canada, the lieutenant-governor of an Atlantic province, the premier of a Prairie province and a French-Canadian university professor of constitutional history. Not a bad committee, had it been one, but not a precedent ever followed again. In 2010 Prime Minister Harper did create what I hope will set a precedent. He formally called together an "advisory committee of experts" to consult widely and produce a short list of candidates. This was a very happy procedure, welcomed by all serious commentators. But it has to be only a first step. Who will choose the committee, next time? Will it be non-partisan? Will the prime minister agree to the recommended list?

True, in their recommendations Prime Ministers Diefenbaker, Pearson, Trudeau, Mulroney, Chrétien and Martin chose felicitously and wisely. As a result, highly deserving men and women of dedication and integrity were chosen. Their previous accomplishments ensured they could – and did – worthily hold the highest and most excellent office in the land. Still, a choice made by a single partisan person is ever at risk of being misunderstood and becoming a serious mistake. (In fact, some previous appointments have been very unfairly described as made "on a whim," or as a political "reward," or again as "payback" to a partisan crony. Similar vocabulary has also been used about the appointments of lieutenant-governors, the fear there being of appointments that would be unworthy of the office.) Prime Minister Harper's precedent-setting initiative in 2010 is obviously a notable contribution. However, it still needs to stand the test of time.

Some have suggested that the governor general be elected by an oligarchy such as the Companions of the Order of Canada – a development, in my view, which would essentially – and harmfully – change the nature of the Order, if not of our whole distinctive (and distinguished) honours system. Others prefer election by a joint session of the Senate and House of Commons, or again by the Council of the Federation.

These changes would practically guarantee its becoming a partisan office. What then of its role to be the unbiased umpire between competing parties, policies and politicians? Besides, every democratic election is divisive. It produces winners and losers – not a good way to choose someone of unassailable public stature whose responsibility it is to create community and consensus. The fact remains that, despite the high credibility and higher visibility, the office of governor general happily acquired during the tenure of Madame Clarkson and of her successor Madame Michaëlle Jean, the office of governor general still needs strengthening, and this especially in its relationship with the Sovereign and with the office of the prime minister.

Both the Sovereign and the prime minister are permanently and inevitably the focus of daily attention in the media. The Queen has been in this situation for well over half a century. The prime minister, at least since John Diefenbaker's days, has been a daily headliner, and more so since the televised Question Period. The governor general, whose public activities are generally not, or very little, covered by the media, is crushed, so to speak, between these two very powerful figures. I believe, however, that the office can be strengthened, and this by more visibly involving the Sovereign and the prime minister in the appointment of the governor general.

My modest proposal is a ritual that uses the constitutional mechanisms and principles already in place. The appointment must clearly continue to be made by the Sovereign on the advice of the prime minister. Any change would require a constitutional amendment. Secondly, it is important that the prime minister (who will be, after all, recommending someone who will have the power to dismiss him and/or refuse his advice) be known to have sought impartial and independent opinions, and then to have exchanged them with the Queen herself. Otherwise the suspicion cannot be lifted of partisan partiality. Third, the appointment should be surrounded with as much respect, evocative symbolism and publicity as the office deserves, which is the highest. The governor generalcy is, after all, the only institution in Canada that has represented Canada uninterruptedly since the beginnings of European settlement here. It has witnessed and had been involved in every moment of our history. It is similar to very few, if any, others in the world. It is one of which we are all, quietly, proud. It is what makes the Crown specifically Canadian.

My proposal respects these conditions and, with the addition of important Canadian references, borrows from the ritual followed in the choice of the only "elected" sovereign left in the world.

It goes like this: at the appropriate time the members of the privy council under the age of eighty – except for an acting prime minister and a substitute – would be summoned by the governor general to a meeting in the East Block, where the original privy council chamber was, and which has been restored to what it was in 1873, with the original offices of Lord Dufferin, Sir John Macdonald and Sir George Cartier. It would be temporarily re-equipped for overnight stays. After being reminded by the president of the privy council of their solemn oath of confidentiality, the councillors would be locked in until after they had prepared a short list of names for the prime minister to discuss with the Queen.

The "lock up" of the East Block is to ensure the confidentiality, the integrity – the mystery – of the election. May I say that it does not add to the stature of an elected head of state that he or she be known to have been chosen on the twenty-third ballot, or to have won the election by two votes after a back-room deal, or again to have been the only person whom the leaders of rival political parties found to be the lesser evil among the competing nominees – all of which examples (and many other such) have actually happened during the Third Republic in France and in other "modern" parliamentary republics. Our privy council is composed mainly of partisan politicians: but since they have been chosen over the years from several partisan parties, and since they are joined in the council by many independent non-partisan appointees, as a whole the council does make for a balanced non-partisan impartiality.

The lock up continues after the short list has been agreed upon. The president of the council, however, communicates in secret with the nominees to ascertain their availability, my assumption being that most would probably not be privy councillors. Simultaneously, the prime minister advises the Queen, who has already taken up residence at Rideau Hall, to come to the East Block to grant him an audience. After her decision, while the governor general-designate is secreted into the lock-up and also granted an audience by the Queen, her standard, previously raised on the East Block as a signal to the outside that an announcement may soon be made, is raised on the Peace Tower to announce that the Sovereign has accepted the prime minister's advice.

Afterwards, the governor general and the participating privy councillors, then the designate, accompanied by the prime minister, then the Queen, proceed to the Hall of Honour, where dignitaries and invited guests await. The prime minister makes the announcement, the Sovereign invests the designate as a Companion of the Order of Canada, and the Sovereign's Canadian secretary reads the proclamation indicating the day, time, and place when the new governor general will be officially installed.

Instead of the East and Central Blocks, the Citadels in Halifax and Quebec could be used on occasion, recalling that two members of the Royal Family, Lord Lorne in 1874 and the Duke of Connaught in 1911, were installed at Halifax and Quebec respectively.

Need I enumerate the advantages of that kind of a ritual? As an event lasting a few days with growing speculation in the media and with popular anticipation (watching for the white smoke!), it will heighten awareness of the governor generalcy and provide from the start a more dramatic profile of the new incumbent. Also it will not only bring the Sovereign to Canada more often and on a regular, predictable, basis but draw attention to the exercise of the royal prerogatives in Canada. (How often has this happened before? The King's "Royal Assent" in 1939; two openings of Parliament in fifty-eight years; the proclamation of the patriated Constitution in 1982.)

The Sovereign could be brought in for lieutenant governors as well and thus happily provide repeated affirmation in person of our own Canadian "compound" Crown. The ritual would have to be adapted, for example, with an *ad hoc* advisory "electoral college" composed, let's say, of members of the provincial cabinet and, perhaps, former lieutenant-governors, chief justices and premiers as well as the prime minister of Canada, who is responsible for "advising" the governor general. The Sovereign might come for the installation and deliver an address.

Despite ever-improving conditions for frequent travel, these short "working" visits may become a burden for an aging Sovereign. If so, the Prince of Wales or Prince William (no less) should be delegated to take her place.

A second, less modest proposal which, I submit, would help to enhance the governor general's office, is that of arranging for a longer term. Contrary to a general perception, there is no fixed term: the governor general is appointed at the Sovereign's pleasure. Since 1940 and until 1974 each one (Lord Athlone, Lord Alexander, Vincent Massey, General Vanier, and Roland Michener) held office for well over six years, Vincent Massey being the longest at seven years and seven months, while General Vanier, who died in office after seven years and six months, had been asked to stay on indefinitely. Since the end of M. Léger's tenure in 1979, however, not one of his six successors has held office for more than five years and a few months. In my view this is much too short. For the incumbent it may be too little time to acquire solid experience in ways to exercise his constitutional duty to be consulted, to encourage, and to warn. Nor is it long enough for the public truly to appreciate the manner in which the governor general is actually helping to keep the "peace, order, and good government" of the country. I suggest the term should at least cover more than the length of one parliament or that of the mandates given to such high and trusted non-partisan officers of parliament and the state, such as the auditor general, or the commissioner of official languages, or the privacy commissioner, or again the chief electoral officer. Much of their credible impartiality with the Canadian public depends on the length of their experience in office.

The Constitution states that lieutenant governors may not be removed from office within five years of their appointment. A rapid check of the lists of lieutenant governors appointed since Confederation indicates that many have very successfully remained in office for as long as ten, thirteen or even fifteen years.

A third suggestion concerning the stature of the governor generalcy is that of its relationship with the office of the prime minister, not to mention the personal relations between the two incumbents. Since Confederation and until 1943, when Lord Athlone gave up his office in the East Block to make room for the wartime expansion of the Department of External Affairs, the governor general and the prime minister were in daily personal contact, their working offices being contiguous on the second floor of the East Block. Afterwards, they grew apart, Mr. Diefenbaker, for instance, meeting Vincent Massey almost exclusively at official public ceremonies or special social events.

A study of Lord Alexander's and Vincent Massey's daily agendas since 1950 reveals that Mr. St. Laurent's and Mr. Diefenbaker's visits to the governor general never reached more than five a year, including the necessary ones to advise a dissolution of parliament in 1953 and 1957. For 1960 there is no evidence of even a single visit. But after March 1963, the number of visits from Mr. Pearson to General Vanier reached a dozen for that year and climbed to an average of eighteen to twenty a year through the Michener and Léger years into the early 1980s. Since then, I am told, the practice has been much less regularly observed. (Even less respected, I am also told, is the like duty between lieutenant-governors and premiers.)

Although the content of these conversations is naturally highly confidential, the fact of their taking place, were it public, would do much, I think, to draw positive attention both to the governor general's exercise of the not-so-well-known right "to be consulted, to encourage, and to warn" as well as to the prime minister's appreciation of how much the governor general can, in fact, be a great help to him. It cannot be other than to his advantage that in preparing government measures for the good of Canadians he is known to have been the beneficiary of the Crown's impartial and disinterested advice.

Is all this the impossible dream of a frustrated choreographer? (or liturgist?) What my suggestions would do, I submit, is help all the partners involved in our compound Crown. If they were followed, the prime minister would be spared any possible accusation of partisan favouritism. The governor general and the lieutenant governors would be much more clearly and closely associated with the Sovereign, who will be seen to be playing, here in Canada, her essential role in the government or our country … most certainly in the process of choosing which Canadian will occupy the highest office in the land.

Royal tours are wonderful. They give the Sovereign and all Canadians magic moments to know and greet each other, and in every part of the country. Such tours should continue. What we need to add now are regular, short, working visits ("prerogative" visits?) of the Sovereign.

My proposal and suggestions are about changes in practice. They require no constitutional or legal measures. They depend only on the political will of the incumbents.

The Sovereign's role, as she reminded us in Quebec in October 1964, is "to personify the democratic state and to guarantee the execution of the people's will." It is to give a human face to the power of law; to link us in an unbroken line of succession to practices and institutions that have stood the test of time; to ideals of dedication, fairness, personal freedom and service that find their source in King Edward I's Model Parliament at Westminster, in Saint Louis' judgments at Vincennes, and into our own times in Louis XIV's and Queen Victoria's treaties with Canada's Native peoples, who for their part had in this land and from time immemorial held to values not unlike our own.

On all of which points, I cannot resist closing with a quotation from my friend John Fraser. He is more eloquent than I can ever be on the contribution that a more frequent and visible presence of the Sovereign would make. At the Accession Day Service in St. James (Anglican) Cathedral in Toronto on February 6, 2000, he said:

> The fact remains that the mystery and magic behind our Constitution is all tied up in an hereditary monarchy. It is our past, which if denied, will confound our future; it is our dignity, which if cast carelessly aside, will make us crasser people; it is the protection of our rights, which if abandoned, could lead to demagogic manipulation. Most important of all, the Crown helps define our uniqueness and is evidence of a mature community that can carry its history forward with pride.

14

ROYAL ASSENT: A TIME FOR CLARITY

HUGH SEGAL

Est-il opportun de recourir aux juges de la Cour suprême du Canada pour donner la sanction royale quand le gouverneur général est indisponible ? Qu'arrive-t-il des lois sanctionnées par un juge qui sont par la suite contestées devant les tribunaux pour cause d'appel ou de renvoi direct ? Pourquoi le Parlement de la Grande-Bretagne, notre modèle fondateur, procède-t-il différemment ? Quelles leçons pouvons-nous tirer de la pratique de la sanction royale en usage au Royaume-Uni ?

In Canada, Royal Assent is defined as the final stage of the legislative process wherein a bill becomes law. Traditionally, the ceremony itself involves the governor general, as representative of the sovereign, seated in the Senate chamber, members of the House of Commons who are summoned to the chamber and the senators themselves. Thus legislative members of both houses of Parliament witness this final stage in the enactment of a law. In truth, the ceremony itself is often sparsely attended and, more often than not, Royal Assent is executed by a judge of the Supreme Court of Canada. In the provinces, a similar substitution of a senior judge for the lieutenant-governor often occurs. Now, as almost any piece of legislation could well be challenged before the high courts in Ottawa or the provinces, it strikes me that we are setting up a problematic context by enabling Royal Assent to be executed in this fashion. Royal Assent is not judicial assent. And judges, however often they are found to assume "administrative roles" *pro tem*, are not part of the Royal Assent purpose.

In the United Kingdom, the *Royal Assent Act of 1967* set out two possible scenarios for the granting of Royal Assent. The first was in the presence of three Lords Commissioners and both Houses of Parliament, as was the norm. However, the second option allowed for each House of Parliament to be notified by the Speaker of that House, while sitting separately, at a convenient time during a sitting, that Royal Assent had been granted. This information would be relayed by the Lords' Commissioner to each chamber. The *Royal Assent Act of 1967* was the result of two separate incidents in the British Parliament in the 1960s. Twice, Members of the House refused to leave their seats to attend Royal Assent as there was a heated debate ongoing within the House relating to bills on the Order Paper.

In Canada, attempts were made to streamline the Royal Assent process. Bill S-34 was introduced in October, 2001 by the then-Leader of the Government in the Senate, the Honourable Sharon Carstairs. The bill would have provided much the same alternative as was being used under the *Royal Assent Act of 1967* in the UK Parliament and was also very similar to the procedure used for many years in Australia. In Australia, after the Governor General has affixed his or her signature to a bill, a message is transmitted to the President of the Senate and the Speaker of the House, who then notify their respective chambers that assent has transpired. Bill S-34 was studied in some detail by the Standing Senate Committee on Rules, Procedures and Rights. It was then sent, with observations and a few amendments, to the House of Commons where it subsequently died on the Order Paper with the prorogation of the 37th Parliament.

The transition to a written process, enabled by legislation in 2004, is not at issue here. That was a modernization of the ceremonial practice which has benefited all concerned. However, in doing it the way we do in Canada by delegating the signing function to a senior judge, who is acting as the "administrator" of Canada in the absence of the governor general, do we really mean to imply that this individual is part of Parliament in the same way as the Crown, House and Senate, which constitute the three-headed essence of Parliament? And if the same judge is called upon to sit on a case that emanated from a bill he in fact assented to on behalf of the Crown, should he recuse himself from those hearings and deliberations? Some will argue that the role is only ceremonial, and at some level that is true. But surely there is ceremonial and ceremonial. Presenting medals to St. John Ambulance volunteers is one kind of ceremonial; assenting to a bill passed and debated by both the elected House and the appointed Upper Chamber is a very different level of ceremonial – a level at the very core of Canadian parliamentary democracy and the role of the Crown as the embodiment of all the institutions of state. It is *not* just another mundane scheduling issue.

The British tradition and convention with respect to Royal Assent emanates from a different source than convenient time and legislative schedule management. Until 1541, the King would attend the House of Lords to give consent to bills. However, the task ended up being assigned to a Royal Commission when Henry VIII did not wish to appear in person and give Royal Assent to the Bill of Attainder which called for the execution of his wife, Catherine Howard. As one of my colleagues in the Senate, Lowell Murray suggested, he did not wish blood-stained hands to be ink-stained as well. Going forward, Lords Commissioner became responsible for giving Royal Assent, although the monarch could appear in person to do so. However, it has been more than 156 years since the last monarch, Queen Victoria, attended in person in order to give Royal Assent. And now, it is not members of the new Supreme Court in the UK who sign but a Designated Commission established by Her Majesty for that same purpose.

The UK Supreme Court officially opened in October 2009 as a result of a bill passed in 2005. It has assumed the jurisdiction of the Appellate Committee of the House of Lords and the devolution jurisdiction of the Judicial Committee of the Privy Council. It is an independent institution, presided over by twelve independently appointed judges, known as Justices of the Supreme Court. And, just to be clear, we should take note of the following introduction to the Court on its official website: "The introduction of a Supreme Court for the United Kingdom provides greater clarity in our constitutional arrangements by further separating the judiciary from the legislature."

In the UK, any bills ready for Royal Assent are brought to the Chamber and to the Lords Commissioner. Former Law Lords are no longer eligible to sit in the House of Lords, they are now Supreme Court judges and, because of the Commission, are ineligible and would never be asked to provide Royal Assent. In fact, this conflict was mentioned prior to the passage of the 2005 Act creating the Supreme Court itself.

What this suggests is that here in Canada, we might be well advised to have Assent granted not by senior judges but by a designated commissioned series of officers specifically assigned for that purpose. They might be present or long-serving senators (perhaps the Dean of the Senate), the Speaker of the Senate or some other individual chosen for that purpose. In so doing we might well obviate, through simple procedure, any untoward appearance of conflict down the road.

This is not about replicating a British procedure. It is about assessing our own practices and ensuring that we do not allow convenience and the vagueness of the vice-regal and Senate schedules to dilute what Royal Assent is meant to achieve. In fact, a fresh look at the issue, in a way that dealt with this potential conflict, could also address matters that have been raised about aspects of this process in the past. Clarity, with respect to Royal Assent, is neither a failure nor a side issue. Royal Assent is at the centre of the practice of responsible government and the relationship between responsible government and the Crown. The procedure that is used to grant Royal Assent should be addressed in a way that reflects this central role.

A change on this front is a small matter but it is through small modernizations and adjustments that we can keep the Maple Crown a vibrant and continuing part of our constitutional and democratic infrastructure of civility here in Canada.

The Crown has appropriate formal aspects but is more than just a formality. It is at the intersection of democracy, responsible government, the role of the state and the trinity of Canada's parliament – House of Commons, Senate and Crown. It reflects how we embraced accountability and shaped Confederation. It is not an afterthought. It is part of who we are.

15

THE CROWN AND PRIME MINISTERIAL GOVERNMENT OR THE SLOW WITHERING OF THE MONARCHICAL INSTITUTION

SERGE JOYAL

Que ce soit à dessein ou par simple ignorance, une Couronne canadienne sans cesse dépréciée ne pourra que dépérir ou disparaître. Telle est la situation actuelle qu'expliquent tout à la fois l'évolution historique, l'indifférence des premiers ministres successifs et certaines décisions complaisantes des titulaires de la charge vice-royale. Ainsi s'est formée une institution hybride qui éloigne le monarque de l'exercice des pouvoirs traditionnellement dévolus à la Couronne. En amoindrissant le rôle constitutionnel du gouverneur général et en imposant des restrictions exercées par le premier ministre, nous avons peu à peu altéré les principes de notre monarchie constitutionnelle et suscité à leur égard une profonde incompréhension. D'où la confusion qui caractérise la perception de notre régime politique et de son évolution.

An institution like the Canadian Crown that is continually depreciated, either by design or through ignorance, will eventually atrophy. It will wither and die, as will an integral part of our constitution with it.

For more than forty years, all Canadian prime ministers have undermined the legitimacy and authority of the Crown in the eyes of both the public and the political class. The trend has followed an uninterrupted downward slope. The lack of majority government in recent years has only served to enhance the trend. The unprecedented use of the prerogative power of prorogation for purely partisan ends offers a dramatic confirmation.

The depreciation of the Crown is not entirely one-sided; it is not simply due to the actions of the prime minister's office (PMO). Initiatives taken by the office of the governor general itself have also weakened the constitutional status and symbolic value of the Crown. Ironically, even the general objective of "Canadianizing" the Crown, laudable in itself, seems to have had the unintended consequence of diminishing the Crown. The appointment of distinguished Canadians as governors general to enhance their role as functional heads of state on behalf of the Queen seems perversely to have decreased the substantive and symbolic value of the Crown. It is way past the time to ask where this development is leading: we know this all too well. But can anything be done to restore an appropriate and meaningful appreciation of the value of the Crown?

Public opinion about the monarchy has evolved in Canada in the last decade, and polls taken in 2009[1] and in May[2] and June[3] 2010 found that, although Canadians respect and admire HM Queen Elizabeth II, a majority of them have reservations about the future of the monarchy in Canada. However, an objective history of the monarchy in Canada remains to be written in either English or French; historians are keeping a respectful distance from the subject. In academia, with very few exceptions (Smith 1995), the topic tends to be avoided, as though it were simpler to leave prejudiced views of the monarchy unexamined rather than to strive for a fuller understanding of what is still one of Canada's defining constitutional features. So we are moving into territory that is not well mapped, where emotion and personal opinions can replace facts and sober reflection. It is almost as though Canada cannot fully mature so long as it is among the few monarchies[4] left in the two Americas.

Canada's Head of State Is Not Resident

The Sovereign, who embodies our state sovereignty, is non-resident. It was not until the tour of King George VI and Queen Elizabeth in 1939 that a reigning monarch came to visit this country, more than 400 years after Canada was claimed by Jacques Cartier in the name of King François Ier in 1534. In other words, Canada became a sovereign nation (after the

---

[1] According to an Ipsos Reid poll from October 2009, 53 percent of respondents nationally would like to sever the country's ties with the monarchy (*National Post* 30 October 2009).

[2] A Léger Marketing poll, conducted May 25–27, 2010, concluded that 39 percent of Canadians welcomed Queen Elizabeth II's visits, while 59 percent of online respondents have little or no interest in Her Majesty's trip (Raj 2010).

[3] In the June 2010 poll conducted by Ipsos Reid, "two in three Canadians agree the Royal family should not have any formal role in Canadian society." However, on a national level, "the Queen's approval rating is at 73 percent" (Minsky 2010); A Canadian Press Harris-Decima survey found that 48 percent of respondents consider the monarchy "a relic of our colonial past that has no place in Canada today" (Canadian Press 29 June 2010).

[4] Nine of the States and Federations in the Caribbean are also constitutional monarchies; in the European Union, Belgium, The Netherlands, Spain, Denmark, Sweden, Norway and Luxemburg are constitutional monarchies.

1931 *Statute of Westminster*) without a reigning sovereign having ever set foot on our soil. For centuries we have thus had a most unusual "arms-length" experience of the national link with the head of state. Since the Sovereign does not live here, we see him or her as remote and somewhat foreign, and often through the eyes of the international press. There are sometimes long intervals between royal visits: King George VI never came back to Canada. It was only with the current Queen that visits were made more regularly, although there have been intervals as long as five years between them (1997–2002, 2005–10). We should bear in mind, though, that by 2012, when the Queen will celebrate 60 years on the throne, she will have come to Canada officially 22 times during her reign, visiting us more often than any other Commonwealth country (Department of Canadian Heritage 2010).

Although her visits have been relatively frequent, the Queen has only very rarely exercised the powers and prerogatives that are hers by right under the Canadian Constitution of 1867. In 1957, she presided over the opening of the first session of the 23rd Parliament; in 1982, she signed the Royal Proclamation of the new *Constitution Act, 1867*. She has never given royal assent to any federal legislation,[5] and even as the Sovereign of the Order of Canada since 1967 she has never personally presented this honour to Canadian citizens, apart from Governor General Jules Léger after his term ended and succeeding governors general immediately before their appointment. Since 2005, ambassadors' credentials and letters of recall have been addressed directly to the governor general, not the Queen. The fact is, that since the Letters Patent of 1947, virtually all the executive and legislative powers vested in Her Majesty under our constitution and its unwritten conventions have been wholly assumed by the governor general.[6] The consequence has been to disenfranchise the Sovereign from the constitutional responsibilities invested in him or her, responsibilities which remain the foundation of our system.

Limited Impact of Royal Visits

Moreover, the symbolism of royal visits is of limited impact. When Her Majesty visits our country, she comes here at the express invitation of the Canadian government. She is also advised by the government on the substance of her public speeches. During her visits she is obliged to carry out activities and attend events that are not necessarily high points of our national life. During this past winter's Olympic Games in Vancouver, for

---

[5] George VI was the only monarch to do so, giving royal assent to nine federal bills on May 19, 1939, during his visit to Canada.

[6] In 1990, under section 26 of the *Constitution Act, 1867*, the Queen appointed eight senators to facilitate the adoption of the bills implementing the GST.

example, when patriotism and pride were at their height, our Sovereign was unable to share in the widespread excitement as someone who belongs to this country too, since she did not attend the event. In the United Kingdom, she can travel as she pleases among royal residences and she exercises all the attributes of her office.

A HYBRID SYSTEM

In Canada, the neutrality, stability and moral authority associated with the Crown take a very different form than they do in other constitutional monarchies. Ever since our first Canadian-born governor general, the Right Honourable Vincent Massey, was appointed in 1952, we have seen a slow slippage in public understanding of the monarch's constitutional role as opposed to the role of the governor general. Prior to his appointment, all previous governors general had been appointed from the British upper classes and aristocracy. Indeed, several were members of the Royal Family. All possessed an understanding and identity with the British Crown which were not shared to the same degree with the subsequent Canadian nominees to the position. In appointing Canadians, we have created a sort of hybrid system, where the actual Crown continues to reign on paper while its representative acts, performs, and exercises the office's powers and attributes.

This hybridization did not happen by accident. If a reigning sovereign does not exercise his or her constitutional roles or does not actually reign, over time the roles appear to become disassociated from his or her person, and the perception grows that these prerogatives and powers are no longer proper to the monarch but rather to the monarch's representative. Over the years, this perception has become a reality in some circles, and it led to the controversial statement in Paris on October 5, 2009 by Governor General Michaëlle Jean that the governor general is Canada's head of state (Jean 2009).

Some expert analysts of government institutions (Franks 2010; Franks 2010a) have responded by coming up with a curious line of reasoning that I will summarize simply, with apologies to them, in this way: since the term "head of state" is not to be found in the text of the Constitution, we are not depriving the Crown of anything by letting the governor general use the expression to describe her status! Of course, there was a hasty effort to retrieve the situation and speak instead of the governor general as the *de facto* head of state, but, as the political analysts say, perception is reality. In other words, to parody a legal dictum, the accessory does not follow, but becomes, its principal. This, however, is quite another debate. It is noteworthy that in his first speech as governor general-designate, David Johnston referred to "the Queen of Canada, who is our country's head of state" (Johnston 2010). In his declaration he recognized his proper role as representative of the Queen.

CURTAILING THE ROLE OF THE GOVERNOR GENERAL

Since the early 1970s, all our prime ministers, the Sovereign's principal advisers, have let their advisory responsibility dwindle into a sort of careless indifference to the governor general. We can recall instances of this in the recent past. Governors general have on several occasions found themselves in the unpleasant position of being prevented first from acting on, and then from countering, public criticism and satisfying public expectations because they were kept dangling by the prime minister and his government.

We all remember how Governor General Jeanne Sauvé waited in vain for a decision by Prime Minister Mulroney's government to reopen the grounds of Rideau Hall, which had been closed for security reasons. This left Madame Sauvé in the untenable position, on the one hand, of being unable to act and, on the other hand, being unable to place the responsibility for her inaction where it belonged. The Prime Minister waited until her successor arrived in 1990 to give the expected authorization. And there was the embarrassing fracas that arose over Governor General Adrienne Clarkson's trip to the circumpolar countries in September and October 2003, a trip instigated and approved by the government of the day, which delegated two cabinet ministers (Stéphane Dion and David Anderson) to accompany Madame Clarkson (Governor General's Office 2003). The trip had been planned for a long time and had the direct involvement of the Department of Foreign Affairs and International Trade and the Prime Minister's Office, since the governor general never travels officially outside the country without the prime minister's approval. However, when public criticism of the trip's cost erupted, neither the Prime Minister nor any of his ministers (least of all the ones who had gone along on the trip), came to the governor general's defence. Only the leader of the NDP, Jack Layton, said, "The Governor General is perhaps being unfairly targeted here ... she's just doing her job as requested by the government" (CTV.ca 2003). All Madame Clarkson could do was to dispatch her chief of staff to answer questions from Members of Parliament who are, as we know, often ready to join in when the media start attacking someone else's spending (Clarkson 2006, 192–93). Governors general are thus left to twist in the wind, able neither to enter into public conflict with the prime minister (and thus redirect public pressure) nor to answer questions about activities recommended and approved by the prime minister. They are condemned to stay mute and helpless in the face of public opinion, incapable of shifting responsibility for decisions back to where it belongs: the prime minister. The leader of the opposition should have defended her.

A Cavalier Treatment

The principal adviser to the governors general thus becomes their puppet-master, with the risk of drawing him or her closer to the field of partisan politics. Let us recall the recent episode of the prorogation of the first session of the 40th Parliament on December 4, 2008, when the prime minister and his staff had to demonstrate to the governor general that they were justified in wanting to prorogue Parliament so soon after an election. The experience apparently left a sour taste in the mouth of the principal adviser to the Queen's representative. When the prime minister decided only a year later to request prorogation of the second session of the same Parliament, on December 30, 2009, he did not do what convention and protocol require by paying a formal visit to the governor general, but casually picked up the phone! Can one imagine a British prime minister asking the Queen to prorogue or dissolve the House of Commons by ringing up Buckingham Palace? He would be roundly criticized for a serious breach of constitutional convention, if not an affront to the Crown. In this country, the media noted the cavalier way the prime minister behaved, but attributed it to so-called "cool" relations between him and the PMO, on the one hand, and the governor general on the other.

In Canada, the prime minister can treat Her Majesty's representative dismissively even when it comes to the exercise of her constitutional prerogatives. For some people, the exercise of these prerogatives merely represents an arcane set of political details. However, in fact the exercise sets a precedent that can have real consequences. The prime minister's dismissiveness can politicize the office of the governor general. The impression is that when a prime minister does not like a governor general, either because the person holding the office was not chosen by him or because he is not pleased with the way the person is carrying out the vice-regal duties, or because the public is criticizing the person's initiatives, he or she can simply let negative perceptions in the media go unchallenged, or more simply turn his or her back on the governor general. The respect and esteem of the Sovereign's representative held by the general public are tarnished by such behaviour. If the prime minister can treat the highest office in the land as an insignificant inconvenience, we can hardly hope that the man in the street will retain any greater respect for it than that.

Disregard of the Constitutional Role of the Governor General

There is more. Our prime ministers have disregarded the constitutional role of the Sovereign's representatives which, according to convention, is "to be consulted, to encourage and to warn" (Jackson 2009). If they can show their displeasure over the way Her Majesty's representative carries out vice-regal duties by not coming to his or her defence and by dragging their feet in situations that are problematic for him or her, they can also decide to stop visiting Government House to hear the governor general's opinions and advice. It is an ancient practice rooted in the prerogatives of the British sovereign. Anyone who saw the 2006 film *The Queen*, directed by Stephen Frears, will remember the scene where Her Majesty receives the red dispatch boxes sent her every week by the prime minister. They contain summaries of cabinet minutes, documents she reads attentively so that during the prime minister's regular visits she can discuss them with him and offer him appropriate advice, the fruit of her long experience and the professionalism that keeps her rigorously outside of partisan politics. In her memoirs, Adrienne Clarkson recalls how Prime Minister Chrétien told her about the cabinet's decision not to send troops to Iraq before announcing it in Parliament, and she encouraged his decision (Clarkson 2006, 200).

Former Senator Eugene Forsey, a constitutional expert, made very clear the position of Her Majesty's representative:

> He [the governor general or the lieutenant-governor of a province] must be kept informed [by the prime minister or the provincial premier]. He can suggest alternatives [to the prime minister or the premier]. He can remonstrate against what he considers glaringly unsuitable appointments or foolish or dangerous policies (Clarkson 2006, 54).

Now, however, our prime ministers have extended their power so far that they exercise prerogatives held until quite recently by Her Majesty's representative. Precedent after precedent has been set from one prime minister down to the next: from P.E. Trudeau and Brian Mulroney through Jean Chrétien and Paul Martin to Stephen Harper, each has sought to make Her Majesty's representative subject to their control and discretion. Again, the Right Honourable Adrienne Clarkson saw this process first-hand. She wrote:

> During my term I observed power being centralized, not to the government or the Cabinet but increasingly to the Prime Minister's Office – a group of people who are supposed to be helping the Prime Minister put forward his political policies but who are, in fact, unelected people with a huge amount of power over everything ... (Clarkson 2006, 204).

It is no secret to anyone that Prime Minister Harper did not regularly visit Governor General Michaëlle Jean for consultation, to discuss his government's decisions, or to receive her advice on the implications of his decisions for national policy. This aspect of the office's prerogatives had no relevance for him, and public opinion was aware of it. If it were otherwise, he would have made that clear publicly.

LIMITED TERM OF OFFICE

Successive prime ministers have found it convenient to limit the term of office of the governor general from seven years to five, beginning with Jules Léger, whose illness ended his term after five years in January 1979. This term can be extended by an additional year or two if the prime minister wishes, as happened in the cases of Jeanne Sauvé and Adrienne Clarkson. Such a trend also has consequences. It contrasts with Vincent Massey, Georges Vanier and Roland Michener, who were in office for at least seven years each. Even the majority of public office holders who are considered "Officers of Parliament" are given terms of at least seven years. This is true of the Senate's Ethics Officer and the House of Commons' Ethics Commissioner, the Commissioner of Official Languages, the Information Commissioner and the Privacy Commissioner, while the Auditor General and the President of the Public Service Commission enjoy a ten-year term.

In fact, when a prime minister does not seem to respect the person who occupies the position, or intends to replace that person with someone of his own choice who shares his convictions, he keeps to the strict five-year limit. The media quoted a "well-informed source" in the PMO as saying that this would be the case with Madame Jean (MacCharles 2010). In fact, her successor was announced almost three months ahead of the end of her term on September 27, 2010,[7] even though she had the approval of a sizeable majority of Canadians – 58 percent at least according to opinion polls released in April and May (Angus Reid Poll 2010; Canadian Press 16 May 2010). It has been many years since any federal politician had a 58 percent approval rating! It is this level of support that prompted the leader of the official opposition on May 2, 2010 to advocate publicly for the extension of the mandate of the current governor general following a private consultation by the prime minister on the potential candidates for appointment to the office (Chase 2010; Presse Canadienne 2010). In doing so, the opposition leader gave rise to a public debate on the selection of the governor general, bringing back the argument that such a decision should be the object of public consultation (Lype 2010; Toronto Star Editorial 2010). His comments had the effect of opening the debate (Bliss 2010) on the selection process.

The issue is not totally new.[8] The previous governor general raised similar ideas in her memoirs (Clarkson 2006, 194–96) without, however,

---

[7] Prime Minister Paul Martin announced that Madame Jean would succeed Adrienne Clarkson as governor general on August 4, 2005, a month and a half before her installation on September 27, 2005.

[8] Bill C-60, introduced at first reading on June 20, 1978, contained provisions from articles 42 to 48 establishing a process for the selection of the governor general, his term in office, his status and the performance of his mandate. It was the first time in the legislative history

properly evaluating the constitutional and political impact that such a change would certainly have on the institution of the Crown. To pretend that there would be none is to ignore the essential neutral nature of the Sovereign and its inherent prerogatives. There is no doubt that if the person to be appointed were chosen by a vote, of whatever kind, an important prerogative of the Crown would be lost. The status of the governor general would slip irretrievably into a republican presidential model; his selection would no longer be a matter of the exercise of the prerogative but rather the result of a vote (Russell 2010). Prime Minister Harper decided to entrust a committee of six persons to get a recommendation on an appropriate candidate. However, the criteria remained elusive (Curry 2010).[9]

In other words, with the term whittled away to less than five years, the prestige of the office of the governor general has been watered down and placed at the mercy of successive changes of government. Obviously, this could never happen in Great Britain. The British prime minister can neither limit the length of the Sovereign's reign nor deny him or her "the right to be consulted, the right to advise and the right to warn" (Forsey 1977, 51–54). The perception created by all this is that the prime minister has the right to decide the length of a governor general's term as he sees fit and for reasons he need not specify, resulting in the diminished credibility of the holder of the office. By cutting back the length of the governor general's term, we have opened the door to still further prime ministerial domination of the appointment's duration and stability. These principles, inherent in the Crown, have been turned on their head: it is now the Crown that is ephemeral and the prime minister who incarnates continuity!

THE BACKGROUND OF AN INCUMBENT IN THE POSITION OF GOVERNOR GENERAL

Another important element pertains to the professional background of an incumbent. The domination of the prime minister of the process for the appointment of the governor general brings it ever more into the partisan political orbit, particularly when the appointees are former politicians or

---

of the country that an attempt was made to codify the function of the representative of the Crown. The bill died after the ruling of the Supreme Court in 1980 on the *ultra vires* nature of its provisions dealing with Senate reform.

[9] Curry writes: "The committee was chaired by Sheila-Marie Cook, who has worked as the secretary and deputy to the governor general since September, 2006. The committee members included University of Calgary political science professor Rainer Knopff; the Senate's Usher of the Black Rod, Kevin MacLeod; McGill University political science professor Christopher Manfredi; Christopher McCreery, private secretary to the Lieutenant-Governor of Nova Scotia; and historian Jacques Monet."

are seen to be ideologically close to the government of the day (Travers 2010; Maher 2010). When the person has had a previous career in public affairs, coupled with a tradition of public non-partisanship, the strength of the relationship with the prime minister takes a different form. However, if former politicians or persons linked to the government of the day are appointed, the office loses some of its inherent neutrality. This is not a small matter, especially considering that three recent prime ministers (Pierre Trudeau, Brian Mulroney and Jean Chrétien) appointed former cabinet colleagues (and in one case, a former premier) to the office. As Professor Peter H. Russell wrote, "Admittedly, much of [the] advantage of the monarchical system is lost in Canada when Prime Ministers recommend partisan colleagues to be appointed Governor General and represent [the Queen] here" (Russell 2009).

THE IMPORTANCE OF INDEPENDENT ADVICE

The governor general must necessarily be wholly independent and completely neutral (non-partisan). The office is designed to follow the example of the Sovereign. In carrying out her responsibilities and to ensure that she remains above the political fray, the Queen is aided by a team of experienced advisers of her choosing. They have the confidence of the Queen to guide her in fulfilling her constitutional duties and exercising her prerogative powers. Financial support in the provision of these advisers comes from the civil list voted on annually by the British parliament.

In Canada, where the governor general is appointed for a limited period of time and often comes into the office without experience or training in the understanding of the role of the Queen's representative, it is even more important that the appointee be supported by capable advisers of his or her own choosing who, like their British counterparts, are independent and without any association with the government of the day and the partisanship of Parliament Hill. Equally, it is essential that appropriate funds be available in the annual budget of the governor general to provide these services.

NO FINANCIAL INDEPENDENCE

Finally, the independence required by the function of the governor general is also framed by its underlying financial conditions. Contrary to Her Majesty, who is the owner of large estates and a vast art collection and moreover enjoys a fortune which ensures a certain level of independence (Ruddick 2010) over and above the Civil List voted on by Parliament, the designated holder of the office of governor general of Canada possesses nothing of the two official residences, title of property or their contents, and nobody expects that a share of the office holder's personal income will be used to maintain the office. The governor general depends entirely on public financial support, hence on Parliament, and on the initiative of the prime minister who decides, according to the given political circumstances and the sensitivity of public opinion, whether or not to commit additional expenditures to the office. On the financial side, then, the governor general is completely dependent in every way on the prime minister and on the will of Parliament. The monitoring of the use of public funds, accessible to the incumbent, is in the hands of the government of the day.

UNDER THE CONTROL OF THE PRIME MINISTER

Does the shrinking status of Her Majesty's representative, who is ever more subordinate to the prime minister and the PMO, serve the interests of the institution that is the cornerstone of our Constitution? Is the institution truly being served when it is made subject to the prime minister? Will Canadians respect the form of their government more if they decide, considering the relentless erosion of the position of governor general, that the institution is less credible than before, has been drawn into Ottawa politics and is no longer the locus of a nation united under the Crown? For some people, these changes may appear timely: anything that might discredit or belittle the institution is one more step toward an eventual regime change. For others, they imply an undermining of the system of government that may bring about a series of unintended consequences. Let us rephrase the question: is it in the nation's interest to strengthen the powers and grip of the prime minister, already so strong, on Parliament and the Crown? Is it in our interest to provide the prime minister with yet more opportunities to develop further what is already an enormous fund of power?

When Canadians were asked in a recent Nanos poll (Clark 2010) about the number one problem with the way their democratic system operates, a majority replied that the PMO had too much power! According to this poll, over a thousand Canadians, or 41.6 percent, thought that the PMO had too much power, while only 13.3 percent – the smallest proportion – thought the House of Commons did. Executive dominance (Smith 1995) is in fact the Achilles heel of Canadian democracy, and it is this tendency towards the hyperconcentration of power in the hands of a single person that should be re-assessed and "recalibrated." Centuries ago, the Parliament in England had as its fundamental aim to limit the royal discretion by forcing the King to accept the decisions of an elected House. Today we are seeing a reverse trend: powers either acquired by the elected House or retained by the Sovereign are being usurped and concentrated in the hands of the prime minister and his office (Savoie 1999).

QUESTIONABLE DECISIONS AT RIDEAU HALL

There are other practices that are distorting Canadians' perception of what the Queen's representative is and does. Some of these result from decisions made at Rideau Hall, some from government agencies, in particular the Bank of Canada and the Royal Canadian Mint.

Absence of Royal Assent

In 2002, following an initiative of the sitting leader of the official op-position in the Senate, Parliament adopted the *Royal Assent Act* which stipulates that the traditional ceremony of acknowledging bills adopted by the Senate and the House of Commons as Acts of Parliament, take place in the Senate at least twice a year and any other royal assent can be performed privately by written declaration at Rideau Hall. It just so happens that the governor general has regularly been absent from Ot-tawa for the public ceremony. According to their official commission, justices of the Supreme Court have at times been substituted for the governor general in the Royal Assent ceremony in the Senate chamber. It is odd that such justices (who are, in principle, in a separate branch of government) should act as the formal head of the legislative branch. At times, it might even put them in an apparent conflict of interest if an acknowledged bill were brought to the Supreme Court for a judgement or a ruling! By being replaced too often in the exercise of this constitu-tional function, the governor general leaves the impression that it is not an important use of his or her time. As well, it blurs the line of separa-tion between the judicial and legislative branches. The replacement of the governor general in the Royal Assent ceremony, as now provided, should be terminated, and a substitute, in the form adopted in Great Britain, should be used instead.[10]

The Symbolic Portrait of the Queen

In recent years, Rideau Hall's symbolic image as the residence of the Sovereign's representative has been diminished. One of the changes, which may appear inconsequential, was the repositioning of the Queen's portrait in the ballroom where official ceremonies take place. The gov-ernor general no longer officiates in front of the image of the Sovereign she represents. Everyone will have noticed that the swearing-in of cabinet and the presentation of national honours have for the past few years

---

[10] See Senator Hugh Segal's proposals in his chapter in this volume entitled "Royal As-sent: A Time for Clarity."

been done not in front of a portrait of Her Majesty, but in front of a large canvas by the Ojibwa painter Norval Morrisseau entitled *Androgyny*. The Queen's portrait by Jean-Paul Lemieux has been moved to another wall and is no longer visible to people watching the ceremonies on television. When the very places where the symbols and history of the Crown should dominate are instead removed and are absent from functions that are the Sovereign's prerogative, especially when that Sovereign is non-resident, the image that the ordinary citizen sees is completely voided of its symbolic significance. In any country, whatever the form of the system of government, residences occupied by the incumbents performing as head of state should reflect the country's history, recall its heroes, and above all embody its stability. It is the particular attribute of our constitutional Crown that guarantees the continuity and stability of our state.

We have been busy in recent years relegating concrete symbols of the Crown anywhere other than where they should be. The decision to shift the Sovereign's portrait from a central position in Rideau Hall to a secondary one, and to remove it entirely from the Citadel, obliterates the symbolic link that exists between the governor general and the Sovereign when the former is carrying out official responsibilities. This secularization, as we might call it, of the office has had very definite repercussions. One may recall that, in December 2003, Prime Minister Paul Martin urged Governor General Clarkson to hold the swearing-in of his new cabinet in the Parliament Buildings instead of at Rideau Hall. If this had happened, a fundamental aspect of the Crown, the seat of the monarchical principle, independent from the government of the day, would have been jeopardized; it would have been assimilated and integrated into partisan political life. The whole set-up would have been presidential. Governor General Clarkson, conscious of the purposes and symbolic aspects of her office, refused (Clarkson 2006, 195).

We even seem to leave it up to each successive occupant of Rideau Hall to rearrange as he or she sees fit the presentation and content of what are called the State Rooms, regardless of the consequences for their institutional image – the image that Canadians see. From one occupant to the next, the decoration changes depending on the incumbent's taste, knowledge or priorities. In 2009, there was the episode of the sale over the Internet of historic silver *objets d'art* that had been lent to Rideau Hall by Buckingham Palace: wedding presents to the then Duke of York (the future King George V) from senior members of the peerage. They were clearly identified, incidentally, by engraved inscriptions. Other heritage items were sold at the same time. We may justly ask who at Rideau Hall is responsible for conserving the elements of our historic heritage and what are the objectives of the policy for managing rooms reserved for official functions. As has already been indicated, the issue is not a trivial one.

Absence of the Title "Queen of Canada"

However, it is not only at Rideau Hall that we are failing to give the Sovereign the position and identity that her status demands. The identity of the Sovereign is even problematic on our own currency. On the 20 dollar bill, there is a portrait of the Queen, but neither her name and her title nor the insignia of royalty appear, while the portraits of Sir Wilfrid Laurier, Sir John A. Macdonald, William L. Mackenzie King and Sir Robert Borden on Canadian 5, 10, 50 and 100 dollar bills, respectively, are well identified with name and title written underneath. Compare this with a British pound. On it the Queen wears the royal diadem and next to her picture appears the cypher *Elizabeth II Queen.* However, the Canadian banknote does not bother to mention that the person depicted is Her Majesty Elizabeth II, Queen of Canada. Absent this name or title, the depiction could be regarded as a generic portrait of a lady who remains unidentified. In fact, the title of "Her Majesty, Queen of Canada" is nowhere to be found in public presentations or in reference to the Sovereign. The title "Queen of Canada" has not even been added to the oath of allegiance that MPs and senators have to swear under the *Constitution Act, 1867.* No wonder a majority of Canadians cannot make the distinction among the titles of Her Majesty when she is acting as Queen of Canada.

Misunderstanding of the Principle of Constitutional Monarchy

More unexpected were the public comments made to the French magazine *L'Express* by the husband of Governor General Michaëlle Jean, Jean-Daniel Lafond, in the closing months of her mandate: "Le Canada britannique est en train de s'effilocher, les liens avec la couronne sont symboliques," tranche-t-il. Lafond affirme avoir profité du mandat de son épouse "pour repousser les murs jusqu'à l'extrême" (Nadeau 2010).[11] These comments were published while the Queen was actually in Canada. What remained unexplained, however, was the reference to "British Canada." Nor is it clear what he meant when he spoke about "pushing the limits." One is led to raise the following question: who in the Privy Council Office was responsible for instructing the occupants of Rideau Hall on the nature of our system of government? More generally, who is responsible for briefing the new incumbent about the positions of governor general or lieutenant governor? Otherwise, persons who hold these offices temporarily may feel entitled to define the mandate for themselves.

---

[11] The first statement was reprinted in the *National Post* a few days later: "British Canada is fraying and the nation's ties to the Crown are purely symbolic" (Hamilton 2010).

A SLIPPERY SLOPE

Recognizing all of these facts is instructive and leads us to ask: what rational approach should we take to a constitutional monarchy? An official Senate document states: "The Crown occupies a central place in our Parliament and our democracy, founded on the rule of law and respect for rights and freedoms; the Crown embodies the continuity of the state and is the underlying principle of its institutional unity. The Crown is fused to all three branches of government" (Senate 2004, Introduction). If we refuse to maintain the principles that define our system of government, and continue thoughtlessly, incrementally, by a series of small repeated oversights, to undermine the very institution that is the cornerstone of our Constitution, we are by default allowing the most powerful player in the system – the prime minister – to tighten a personal and partisan stranglehold around the office of the governor general. The changes are often silent, even insidious. They seep into the system surreptitiously, without fanfare, but their effect is to undermine our system of government and dilute the principle of constitutional monarchy to the point where it will bear the name of one and nothing more, and its democratic character will be much weaker.

It is extremely short-sighted to think that what the Sovereign loses in the way of power and prestige directly benefits and strengthens the country's democratic character. The recent episodes of the prorogations, agreed to by the governor general, did not end in greater powers for the House of Commons or for MPs. They simply confirmed the dominance of the executive branch over the elected House.

How are we to stop the progressive weakening of the monarchical principle, taking into account that the "Crown is like a trust in which powers are kept for safekeeping?" (MacKinnon 1976, 73). If we eviscerate the Crown's powers and drain its relevance, without clearly formulating the alternative we would prefer, we will only accentuate the current deformations of our system of government and our democratic life will be enfeebled, without Canadians finding themselves any better governed. Every successful democratic political system is made up of checks and balances. No single one of its components should have all the powers to hold the others to ransom: "The power [of the Crown] lies in the unspoken, the unexercised [...] Our political system is very vulnerable, and tinkering with it out of ignorance or attempting to make radical changes in it for vainglorious reasons would require a whole rethinking of our structures, our Parliament, our judicial system" (Clarkson 2006, 187, 195). If Canadians ever decide that they want to modify the fundamental principles of their system, they should do so with their eyes open, after informed debate and full awareness of the stakes involved. They should not be tricked into endorsing radical change little by little.

In recent years, the only office, the power of which has increased in Canada, is that of the prime minister at the expense of Parliament and the Crown. Madame Clarkson writes:

> The Crown represents everything that is stable in our society, and as the representative of the Crown in Canada, the Governor General has an obligation to make sure that the respected institutions continue to be meaningful (Clarkson 2006, 196–97).

Should the House of Commons have a responsibility in monitoring the exercising of the prerogatives of the Crown? (Thomas 2010). How can it do so while respecting the integrity of those prerogatives? Or how can we protect the principle of responsible government which is at the heart of our democratic system, as Speaker Milliken stated in his 2009 decision on the parliamentary privilege of access to government documents (Milliken 2010)? Eugene Forsey wrote: "Only the Queen can stop irresponsible government" (Forsey 1966, 11). It is only by fully understanding the principles and the spirit that overarch and underlie our constitutional scaffolding – principles and a spirit that have so far enabled us to maintain a high standard of democratic life – that our country can reach higher still.

The idea of the "Canadianization" of the Crown, formulated in the middle of the preceding century, lay beneath an objective which was spontaneously endorsed by the majority of Canadians: to adapt the Crown into an institution which reflected the particular identity and nature of our country. In spite of the best of intentions, the unintended consequence of the Canadianization of the Crown has been to weaken one of the essential elements that act as a counterweight to the now excessive power of the prime minister. It has become urgent to include this element of reflection in the more global objective of strengthening the democratic nature of our parliamentary system.

REFERENCES

Scholarly Books and Articles

Clarkson, A. 2006. *Heart Matters*. Toronto: Viking Canada.

Forsey, E. 1977. "The Monarchy and the Canadian Constitution." In *The Silver Jubilee: Royal Visit to Canada*. Ottawa: Deneau and Greenberg.

— 1966. *Canada: Monarchy or Republic?* Ottawa: Library of Parliament.

Jackson, D.M. 2009. "The Crown in Saskatchewan: An Institution Renewed." In *Saskatchewan Politics: Crowding the Centre*, ed. H.A. Leeson. Regina: CPRC Press, University of Regina.

MacKinnon, F. 1976. *The Crown in Canada*. Calgary: Glenbow Alberta Institute.

Savoie, D.J. 1999. *Governing from the Centre: The Concentration of Power in Canadian Politics*. Toronto: University of Toronto Press.

Smith, D.E. 1995. *The Invisible Crown: The First Principle of Canadian Government.* Toronto: University of Toronto Press.

Newspaper and Magazine Articles

Bliss, M. 2010. "Selecting a Governor General." *The Globe and Mail.* 5 May, A17.

"Canadians apathetic about Prince Charles: poll." 2009. *CBC news.* 27 October. Accessed online at http://www.cbc.ca/canada/story/2009/10/26/prince-charles-poll.html

Canadian Press. 2010. "Poll shows Canadians bored with monarchy." *The Guardian* (Charlottetown). 29 June, A7.

Chase, S. 2010. "Ignatieff calls for Jean's term to be extended." *The Globe and Mail.* 3 May, A6.

Clark, C. 2010. "PMO Too powerful, Canadians say." *The Globe and Mail.* 25 March, A16.

CTV.ca News Staff. 2003. "Gov. Gen. Clarkson defends her spending." *CTV. ca Montreal.* 24 September. Accessed online at http://www.ctv.ca/servlet/ArticleNews/scfcn/CTVNews/20030924/clarkson_trip030919/CTV NewsAt11/

Curry, B. 2010. "Harper's quest for a new GG: Partisans need not apply." *The Globe and Mail.* 12 July, A4.

Franks, C.E.S. 2010. "Crown and Country: Keep Queen and choose another head of state." *The Globe and Mail.* 10 April, A21.

— 2010a. "Governor General stages tactful absence." *Ottawa Citizen.* 1 July, C3.

Hamilton, G. 2010. "Rideau Hall turncoat takes aim at separatism." *National Post.* 6 July, A1.

Johnston, D. 2010. "Text of David Johnston's speech." *National Post.* 9 July, A2.

"Lift veil on GG selection." 2010. *Toronto Star.* 5 May, A18.

Lype, M. 2010. "Reconsider replacing Jean as G-G: Ignatieff." *National Post.* 3 May, A4.

MacCharles, T. 2010. "Jean coy about her future after vice-regal post ends." *Toronto Star.* 16 April, A12.

Maher, S. 2010. "Airbus worked out well for PM, thanks to Johnston." *The Chronicle Herald.* 10 July, B1.

"Michaëlle Jean conserve la faveur populaire." 2010. *Canadian Press.* 16 May, 23.

"Michaëlle Jean devrait rester en poste, estime Ignatieff." 2010. *Presse Canadienne.* 3 May, A6.

Minsky, A. 2010. "We love the Queen, but want ties to monarchy cut, poll finds." *Ottawa Citizen.* 16 June, C10.

Nadeau, J.-F. 2010. "Jean-Daniel Lafond en entrevue à L'Express - Le séparatisme est mort, la monarchie dépassée." *Le Devoir.* 3 July, A3.

Raj, A. 2010. "One in five Canadians think the Queen should stay home: poll." *Ottawa Sun.* 1 June. Accessed online at http://www.ottawasun.com/news/canada/2010/05/31/14206021.html

Ruddick, G. 2010. "Queen set to sell part of prized Regent Street." *The Daily Telegraph.* 15 July, Business 4.

Russell, P.H. 2009. "Grow up Canada, keep the monarchy…" *Toronto Star.* 5 November, A27.

Russell, P.H. and H. Thorburn. 2010. "G-Gs in a political world." *The Globe and Mail*. Letters to the Editor. 6 May, A16.

Travers, J. 2010. "Fadden, Johnston both pose risk for Harper." *Toronto Star*. 7 July, A10.

"What you need to know about the royal visit." 2009. *National Post*. 30 October. Accessed online at http://www.nationalpost.com/related/topics/What+need+know+about+royal+visit/2165509/story.html

Government Documents

Canada. 2004. *Canada, A Constitutional Monarchy*. Leaflet distributed to Senate visitors. Accessed online at http://www.parl.gc.ca/information/about/people/senate/Monarchy/SenMonarchy_00-e.htm

— 2009a. *Debates of the Senate*. Motion introduced by Senator Serge Joyal "to Urge the Preservation of Canadian Heritage Artifacts." 28 May, Vol. 146, issue 39. Accessed online at http://www.parl.gc.ca/40/2/parlbus/chambus/senate/deb-e/039db_2009-05-28-E.htm?Language=E&Parl=40&Ses=2

— 2009b. *Debates of the Senate*. Senator Serge Joyal speech on the motion. 9 June, Vol. 146, issue 43. Accessed online at http://www.parl.gc.ca/40/2/parlbus/chambus/senate/deb-e/043db_2009-06-09-

—2009c. *Debates of the Senate*. Senator Donald H. Oliver speech, 6 October 2009. Vol. 146, issue 57. Accessed online at http://www.parl.gc.ca/40/2/parlbus/chambus/senate/deb-e/057db_2009-10-06-E.htm?Language=E&Parl=40&Ses=2E.htm?Language=E&Parl=40&Ses=2

— 2010. Department of Canadian Heritage website. "Royal Visits to Canada." Accessed online at http://www.pch.gc.ca/pgm/ceem-cced/fr-rf/visit-eng.cfm

— 2010a. *Debates of the House of Commons*. The Hon. Peter Milliken, Speaker of the House of Commons, *Provision of Information to Special Committee on the Canadian Mission in Afghanistan – Speaker's Ruling*. 27 April. Accessed online at http://www2.parl.gc.ca/HousePublications/Publication.aspx?Language=E&Mode=1&Parl=40&Ses=3&DocId=4470112

— 2010b. *Debates of the Senate*. Motion introduced by Senator Serge Joyal "to Urge Government to Revise Twenty Dollar Banknote." 17 June 2010, Vol. 147, Issue 40. Accessed online at http://www.parl.gc.ca/40/3/parlbus/chambus/senate/deb-e/040db_2010-06-17-E.htm?Language=E&Parl=40&Ses=3

— 2010c. *Debates of the Senate*. Senator Serge Joyal speech on the motion. 22 June 2010, Vol.147, issue 42. Accessed online at http://www.parl.gc.ca/40/3/parlbus/chambus/senate/deb-e/042db_2010-06-22-E.htm?Language=E&Parl=40&Ses=3

Documents from the Office of the Governor General

Jean, Michaëlle. Speech given to the members of UNESCO's Executive Council, Paris. 5 October 2009. http://www.gg.ca/document.aspx?id=13278

Press release. "Exceptional Lineup of Canadians to Accompany Governor General on State visits to Russia, Finland and Iceland." 10 September 2003. http://archive.gg.ca/media/doc.asp?lang=e&DocID=4017

Other Sources

Angus Reid Poll. 2010. "Canadians Approve of Michaëlle Jean; Split on Extending Her Term." 3 April. Accessed online at http://www.visioncritical. com/2010/04/canadians-approve-of-michaelle-jean-split-on-extending-her-term/

Thomas, P.G. 2010. "Be Careful What You Wish For: Placing Limits on the Power of the Prime Minister." Speaking notes to the House of Commons Standing Committee on Procedure and House Affairs, 13 May.

BIBLIOGRAPHY

Books

Ajzenstat, J. 2007. *The Canadian Founding: John Locke and Parliament*. Montreal and Kingston: McGill-Queen's University Press.

— 2003. *The Once and Future Canadian Democracy. An Essay in Political Thought*. Montreal and Kingston: McGill-Queen's University Press.

Ajzenstat, J., P. Romney, I. Gentles and W. Gairdner, eds. 2003. *Canada's Founding Debates*. Toronto: University of Toronto Press.

Ajzenstat, J. and P.J. Smith, eds. 1997. *Canada's Origins: Liberal, Tory, or Republican?* Ottawa: Carleton University Press.

Bagehot, W. 1961. *The English Constitution*. London: Oxford University Press.

Barnett, A., ed. 1994. *Power and the Throne: The Monarchy Debate*. London: Vintage.

Batt, E. 1976. *Monck, Governor General, 1861–1868: A Biography*. Toronto: McClelland & Stewart.

Bissell, C. 1986. *The Imperial Canadian: Vincent Massey in Office*. Toronto: University of Toronto Press.

Black, C.E.D. 1903. *The Marquess of Dufferin and Ava … Diplomatist, Viceroy, Statesman*. London: Hutchinson.

Black, E. 1975. *Divided Loyalties: Canadian Concepts of Federalism*. Montreal and Kingston: McGill-Queen's University Press.

Blakeney, A. 2008. *An Honourable Calling: Political Memoirs*. Toronto: University of Toronto Press.

Blatherwick, J. 2003. *Canadian Orders, Decorations and Medals*. 5th ed. Toronto: The Unitrade Press.

Bogdanor, V. 1995. *The Monarchy and the Constitution*. London: Oxford University Press.

Bousfield, A. and G. Toffoli. 2002. *Fifty Years the Queen: A Tribute to Elizabeth II on Her Golden Jubilee*. Toronto: Dundurn Press.

— 2010. *Home to Canada: Royal Tours 1786–2010*. Toronto: Dundurn Press.

— 2002. *The Queen Mother and Her Century: An Illustrated Biography of Queen Elizabeth The Queen Mother on Her 100th Birthday*. Toronto: Dundurn Press.

— 1991. *Royal Observations: Canadians and Royalty*. Toronto: Dundurn Press.

— 1989. *Royal Spring: The Royal Tour of 1939 and the Queen Mother in Canada*. Toronto: Dundurn Press.

Boyce, P. 2008. *The Queen's Other Realms: The Crown and Its Legacy in Australia, Canada and New Zealand.* Sydney: The Federation Press.

Bradford, S. 1996. *Elizabeth: A Biography of Her Majesty The Queen.* Toronto: Key Porter Books.

Buckner, P., ed. 2005. *Canada and the End of Empire.* Vancouver: University of British Columbia Press.

Buckner, P. and R.D. Francis, eds. 2006. *Canada and the British World.* Vancouver: University of British Columbia Press.

Butler, D. and D.A. Low, eds. 1991. *Sovereigns and Surrogates: Constitutional Heads of State in the Commonwealth.* London: Macmillan.

Canada. Privy Council Office. 1968. *Manual of Official Procedure of the Government of Canada.* Henry F. Davis and André Millar. Ottawa: Government of Canada.

The Canadian Press. 2008. *Canada's Queen. Elizabeth II: A Celebration of Her Majesty's Friendship with the People of Canada.* Toronto: John Wiley & Sons.

Cardinal, H. and W. Hildebrandt. 2000. *Treaty Elders of Saskatchewan: Our Dream Is That Our Peoples Will One Day Be Clearly Recognized As Nations.* Calgary: University of Calgary Press.

Cardinal, L. and D. Heaton, eds. 2002. *Shaping Nations: Constitutionalism and Society in Australia and Canada.* Ottawa: University of Ottawa Press.

Champion, C.P. 2010. *The Strange Demise of British Canada: The Liberals and Canadian Nationalism, 1964–1968.* Montreal and Kingston: McGill-Queen's University Press.

Cheffins, R. and R. Tucker. 1976. *The Constitutional Process in Canada.* 2nd ed. Toronto: McGraw-Hill Ryerson.

Clarkson, A. 2006. *Heart Matters.* Toronto: Viking Canada.

Coady, M.F. 2011. *Georges and Pauline Vanier: Portrait of a Couple.* Montreal and Kingston: McGill-Queen's University Press.

Cotton, P.N. 1981. *Vice-Regal Mansions of British Columbia.* Vancouver: Elgin Publications.

Cowan, J. 1965. *Canada's Governors General, Lord Monck to General Vanier.* Toronto: York Publishing.

Cox, N. 2008. *A Constitutional History of the New Zealand Monarchy: The Evolution of the New Zealand Monarchy and the Recognition of an Autochthonous Polity.* Saarbrücken: VDM Verlag Dr. Müller.

Creighton, D. 1964. *The Road to Confederation: The Emergence of Canada, 1863–1867.* Toronto: Macmillan of Canada.

Dawson, R.M. 1933. *Constitutional Issues in Canada, 1900–1931.* London: Oxford University Press.

— 1970. *The Government of Canada.* 5th ed. Revised by Norman Ward. Toronto: University of Toronto Press.

Dempsey, L.J. 1999. *Warriors of the King: Prairie Indians in World War I.* Regina: Canadian Plains Research Center, University of Regina.

Dicey, A.V. 1962. *Law of the Constitution,* 10th ed. Introduction by E.C.S. Wade. London: Macmillan and Co.

Diefenbaker, J.G. 1972. *Those Things We Treasure.* Toronto: Macmillan of Canada.

Dimbleby, J. 1994. *The Prince of Wales: A Biography.* New York: William Morrow and Company.

Evatt, H.V. 1987. *The Royal Prerogative.* Sydney: Law Book Company.

Evatt, H.V. and E.A. Forsey. 1990. *Evatt and Forsey on the Reserve Power*. A complete and unabridged reprint of H.V. Evatt, *The King and his Dominion Governors* (2nd ed., 1967) and E.A. Forsey, *The Royal Power of Dissolution of Parliament in the British Commonwealth*, 1968 reprint together with a new introduction by Dr. Forsey. Sydney: Legal Books.

Farthing, J. 1957. *Freedom Wears a Crown*. Toronto: Kingswood House.

Forsey, E.A. 1974. *Freedom and Order: Collected Essays*. Toronto: McClelland and Stewart.

— 1990. *A Life on the Fringe: The Memoirs of Eugene Forsey*. Toronto: Oxford University Press.

— 1943. *The Royal Power of Dissolution of Parliament in the British Commonwealth*. Toronto: Oxford University Press. Reprinted in paperback with corrections in 1968.

Fraser, A. 1990. *The Spirit of the Laws: Republicanism and the Unfinished Project of Modernity*. Toronto: University of Toronto Press.

Fraser, J. 2000. *Eminent Canadians: Candid Tales of Then and Now*. Toronto: McClelland & Stewart.

— 2012. *The Secret of the Crown: Canada's Affair with Royalty*. Toronto: House of Anansi Press.

Grant, G. 1970. *Lament for a Nation: The Defeat of Canadian Nationalism*. Third Reprint. Toronto: McClelland & Stewart.

Hall, T. 1989. *Royal Canada: A History of Royal Visits to Canada since 1786*. Godalming, Surrey, UK: Archive Publishing.

Happy & Glorious. A Celebration of the Life of HM Queen Elizabeth II. 2006. London: Cassell Illustrated.

Hardman, R. 2007. *A Year with The Queen*. New York: Simon & Schuster.

Heard, A. 1991. *Canadian Constitutional Conventions: The Marriage of Law and Politics*. Toronto: Oxford University Press.

Hnatyshyn, G. and P. Lachapelle-Bélisle. 1994. *Rideau Hall: Canada's Living Heritage*. Ottawa: Friends of Rideau Hall.

Hogg, P. 2001. *Constitutional Law of Canada: 2001 Student Edition*. Toronto: Carswell.

— 1989. *Liability of the Crown*. 2nd ed. Toronto: Carswell.

Hryniuk, M. and G. Pugh. 1991. *"A Tower of Attraction": An Illustrated History of Government House, Regina, Saskatchewan*. Regina: Government House Historical Society / Canadian Plains Research Center, University of Regina.

Hubbard, R.H. 1989. *Ample Mansions: The Viceregal Residences of the Canadian Provinces*. Ottawa: University of Ottawa Press.

— 1977. *Rideau Hall: An Illustrated History of Government House, Ottawa*. Montreal and London: McGill-Queen's University Press.

Jackson, M., ed. 2007. *Honouring Commonwealth Citizens: Proceedings of the First Conference on Commonwealth Honours and Awards, Regina, 2006*. Toronto: Ontario Ministry of Citizenship and Immigration.

Joyal, S., ed. 2003. *Protecting Canadian Democracy: The Senate You Never Knew*. Montreal and Kingston: McGill-Queen's University Press, for Canadian Centre for Management Development / Centre canadien de gestion.

Keith, A.B. 1933. *The Constitutional Law of the British Dominions*. London: Macmillan and Co.

— 1936. *The King and the Imperial Crown: The Powers and Duties of His Majesty*. London: Longmans, Green & Co.

Kennedy, W.K. 1926. *Lord Elgin*. London: Oxford University Press.

— 1929. *The Sovereignty of the British Dominions*. London: Macmillan and Co.

Léger, J. 1989. *Jules Léger: gouverneur-général du Canada, 1974–1979: Textes et réflexions sur le Canada / Jules Léger: Governor General of Canada, 1974–1979: A Selection of His Writings on Canada*. Montréal: Éditions de l'Hexagone.

Lemieux, F., C. Blais et P. Hamelin. 2005. *L'histoire du Québec à travers ses lieutenants-gouverneurs*. Québec: Les Publications du Québec.

Lennox, D. 2009. *Now You Know Royalty*. Toronto: Dundurn Press.

Lipset, S.M. 1990. *Continental Divide: The Values and Institutions of the United States and Canada*. New York: Routledge.

Low, A. 1988. *Constitutional Heads and Political Crises*. London: Macmillan.

Lownie, A. 2004. *John Buchan: The Presbyterian Cavalier*. Toronto: McArthur & Company.

MacDonnell, T. 1989. *Daylight Upon Magic: The Royal Tour of Canada – 1939*. Toronto: Macmillan.

MacKinnon, F. 1976. *The Crown in Canada*. Calgary: Glenbow Alberta Institute / McClelland and Stewart West.

MacMillan, M., M. Harris and A.L. Desjardins. 2004. *Canada's House: Rideau Hall and the Invention of a Canadian Home*. Toronto: Alfred A. Knopf Canada.

Mallory, J.R. 1984. *The Structure of Canadian Government*. Revised ed. Toronto: Gage.

Marshall, G. 1984. *Constitutional Conventions: The Rules and Forms of Political Accountability*. Oxford: Oxford University Press.

Massey, V. 1948. *On Being Canadian*. Toronto: Dent.

— 1963. *What's Past is Prologue: The Memoirs of Vincent Massey*. Toronto: Macmillan.

McCreery, C. 2010. *The Canadian Forces' Decoration / La Décoration des Forces canadiennes*. Ottawa: Department of National Defence / Ministère de la Défense nationale.

— 2005. *The Canadian Honours System*. Toronto: Dundurn Press.

— 2008. *On Her Majesty's Service: Royal Honours and Recognition in Canada*. Toronto: Dundurn Press.

— 2005. *The Order of Canada: Its Origins, History and Development*. Toronto: University of Toronto Press.

McKenna, M. 1996. *The Captive Republic: A History of Republicanism in Australia 1788-1996*. Melbourne: Cambridge University Press.

McWhinney, E. 2005. *The Governor General and the Prime Ministers: The Making and Unmaking of Governments*. Vancouver: Lonsdale Press.

Messamore, B.J. 2006. *Canada's Governors General, 1847–1878: Biography and Constitutional Evolution*. Toronto: University of Toronto Press.

Michelmann, H.J., and C. de Clercy, eds. 2006. *Continuity and Change in Canadian Politics: Essays in Honour of David E. Smith*. Toronto: University of Toronto Press, 2006.

Monahan, P.J. 2006. *Constitutional Law*. 3rd ed. Toronto: Irwin Law.

Monet, J. 1979. *The Canadian Crown*. Toronto: Clarke, Irwin & Company.

— 1969. *The Last Cannon Shot: A Study of French-Canadian Nationalism, 1837–1850*. Toronto: University of Toronto Press.

— 1979. *La Monarchie au Canada*. Ottawa: Le Cercle du livre de France.

Morton, W.L. 1965. *The Canadian Identity*. Toronto: The University of Toronto Press; Madison: The University of Wisconsin Press.

— 1963. *The Kingdom of Canada: A General History from Earliest Times*. Toronto: McClelland & Stewart.

Mowatt, C. 1992. *Pomp and Circumstances*. Toronto: McClelland & Stewart.

Munro, K. 2005. *The Maple Crown in Alberta: The Office of Lieutenant-Governor, 1905–2005*. Victoria: Trafford Publishing.

Noonan, J. 2002. *Canada's Governors General at Play: Culture and Rideau Hall from Monck to Grey, With an Afterword on their Successors, Connaught to LeBlanc*. Ottawa: Borealis.

Noonan, P.W. 1998. *The Crown and Constitutional Law in Canada*. Calgary: Sripnoon.

Nuendorff, G. 1942. *Studies in the Evolution of Dominion Status. The Governor Generalship of Canada and the Development of Canadian Nationalism*. London: George Allen & Unwin.

Oliver, P. 2005. *The Constitution of Independence: The Development of Constitutional Theory in Australia, Canada, and New Zealand*. Oxford: Oxford University Press.

Olmsted, R.A., ed. 1954. *Decisions of the Judicial Committee of the Privy Council Relating to the British North America Act, 1867, and the Canadian Constitution, 1867–1854*. 3 vols. Ottawa: Queen's Printer.

Pike, C.A.W. and C. McCreery. 2011. *Canadian Symbols of Authority: Maces, Chains and Rods of Office*. Toronto: Dundurn Press.

Pimlott, B. 1996. *The Queen: A Biography of Elizabeth II*. London: HarperCollins.

Radforth, I.W. 2004. *Royal Spectacle: The 1860 Visit of the Prince of Wales to Canada*. Toronto: University of Press.

Ray, A.J., J. Miller and F. Tough. 2000. *Bounty and Benevolence – A History of Saskatchewan Treaties*. Montreal and Kingston: McGill-Queen's University Press.

Romney, P. 1999. *Getting It Wrong: How Canadians Forgot Their Past and Imperilled Confederation*. Toronto: University of Toronto Press.

Russell, P.H. 1992. *Constitutional Odyssey: Can Canadians Be a Sovereign People?* Toronto: University of Toronto Press.

Russell, P.H. and L. Sossin, eds. 2009. *Parliamentary Democracy in Crisis*. Toronto: University of Toronto Press.

Russell, P.H. and C. Milne. 2011. *Adjusting to a New Era of Minority Government: Report of a Workshop on Constitutional Conventions*. Toronto: University of Toronto, David Asper Centre for Constitutional Rights.

Saywell, J.T. 2002. *The Lawmakers: Judicial Power and the Shaping of Canadian Federalism*. Toronto: University of Toronto Press, for The Osgoode Hall Law Society.

— 1957. *The Office of Lieutenant Governor: A Study in Canadian Government and Politics*. Toronto: University of Toronto Press, 1957; Revised Edition, Toronto: Copp Clark Pitman, 1986.

Segal, H. 2011. *The Right Balance: Canada's Conservative Tradition*. Toronto: Douglas & McIntyre.

Senior, H. and E.K. Senior. 2009. *In Defence of Monarchy*. Toronto: Fealty Enterprises.

Shea, K. and J.J. Wilson. 2006. *Lord Stanley: The Man Behind the Cup*. Bolton, ON: Fenn Publishing Company.

Smith, D. 2005. *Head of State: the Governor-General, the Monarchy, the Republic and the Dismissal*. Sydney: Macleay Press.

Smith, D.E. 2003. *The Canadian Senate in Bicameral Perspective*. Toronto: University of Toronto Press.

— 2010. *Federalism and the Constitution of Canada*. Toronto: University of Toronto Press.

— 1995. *The Invisible Crown: The First Principle of Canadian Government*. Toronto: University of Toronto Press.

— 2007. *The People's House of Commons: Theories of Democracy in Contention.* Toronto: University of Toronto Press.

— 1999. *The Republican Option in Canada, Past and Present.* Toronto: University of Toronto Press.

Smith, G. 1891. *Canada and the Canadian Question.* Toronto: Hunter Rose Co. New edition edited by Carl Berger, University of Toronto Press, 1971.

Smith, J.A. 1965. *John Buchan: A Biography.* Toronto: Little, Brown and Company.

Speaight, R. 1970. *Vanier, Soldier, Diplomat and Governor General. A Biography.* Toronto: Collins.

Stamp, R.M. 1987. *Kings, Queens and Canadians: A Celebration of Canada's Infatuation with the British Royal Family.* Toronto: Fitzhenry & Whiteside.

— 1988. *Royal Rebels: Princess Louise & the Marquis of Lorne.* Toronto: Dundurn Press.

Stursburg, P. 1989. *Roland Michener, The Last Viceroy.* Toronto: McGraw-Hill Ryerson.

Sunkin, M. and S. Payne. 1999. *The Nature of the Crown: A Legal and Political Analysis.* New York: Oxford University Press.

Swan, C. 1977. *Canada: Symbols of Sovereignty.* Toronto: University of Toronto Press.

— 2005. *A King from Canada.* Stanhope, Durham, UK: The Memoir Club.

Tidridge, N. 2011. *Canada's Constitutional Monarchy.* Toronto: Dundurn Press.

Tizard, C. 1977. *The Role of the Governor-General of New Zealand.* Wellington: Government House.

Treaties as a Bridge to the Future. 1998. Saskatoon: Office of the Treaty Commissioner.

Treaty Implementation: Fulfilling the Covenant. 2007. Saskatoon: Office of the Treaty Commissioner.

Twomey, A. 2006. *The Chameleon Crown: The Queen and Her Australian Governors.* Sydney: The Federation Press.

Vanier, M. and G. Cowley, eds. 1970. *Only to Serve: Selections of Addresses by Governor General Georges P. Vanier.* Toronto: University of Toronto Press.

Vipond, R.C. 1991. *Canadian Federalism and the Failure of the Constitution.* Albany, NY: State University of New York Press.

Ward, N. 1987. *Dawson's Government of Canada.* Toronto: University of Toronto Press.

Weston, H. 2007. *No Ordinary Time: My Years as Ontario's Lieutenant-Governor.* Toronto: Whitfield Editions.

Wheare, K. 1960. *The Constitutional Structure of the Commonwealth.* Oxford: Clarendon Press.

— 1953. *The Statute of Westminster and Dominion Status.* 5th ed. London: Oxford University Press.

Williams, J. 1992. *Byng of Vimy. General and Governor General.* Toronto: University of Toronto Press.

Winterton, G. 1986. *Monarchy to Republic.* Melbourne: Oxford University Press.

— 1983. *Parliament, the Executive and the Governor-General.* Melbourne: Melbourne University Press.

Woods, S.E. 1986. *Her Excellency Jeanne Sauvé.* Toronto: Macmillan.

Educational Booklets

Aird, J.B. 1985. *Loyalty in a Changing World: The Contemporary Function of the Office of Lieutenant Governor of Ontario.* Toronto: Office of the Premier.

*Canadian Honours and Awards Bestowed Upon Members of the Canadian Forces /
Distinctions honorifiques conférées aux membres des Forces canadiennes.* 2011.
Ottawa: Canadian Forces / Les Forces canadiennes.

Découvrir le Canada. 2011. *Les droits et responsabilités liés à la citoyenneté. Guide d'étude.*
Ottawa: Ministre des Approvisionnements et Services Canada.

Discover Canada. 2011. *The Rights and Responsibilities of Citizenship. Study Guide.*
Ottawa: Minister of Public Works and Government Services Canada.

Forsey, E.A. 2010. *Les Canadiens et leur système de gouvernment.* Septième édition.
Ottawa: Ministre des Approvisionnements et Services Canada.

— 2010. *How Canadians Govern Themselves.* 7th ed. Ottawa: Minister of Supply
and Services Canada.

Jackson, D.M. 1990. *The Canadian Monarchy in Saskatchewan.* 2nd ed. Regina: Government of Saskatchewan.

— 2002. *Images of a Province: Symbols of Saskatchewan / Images d'une province: les
symboles de la Saskatchewan.* Regina: Government of Saskatchewan.

— 2007. *Royal Saskatchewan: The Crown in a Canadian Province.* Regina: Government of Saskatchewan.

— 2007. *La Saskatchewan royale: la Couronne dans une province canadienne.* Regina:
Gouvernement de la Saskatchewan.

MacLeod, K.S. 2008. *La Couronne canadienne: La monarchie constitutionnelle au
Canada.* Ottawa: Ministère du Patrimoine canadien.

— 2008. *A Crown of Maples: Constitutional Monarchy in Canada.* Ottawa: Department of Canadian Heritage.

Pomp & Circumstance: An Historical Celebration of Queen's Park. 1984. Toronto:
Legislative Assembly of Ontario.

Silver Jubilee: Royal Visit to Canada, Six Days in the Life of the Queen. 1977. Ottawa:
Deneau & Greenberg.

Stanley, G.F.G. 1992. *The Role of the Lieutenant-Governor / Le rôle du lieutenant-
gouverneur.* Fredericton: Legislative Assembly of New Brunswick / Assemblée
législative du Nouveau-Brunswick.

Symbols of Canada / Les symboles du Canada. 2008. Ottawa: Department of Canadian
Heritage / Ministère du Patrimoine canadien.

Chapters in Books

Arnot, D. 2009. "We Are All Treaty People." In *Saskatchewan Politics: Crowding the
Centre,* ed. H.A. Leeson. Regina: Canadian Plains Research Center, University
of Regina.

Bercuson, D.J. and B. Cooper. 1992. "From Constitutional Monarchy to Quasi
Republic: The Evolution of Liberal Democracy in Canada." In *Canadian Consti-
tutionalism, 1791–1991,* ed. J. Ajzenstat. Ottawa: Canadian Study of Parliament
Group.

Haverstock, L.M. 2007. "Bestowing Honours: The Other Side." In *Honouring Commonwealth Citizens: Proceedings of the First Conference on Commonwealth Honours
and Awards, Regina, 2006,* ed. Michael Jackson. Toronto: Ontario Ministry of
Citizenship and Immigration.

Hubbard, R.H. 1968. "Viceregal Influences on Canadian Society." In *The Shield
of Achilles: Aspects of Canada in the Victorian Age,* ed. W.L. Morton. Toronto:
McClelland & Stewart.

Jackson, D.M. 2009. "The Crown in Saskatchewan: An Institution Renewed." In *Saskatchewan Politics: Crowding the Centre*, ed. H.A. Leeson. Regina: Canadian Plains Research Center, University of Regina.

— 2001. "Political Paradox: The Lieutenant Governor in Saskatchewan." In *Saskatchewan Politics: Into the Twenty-First Century*. ed. H.A. Leeson. Regina: Canadian Plains Research Center, University of Regina.

Monet, J. 1968. "The Personal and Living Bond." In *The Shield of Achilles: Aspects of Canada in the Victorian Age*, ed. W.L. Morton. Toronto: McClelland & Stewart.

— 1995. "La Couronne." In *Le Système parlementaire canadien*, eds. M. Tremblay et M. Tremblay. Québec: Les Presses universitaires Laval.

Morton, W.L. 1970. "Lord Monck, His Friends, and the Nationalizing of the British Empire." In *Character and Circumstance*, ed. J.S. Moir. Toronto: Macmillan.

Murray, L. 2003. "Which Criticisms Are Founded?" In *Protecting Canadian Democracy: The Senate You Never Knew*, ed. S. Joyal. Montreal and Kingston: McGill-Queen's University Press.

Poelzer, G. and K. Coates. 2006. "Aboriginal Peoples and the Crown in Canada: Completing the Canadian Experiment." In *Continuity and Change in Canadian Politics: Essays in Honour of David E. Smith*, eds. H.J. Michelmann and C. de Clercy. Toronto: University of Toronto Press.

Smith, D.E. 2001. "Saskatchewan and Canadian Federalism." In *Saskatchewan Politics: Into the Twenty-First Century*, ed. H.A. Leeson. Regina: Canadian Plains Research Center, University of Regina.

Articles

Aucoin, P. and L. Turnbull. 2004. "Electoral Reform, Minority Government, and the Democratic Deficit: Removing the Virtual Right of First Ministers to Demand Dissolution." *Canadian Parliamentary Review* 27, no. 2.

Benoit, P. 1999. "A Job for Mrs. Clarkson." *Policy Options* 20, no. 9.

— 2002. "Parliament and Democracy in the 21st Century: The Crown and the Constitution." *Canadian Parliamentary Review* 25, no. 2.

— 1996. "The Queen's Prerogatives." *The Literary Review of Canada* 5, no. 7.

— 1982. "Remembering the Monarch." *Canadian Journal of Political Science* 15, no. 3.

Boily, F. 2009. "La « crise de la prorogation » vue du Québec. *Constitutional Forum constitutionnel* 18, no. 1.

Bowden, J.W.J. and N.A. MacDonald. 2012. "Writing the Unwritten: The Officialization of Constitutional Conventions in the Core Commonwealth." *Journal of Parliamentary and Political Law* 6, no.1.

Boyce, P. 2006. "Review of *Head of State*." *Australian Journal of Public Administration* 6, no. 2.

Cheffins, R.I. 2000. "The Royal Prerogative and the Office of Lieutenant Governor." *Canadian Parliamentary Review* 23, no. 1.

Craven, G. 2004. "The Developing Role of the Governor-General: The Goldenness of Silence." *Federal Law Review* 32, no. 2.

Davison, C.B. 2009. "Prorogation: A Powerful Tool Forged by History." *Law Now* 34, no. 2.

Desserud, D.A. 2009. "The Governor General, the Prime Minister and the Request to Prorogue." *Canadian Political Science Review* 3, no. 3.

Forsey, E.A. 1953. "The Crown and the Constitution." *Dalhousie Review* (Spring).
— 1979. "The Role of the Crown in Canada since Confederation." *The Parliamentarian* 60, no. 1.
Guly, C. 2010. "The Perils of Prorogation." *The Lawyer's Weekly* 29, no. 6.
Heard, A. 2009. "The Governor General's Decision to Prorogue Parliament: A Chronology & Assessment." *Constitutional Forum constitutionnel* 18, no. 1.
Hicks, B. 2010. "British and Canadian Experience with the Royal Prerogative." *Canadian Parliamentary Review* 33, no. 2.
— 2010. "The Crown's 'Democratic' Reserve Powers." *Journal of Canadian Studies* 44, no. 2.
— 2009. "Guiding the Governor General's Prerogatives: Constitutional Convention Versus an Apolitical Decision Rule." *Constitutional Forum constitutionnel* 18, no. 2.
— 2009. "Lies My Fathers of Confederation Told Me: Are the Governor General's Reserve Powers a Safeguard of Democracy?" *Inroads* 25.
Hurley, J.R. 2000. "The Royal Prerogative and the Office of Lieutenant Governor: A Comment." *Canadian Parliamentary Review* 23, no. 2.
Hogg, P. 2010. "The 2008 Constitutional Crisis: Prorogation and the Power of the Governor General." *National Journal of Constitutional Law* 27.
Jackson, D.M. 1995. "How the Monarchy Protects Canadian Values." *Canadian Speeches: Issues of the Day* 9, no. 2.
Kirk-Greene, A.H.M. 1977. "The Governors-General of Canada, 1867–1952: A Collective Profile." *Journal of Canadian Studies/Revue d'études canadiennes* 12, no. 4.
MacDonald, N.A., and J.W.J. Bowden. 2011. "No Discretion: On Prorogation and the Governor General." *Canadian Parliamentary Review* 34, no. 1.
— 2011. "The Manual of Official Procedure of the Government of Canada: An Exposé." *Constitutional Forum constitutionnel* 20, no. 1.
Mallory, J.R. 1960. "The Appointment of the Governor General: Responsible Government, Autonomy and the Royal Prerogative." *Canadian Journal of Economics and Political Science* (February).
McWhinney, E. 2009. "The Constitutional and Political Aspects of the Office of the Governor General." *Canadian Parliamentary Review* 32, no. 2.
— 2008. "Fixed Election Dates and the Governor General's Power to Grant Dissolution." *Canadian Parliamentary Review* 31, no. 1.
Messamore, B.J. 2005. "'The Line Over Which He Must Not Pass': Defining the Office of Governor General, 1878." *The Canadian Historical Review* 86, no. 3.
— 1998. "'On A Razor Edge': The Canadian Governors-General, 1888–1911." *British Journal of Canadian Studies* 13, no. 2.
Monet, J. 1976. "La Couronne du Canada." *Journal of Canadian Studies/Revue d'études canadiennes* 11, no. 4.
Munro, K. 2009. "The Turmoil Surrounding the Prorogation of Canada's 40th Parliament & Crown." *Constitutional Forum constitutionnel* 18, no. 1.
Neitsch, A.T. 2007. "A Tradition of Vigilance: The Role of Lieutenant Governor in Alberta." *Canadian Parliamentary Review* 30, no. 4.
Neary, P. 2009. "Confidence: How Much Is Enough?" *Constitutional Forum constitutionnel* 18, no. 1.
O'Connell, D.P. 1979. "Canada, Australia, Constitutional Reform and the Crown." *The Parliamentarian* 60, no. 1.

O'Donnell, D. 1991. "Lord Lisgar: From Governor of New South Wales to Governor-General of Canada." *Journal of the Royal Australian Historical Society* 76.

Patmore, G.A. and J.D. Whyte. 1997. "Imagining Constitutional Crises: Power and (Mis)behaviour in Republican Australia." *Federal Law Review* 25.

Roberts, E. 2009. "Ensuring Constitutional Wisdom During Unconventional Times." *Canadian Parliamentary Review* 32, no. 1.

Russell, P.H. 2011. "Discretion and the Reserve Powers of the Crown." *Canadian Parliamentary Review* 34, no. 2.

Smith, D.E. 1995. "Bagehot, the Crown and Canadian Constitutionalism." *Canadian Journal of Political Science* 28, no. 4.

— 1991. "Empire, Crown and Canadian Federalism." *Canadian Journal of Political Science* 24, no. 3.

— 2000. "RE: The Royal Prerogative and the Office of Governor General." *Canadian Parliamentary Review* 23(3).

Stacey, C.P. 1934. "Lord Monck and the Canadian Nation." *Dalhousie Review* 14.

Stilborn, J. 2009. "The Role of the Governor General: Time to Revisit the Visits." *Policy Options* 30, no. 7.

Tremblay, G. 2010. "Limiting the Government's Power to Prorogue Parliament." *Canadian Parliamentary Review* 33, no. 2.

Whitelaw, W.M. 1940. "Lord Monck and the Canadian Constitution." *Canadian Historical Review* 2.

— 1932. "Responsible Government and the Irresponsible Governor." *Canadian Historical Review* 13.

Whyte, J.D. 1993. "The Australian Republican Movement and Its Implications for Canada." *Constitutional Forum* 4, no. 3.

Unpublished Papers and Theses

Jackson, D.M. 1990. "The Development of Saskatchewan Honours." Research paper for the Senior Management Development Program, Saskatchewan Public Service Commission.

Miller, C.I. 1970. "The Public Career of the 4th Earl Minto in Canada." PhD thesis, University of London.

Neitsch, A.T. 2006. "In Loco Regis – The Contemporary Role of the Governor General and Lieutenant Governor in Canada." MA thesis, University of Alberta.

Palmer, S. 2010. "The Ramifications of Sharing a Head of State: A Study in the Implications of a Structure." PhD thesis, Auckland University of Technology.

Rasmussen, M.D. 1994. "The Decline of Parliamentary Democracy in Saskatchewan." MA thesis, University of Regina.

Queen's Policy Studies
Recent Publications

The Queen's Policy Studies Series is dedicated to the exploration of major public policy issues that confront governments and society in Canada and other nations.

Manuscript submission. We are pleased to consider new book proposals and manuscripts. Preliminary enquiries are welcome. A subvention is normally required for the publication of an academic book. Please direct questions or proposals to the Publications Unit by email at spspress@queensu.ca, or visit our website at: www.queensu.ca/sps/books, or contact us by phone at (613) 533-2192.

Our books are available from good bookstores everywhere, including the Queen's University bookstore (http://www.campusbookstore.com/). McGill-Queen's University Press is the exclusive world representative and distributor of books in the series. A full catalogue and ordering information may be found on their web site (http://mqup.mcgill.ca/).

School of Policy Studies

Life After Forty: Official Languages Policy in Canada/Après quarante ans, les politiques de langue officielle au Canada, Jack Jedwab and Rodrigue Landry (eds.) 2011.
ISBN 978-1-55339-279-8

From Innovation to Transformation: Moving up the Curve in Ontario Healthcare,
Hon. Elinor Caplan, Dr. Tom Bigda-Peyton, Maia MacNiven, and Sandy Sheahan 2011.
ISBN 978-1-55339-315-3

Academic Reform: Policy Options for Improving the Quality and Cost-Effectiveness of Undergraduate Education in Ontario, Ian D. Clark, David Trick, and Richard Van Loon 2011.
ISBN 978-1-55339-310-8

Integration and Inclusion of Newcomers and Minorities across Canada, John Biles, Meyer Burstein, James Frideres, Erin Tolley, and Robert Vineberg (eds.) 2011.
ISBN 978-1-55339-290-3

A New Synthesis of Public Administration: Serving in the 21st Century, Jocelyne Bourgon, 2011. Paper ISBN 978-1-55339-312-2 Cloth ISBN 978-1-55339-313-9

Recreating Canada: Essays in Honour of Paul Weiler, Randall Morck (ed.), 2011.
ISBN 978-1-55339-273-6

Data Data Everywhere: Access and Accountability? Colleen M. Flood (ed.), 2011.
ISBN 978-1-55339-236-1

Making the Case: Using Case Studies for Teaching and Knowledge Management in Public Administration, Andrew Graham, 2011. ISBN 978-1-55339-302-3

Canada's Isotope Crisis: What Next? Jatin Nathwani and Donald Wallace (eds.), 2010.
Paper ISBN 978-1-55339-283-5 Cloth ISBN 978-1-55339-284-2

Pursuing Higher Education in Canada: Economic, Social, and Policy Dimensions,
Ross Finnie, Marc Frenette, Richard E. Mueller, and Arthur Sweetman (eds.), 2010.
Paper ISBN 978-1-55339-277-4 Cloth ISBN 978-1-55339-278-1

Canadian Immigration: Economic Evidence for a Dynamic Policy Environment,
Ted McDonald, Elizabeth Ruddick, Arthur Sweetman, and Christopher Worswick (eds.), 2010. Paper ISBN 978-1-55339-281-1 Cloth ISBN 978-1-55339-282-8

Taking Stock: Research on Teaching and Learning in Higher Education, Julia Christensen Hughes and Joy Mighty (eds.), 2010. Paper ISBN 978-1-55339-271-2
Cloth ISBN 978-1-55339-272-9

Centre for the Study of Democracy

Jimmy and Rosalynn Carter: A Canadian Tribute, Arthur Milnes (ed.), 2011.
Paper ISBN 978-1-55339-300-9 Cloth ISBN 978-1-55339-301-6

Unrevised and Unrepented II: Debating Speeches and Others By the Right Honourable Arthur Meighen, Arthur Milnes (ed.), 2011. Paper ISBN 978-1-55339-296-5
Cloth ISBN 978-1-55339-297-2

Centre for International and Defence Policy

Security Operations in the 21st Century: Canadian Perspectives on the Comprehensive Approach, Michael Rostek and Peter Gizewski (eds.), 2011. ISBN 978-1-55339-351-1

Europe Without Soldiers? Recruitment and Retention across the Armed Forces of Europe, Tibor Szvircsev Tresch and Christian Leuprecht (eds.), 2010.
Paper ISBN 978-1-55339-246-0 Cloth ISBN 978-1-55339-247-7

Mission Critical: Smaller Democracies' Role in Global Stability Operations, Christian Leuprecht, Jodok Troy, and David Last (eds.), 2010. ISBN 978-1-55339-244-6

John Deutsch Institute for the Study of Economic Policy

The 2009 Federal Budget: Challenge, Response and Retrospect, Charles M. Beach, Bev Dahlby and Paul A.R. Hobson (eds.), 2010. Paper ISBN 978-1-55339-165-4
Cloth ISBN 978-1-55339-166-1

Discount Rates for the Evaluation of Public Private Partnerships, David F. Burgess and Glenn P. Jenkins (eds.), 2010. Paper ISBN 978-1-55339-163-0 Cloth ISBN 978-1-55339-164-7

Institute of Intergovernmental Relations

The Federal Idea: Essays in Honour of Ronald L. Watts, Thomas J. Courchene, John R. Allan, Christian Leuprecht, and Nadia Verrelli (eds.), 2011. Paper ISBN 978-1-55339-198-2
Cloth ISBN 978-1-55339-199-9

Canada: The State of the Federation 2009, vol. 22, *Carbon Pricing and Environmental Federalism*, Thomas J. Courchene and John R. Allan (eds.), 2010.
Paper ISBN 978-1-55339-196-8 Cloth ISBN 978-1-55339-197-5

Our publications may be purchased at leading bookstores, including the Queen's University Bookstore (http://www.campusbookstore.com/) or can be ordered online from: McGill-Queen's University Press, at **http://mqup.mcgill.ca/ordering.php**

For more information about new and backlist titles from Queen's Policy Studies, visit http://www.queensu.ca/sps/books or visit the McGill-Queen's University Press web site at: **http://mqup.mcgill.ca/**